THE EGO MILL

By James A. Howard, Ph.D.

People's feelings about mental illness have gone from fear to fad to fact in two generations. Behind those generations lie centuries of neglect, abuse, and the shameful exploitation of the emotionally disturbed. With the advent of community mental health centers, help for all the troubled is becoming a reality.

This book samples the day-to-day work of a psychologist in such a clinic. It takes the reader directly into the pains and problems of patients struggling in the mazes of their minds and the crucibles of their feelings.

Intimate interviews between the patient and the psychologist, as well as the faithful recreation of traumatic events in onstage scenes, combine to reveal five human beings and their struggles to understand themselves.

Anger and disenchantment with living drove Laurel—a twice-married arsonist in constant conflict with family, friends, and lovers—into the lesbian world, only to frustrate her hopes for even this realization of herself.

David—caught in the loss of his music when the big-band era passed—tried to

g of being a man
age, speech disable-
al frustration.

an untenable mar-
otect her children
husband and a vin-

visits from Christ
izophrenic youth—
ny teen-ager should

from conceiving her
ing from the past by
rself in the present,
ed by her therapist's
nt.

en: A boy fights back
A woman chooses
uld have millions? A
lackmails his son's
arries to try for a
A man loses control
ir he will scream his
ntly, how do these
vhat can be done to
ee themselves from
ped emotions?

is Dr. Howard meets
HE EGO MILL. By
mbination of fictional
chniques, the events
dramatic coloration,
impact of a powerful

The
EGO MILL

Five Case Studies
in Clinical Psychology

*

JAMES A. HOWARD, Ph.D

COWLES BOOK COMPANY, INC.
A Subsidiary of Henry Regnery Company

Cowles Book Company, Inc.

A subsidiary of Henry Regnery Company

114 West Illinois Street, Chicago, Illinois 60610

Published simultaneously in Canada by

  General Publishing Company, Ltd.,

    30 Lesmill Road, Don Mills, Toronto, Ontario

Manufactured in the United States of America

First Edition

CONTENTS

Foreword   vii

Introduction   ix

PART ONE   1
LAUREL
Long Journey in a Small Room

PART TWO   59
DAVID
Play Melancholy, Baby

PART THREE   115
KAREN
Hostages to Fortune

PART FOUR   157
JOSEPH
Weigh a Pound of Fog

PART FIVE   207
JULIA
". . . and sweet the wines of May . . ."

FOREWORD

by George Dillinger, M.D.

MEDICAL DIRECTOR, THE DOUGLAS YOUNG CLINIC

SAN DIEGO, CALIFORNIA

WHILE THERE ARE MANY PEOPLE WHO EFFECTIVELY PRACTICE the art of psychotherapy, there are very few who have the ability to write clearly and simply about what happens in the therapeutic experience. Jim Howard is one of the few who have that ability. What is most delightful to me in Dr. Howard's book is the fact that, because of his writing skill, words become like actual situations. I find myself feeling that I am actually with him and his patients—that I feel as they felt in the various experiences he describes.

Psychotherapy is an art, and has many forms. I believe that there are as many different ways to practice this art as there are therapists in the practice of it. Each sets his own pattern in working with the patient or client. That makes each treatment situation different. It is a thing shaped to the needs, feelings, and problems of the particular person. That is why this book will not teach one to be a psychotherapist, or to be the patient of a psychotherapist.

I feel equally strongly, however, that there is something always present in all types of psychotherapy. That thing in common is the situation in which two people try to share what they are. From this sharing, at times, a mutual benefit is derived. We think of these as rewarding situations, while those in which our sharing is incomplete or nonexistent are the attempts we consider to be "failures."

What makes the difference between effective and noneffective therapy, I do not know. Perhaps special selective factors operate within some people to give them the courage to face themselves as they really are. It may also be that some therapists show a better capacity to help people be open with themselves and thus *gain* the courage to confront their personal problems so they can be satisfactorily resolved.

In the cases contained in this book, real people emerge. There are, of course, the five particular people whose treatment Dr. Howard is reporting. There is also a sixth person—Dr. Howard himself—who emerges as one of the humans in these cases. While the reader may not agree with what he did in the various situations of Laurel, David, Karen, Joseph, and Julia, that same reader cannot help but be impressed by the incredible drama and excitement of these people's lives.

After reading the book, you cannot expect to know how Dr. Howard achieved his outlined results. You can expect, however, to get a real glimpse of the challenges and rewards of the process of psychotherapy. In that expectation, I do not feel you will be disappointed.

A graduate of Yale University Medical School, Dr. Dillinger took his psychiatric training at the Menninger School of Psychiatry. In practice for fifteen years, he is a Diplomate of the American Board of Psychiatry and Neurology, and staff adviser to KAIROS, an ongoing training and developing institute dealing with human and social problems.

He is the current Vice-President of the San Diego Gestalt Therapy Institute. His position as Medical Director of the Douglas Young Clinic in San Diego has made him Dr. James Howard's immediate supervisor for the past three years, giving him a unique position to evaluate the work of the author of THE EGO MILL. *Dr. Dillinger maintains a private psychiatric practice in La Jolla, California.*

James A. Howard has been a professional psychologist since 1949, although he had an earlier career as a newspaper reporter for the *Toledo Morning Times* and the *Peoria Morning Star*. He has also written a number of successful suspense novels.

He has taught psychology at Auburn, UCLA, and California Western University, and currently teaches, as time permits, at San Diego State College. He also taught creative writing at Los Angeles State College.

His background of experience includes the design and direction of the first study of the industrial rehabilitation of hemiplegia victims for the Office of Vocational Rehabilitation of the Department of Health, Education, and Welfare.

Several years ago he was Clinical Psychologist and Research Director of one of Minnesota's mental health centers at Luverne, Minnesota. For the past six years, he has been Clinical Psychologist of the Douglas Young Clinic in San Diego, California. He also maintains a private practice of psychology in San Diego.

that show similarities to the experience of others. We weave these into a most unique life-style and can show uniformities, though never identities.

The persons in this book are real. The gains and losses in the therapeutic struggle were, and are, of intense concern to them, and to me. By reporting the struggle, it may be that future mistakes can be reduced, future gains enhanced. It is for this reason that I give my subjective account of what took place with these valuable people. Perhaps, in writing of them, I shall learn more of how to be a therapist. Perhaps, in reading of them, some resonance will be felt that might be of help to others—practitioners and patients.

A caution must be sounded. The reader must not expect that treatment always ends in complete, shining success. Goals are often limited, their attainment only partial. No automatic shielding from future stress, nor unshakable and unbreakable happiness, is created in successful therapy. A more effective individual, meeting his unique world and its demands with increased resources, is the goal of therapy. Life is a process, not a condition achieved and invariant. As such, our function in that process is inconstant. Life touches, withdraws, grasps, strikes, squeezes, shrinks from, caresses, or stabs with varying effect.

Ultimately, no one teaches a subject. He can teach only his view of a subject. So this volume represents my particular view of the task of therapy. No apology is extended for that view. At times, my personal philosophy can be seen in my handling of these situations, as well as the experiential shaping by training and years of practice. This may well be a thing that was not intended by the many psychologists—splendid teachers—from whom I learned. In fact, some of these teachers may well take exception to the things that fit my operational system in psychotherapy.

A final word to my patients, past and present. I am most grateful for the opportunity you give me to learn more and to gain the gratifications that my work provides. This book is for you and for me, just as our therapy is joint, personal, and intense.

James A. Howard, Ph.D.

February, 1971
San Diego, California

PART ONE

* LAUREL *

Long Journey
in a Small Room

IT WAS NINE O'CLOCK IN THE MORNING, BUT THE SILVER BLUE eye shadow said that all of the clocks in the world were wrong. The sun had risen at dusk. Her eyes were carefully made up— intensely, almost ornately so. Her brows were stenciled on with the precision of Japanese paintings. Blue lines edged her eyelids delicately, extending their margins to cross at their outermost folds into tiny fishtails.

For a moment, it seemed that there was no other feature of the woman who had entered my office. Her lipstick was pale in shade and sparingly applied. Her hair, though plentiful and a glossy reddish brown, was done with utmost simplicity. The face showed no other cosmetic, revealing only a consistent and healthy skin color. In body, she was well proportioned, though lacking enough height to carry the few extra pounds that pressed at her blouse and at the tight capri pants she wore on the first of her many visits to my office.

She looked at me for a long time, sitting in her chair with an almost insolent exaggeration of relaxation. Then, quite abruptly, she spoke.

"I suppose you're going to ask me what my problem is, too." Her voice was even and low toned, though the inflection gave her words an edge. "Everybody else does."

When I did not reply, she seemed to be taken aback. She held my eyes expectantly for a moment, then nodded toward the file folder on my desk. "You've got it all there, anyhow."

1

"Papers aren't a person, Mrs. Mount."

"Haven't you even read them?"

"Not yet."

The pause was brief, yet it was apparently one of shock. I continued with some usual words. "I prefer to meet the person first. There will be time for pieces of paper later. Suppose we just talk for a time, and let the questions come as they may."

These words, or similar ones, sometimes help a patient to feel less threatened by a new therapist. I might have recognized, if I had read the papers that preceded the woman to my office, that Laurel Mount was an instinctive attacker. If she were given an opening, she would move within it not at all. Rather, she would almost certainly move against it.

"All the other people here asked me what was wrong and how to help," she snapped. "Hell, if I knew that, I wouldn't even be here. I told Doctor Barnes I was tired of being asked to perform my own diagnosis."

I had accepted Laurel on transfer from Dr. Gerald Barnes, whose intention to leave the clinic meant the transfer to other staff men of those patients he felt were in need of further care. Jerry had seen her twice, diagnostically, following the social worker's initial intake interviews.

"You're tired of being asked what's wrong?" I tried to make it more of an observation than a question.

She lighted a cigarette, allowing me to notice that her nails were long and well kept. The hands were precise in motion and well shaped. "Everybody asks me what my problem is, so I'll tell you." She looked directly at me, holding the burning match with which she had lighted her cigarette. "It's very simple, Doctor Howard. I get mad and then I set things on fire."

She leaned forward, across the corner of the desk, still holding the match before her. At the latest possible moment, she pursed her lips and blew out the flame. "That's why I got sent to Dellwood State Hospital and was kept locked up for five months." She nodded toward the folder again. "It's all in there, I guess."

I nodded, thinking again of the hurried conference Dr. Barnes and I had held, with its regrettably small segment of time for each of the several patients he had referred to me. "The outline is there, I suppose."

2

"What's to tell beyond the outline? Isn't everybody a prostitute at fourteen?" She corrected herself quickly. "Except for the ones who can't pass the physical—we call them pimps."

It had been a broadside blast, coming so early in a first interview. Laurel Mount was spitting at the world. I just happened to represent the part of that world upon which she most wanted to spit. The most natural thing I felt was the grin I was wearing, but she seemed to misinterpret it.

"So you never doubt it—*don't laugh at me!*" Her voice was raw and cold.

"I'm laughing at what you said. You say just what you think, don't you?"

"I always have. Too damned many people don't." She paused, and for a moment the knives were gone from her voice. "Maybe I make a lot of trouble for myself when I do."

"Ummm."

"Oh," she said, quickly reverting to her verbal weapons. "Now you're going to give me the nondirective reflection—is that it?"

"Not exactly. I guess I do agree. Sometimes people make a great deal of trouble for themselves when they say exactly what they mean or feel."

"You, too?"

"At the risk of being misunderstood, yes."

For the first time since she had come in, Laurel Mount smiled. The smile broke evenly, revealing good teeth and a capacity for nonvindictive humor. This first interview went a bit more smoothly after that. She kept her weapons at hand, but proceeded guardedly. She added some details in response to my questions, but it was apparent that she was appraising me.

It is equally apparent that she was not in any hurry to decide whether or not she had been transferred to the wrong man. The session was less spontaneous, both in offering and in replies to my queries, than most first interviews. Usually, people's griefs and angers need unloading to allow some feeling of relief and adjustment to a new therapist. Laurel had lived with her burden of grief for a long time and was not yet ready to share those sore spots.

Before my next interview with her, I did my homework. I

studied the case record of Laurel Mount closely. I was able to shape my impressions of the woman I had seen to the information and observations of others who had touched her life. Yet there was not a consistent pattern or a feeling of preliminary understanding such as I might expect to get from such a wealth of data. I went over the reports of social workers, probation officers, police, the Dellwood Hospital staff men, and especially the members of our own clinic team who had seen her before me.

While I could not unify them into a theme, the realities and the fictions of Laurel Mount began taking shape. For three years prior to coming to our clinic, she had been followed closely. There were the usual footprints—psychological test scores, physical examination reports, a bankruptcy petition, an arrest and detention order, then a commitment order.

These were the realities, the structure on which the flesh of the fictions could be added. Those fictions were the impressions and the subjective reactions of those who had tried to know Laurel. They are not fictions in the literary sense, but in the psychiatric sense. One quickly learns that trying to relive another's experiences is not reality, but a reflection in the trick mirrors of one's own feelings, with no immediate way of measuring the image distortion.

Laurel was the second of four children born to a practical nurse. A sister was older, and two half brothers were from a second marriage of her mother. Her natural father was never known to her. She was reared by her mother and an alcoholic stepfather who died when she was nineteen. She had thought him to be her father until her early teens.

Other interviewers had run into anger in response to questions about her natural father. As the story was pieced together, it was established that the mother's husband had deserted her when she became pregnant in an affair with a military attaché from another country—the pregnancy that resulted in Laurel's birth.

It was some time later that I was able to tap Laurel's feelings about the matter.

"They call me the Mad Russian," she said. "That's what my father was supposed to have been. I don't know if it's true, but I guess it is. The only father I ever knew was my stepfather. When he wasn't drunk, he was a pretty good guy, I guess. He took off when I was about twelve—maybe thirteen. That's when I found out he wasn't my old man."

"Mother copped out?"

"Yeah." The smile was bitter. "She told me a lot of things then. She was bitchin' to anyone who would listen."

As she talked in this sixteenth session, I tried to visualize the confrontation and wounding of Laurel as a child. The words of the angry, adult Laurel were like the charcoal strokes of a speed artist, but the feelings could only be understood by adding the shading and toning—the coloration of conjecture.

"I put daddy's supper in the oven, momma. Is that all right?"

"Feed it to your goddamn cat!" The stubby fingers clenched and unclenched, catching bits of the old oilcloth on the kitchen table, wrinkling it and letting it spring back. "Don't ever try to save a damned thing for a man."

Laurel froze like a startled fawn, her freckles looking like its dappled camouflage. It took a few seconds for her to realize that this was something different from the arguments and aftermaths of spats she had seen before. She had not seen this cold fury in twelve years of knowing her mother's moods. She looked for an easy way to move away.

"I'll do the dishes, momma."

"He's gone. The son of a bitch packed up and left. He took every penny."

The girl stood, half-turned between sink and table. "It'll be all right, momma. He'll come back. He'll bring more money."

"Shit!" The word split the air, and Laurel froze still more tightly to the spot. The mother looked at her with hard eyes, pinning her like a spotlighted animal. "The only reason he didn't take the car was that I had it at work!"

Silence lay there, an awesome thing to Laurel. She fumbled for something to fill the vacuum.

"Daddy wouldn't do that. He wouldn't just leave—not without sayin' good-bye or anything."

The mother uncoiled her stubby frame from the chair like a short spring escaping its bindings. She rounded the table and stood directly in front of the girl. At thirty-seven, she was the hard-used remnant of a woman, drawn in jaw and throat, showing the scars of her own ill-usage on the remains of a well-structured face.

"Look at me! Look!" She commanded the girl's eyes. "I gave that bastard everything I had. I tried to make it up to him—every damned day I tried to make it up to him. What do I get for it? Nothing! The drunken bastard runs out with the money."

She took the girl by the shoulders, fingers driving into Laurel's upper arms, squeezing the shapeless sweat shirt.

"I've got four kids to feed and not a damned cent to do it with! That dirty, no-good bastard!"

"Don't talk like that, momma. My daddy wouldn't—"

"He's not your daddy! Don't call him that! Your daddy was the only real man I ever knew!" Anger rose to fever and burst forth like live steam. "You're the only good thing I ever got from a man! Ada's father was a woman-chasing louse—the thing you've called your daddy left me with the two boys. Isn't that a hell of a thing to have to remember the son of a bitch by? Two goddamn boys to diaper?" The frantic clutch on Laurel's arms tightened still further. "Isn't it? Answer me!"

Laurel's answer was in her stricken face, but it took that stricken look a very long time to penetrate the mother's rage. Time was frozen. The girl fought to find denial, tried to ask for it, sought words to plead for it. No words came.

When time thawed and could move again, the mother pulled her daughter close to her. Tears broke through her rage. Her own great pain welled and overflowed. It was her own words that tore down the last of her defenses.

"Forgive me, honey. I didn't want to hurt you. I'm just so hurt myself I don't know what to say. I didn't want you ever to know!"

She held the girl close, trying to feel something in the rigid, nonbreathing stiffness of the twelve-year-old body within her arms. She sought for something, anything to say that might help the girl to understand.

"When I found out my husband—Ada's father—was running around on me, I was hurt and angry. I set out to get even with him. That was when I met your—when I met Feodor. He was a Russian officer sent over here to get navy training. It was wartime then. We were young, and . . ." She looked at the girl. "I loved him, Laurie. You've got to believe that. I really did love him. He was so very special—so very special."

The body did not relax. "It wasn't anything bad, Laurie. It was the most wonderful thing that ever happened to me." Tears were streaming down the mother's furrowed cheeks. "Then he had to go away. We had so very little. It was so precious, and . . . then it was over."

The girl's voice was suddenly old. "And I'm a—*bastard.*"

"Don't say that, honey. Don't ever say that!"

"Why not? It's true, isn't it?"

As I followed the adult Laurel's words, fleshing in the details from her cryptic telling of the story, I was suddenly struck by the way in which she was reciting the discovery of her illegitimacy. She was speaking as coldly as she would speak in reading the directions for a new kitchen appliance to someone.

"That's the way it happened?"

"More or less."

"How did you feel about it, when you found out?"

"That's the same question everyone asks." She paused and lighted a cigarette. There was a faint tremor in her hand. "How in the hell are you supposed to remember what you felt yesterday? Let alone something from fifteen years ago?"

I waited, saying nothing. Laurel looked at me as if she expected me to make a comment or give some sort of explanation.

"She kept begging me to understand—to forgive her and love her. I don't think I could feel anything then. It must have hit me a little later, I guess. That was when I first ran away from home. I think I was twelve. I wound up in the Hall."

"You were taken to Juvenile Hall then? Had you ever been in trouble before? Like running away?"

"A couple of times, I guess. But those were kid affairs. I'd be gone a couple of hours or something—one time for most of a day. I'd always take my medicine with me. I had convulsions when I was little. They called me an epileptic. I had to take little red and white capsules every day. I didn't stop that till I was about nineteen and ran out of them one time. Never had a seizure, either. I guess I wasn't really an *emptileptic, huh?*"

"I don't know. You didn't have seizures, so maybe not. But what was that you said—an *emptileptic*?"

"I couldn't pronounce it when I was a kid." The appraising look came back into her eyes. I had the impression that Laurel had said more than she was ready to say about her mother and the feelings between the two of them. We ended the session.

Several meetings later, the subject of running away came up again.

"When you ran away, you said you took your medicine along?"

"Sure. Who wants to get sick among strangers?"

"When you ran away, after the first time, where did you go, Laurel?"

"Different places. After the first time, I'd go farther and stay away longer."

"Did you ever get sick among strangers?"

I had no idea, when I posed the question, that Laurel's response would be so massive. She straightened in the chair as if I had touched her with high-tension current. For a moment she did not seem to breathe. Silence lay between us like a resinous fog.

"I've been among strangers all my life. Even if you think there's someone close or friendly, you find them a stranger if you get sick." She lighted another cigarette from the stub of the one she held. "Nobody gives a particular damn about anyone—not when it counts."

"It sounds as if you have something particular in mind."

Her voice was brittle. "Yeah, I have. Something very particular. In fact, I could give you chapter and verse with a hell of a lot of particulars."

"It's your session."

"Goddamn! You just never let up, do you?" She stared at me for a time, seeming to assay my intention. "You keep throwing the ball back to me. I guess I don't always want to handle it."

"Particular?"

The breath was deep and shuddering. It seemed to be one she did not intend to exhale.

"I told you I was a whore at fourteen. I was taking all comers in a Texas motel with my *friends* collecting the money and managing to feed me once in a while. It went on like that for about five or six weeks—till I got burned."

"Burned?"

"I woke up one morning with a fever of a hundred and four and an infection that just wouldn't quit. Christ, I was sick! Just a damned know-nothing kid. I could have died there."

She snapped ashes from her cigarette onto the rug, looking to see if I would offer objection or criticism. *"My friends.* Let me tell you, doc. They were quite noticeable by their absence. I lay there for three damned days like that. I didn't see one of the bastards."

She looked at me with cutting contempt, as a representative of all men. "I had nothing to eat and probably couldn't have held it down if I had. Finally, the old bitch who ran the motel and pretended not to know what was going on came pounding on the door for the rent. I was so sick that even she had to do something or else explain a corpse.

"She did something, all right. She sent for some damned quack who put me into a charity hospital. I was there for nineteen days. When I finally could walk without my guts falling out, the generous county gave me a bus ticket and told me to get the hell out of the state or go to a reformatory."

"What about these . . . er . . . *friends?*" I tried to match her inflection, searching for some kind of visualization of the pressures that had led her to prostitution at an age when most girls are wheedling for permission to use lipstick and pressing to go steady with somebody. Laurel's vivid and angry description again came to my aid. The clinic and the present faded to another, earlier and more urgent time.

"I learned about hustling men when I was in the Hall. I was big for twelve—almost thirteen. I guess Rita taught me—at least she introduced me to Stan. . . ."

"You and Rita were pretty close?"

"I *thought* she was my friend. She taught me how to be warm in somebody's arms. When I was scared, that first week in the Hall, she'd hold me and cuddle me. She even taught me to get excited, and how."

"She was your introduction to sex?"

She nodded. I could almost see her moving back to another time in her life. There was a momentary flash of tenderness, then her face hardened.

"I found out it wasn't all warm and good. I got my introduction to whoring after we were out of the Hall. Rita went for men, when she could get them. We hooked up with a couple of guys and ran away."

The faraway look came back to her face, and she began to tell me about it. . . .

"Can't we just leave, Stan? We've got the car. Can't we just go? Just get out of here?"

"Baby, you think I don't want it some other way?" He put his arm around her shoulders, trying hard to fight her back from the edge of panic. "You think I don't know? But six hundred bucks, baby. We owe the man six hundred dollars. You know what that means? The damned spik will kill me before he'd let me leave town. You saw him—you heard him talk. If we don't get some money by tomorrow, I'm gonna be lyin' in an alley with my guts cut out!"

Rita lifted herself out of the chair with the broken springs, smoothing her skirt. "Me 'n' Danny already talked it over. It's what we gotta do, you and me." She came toward Laurel and Stan, taking the girl's face between her hands. "Ain' none of us like it."

Laurel twisted her head, ripping her face from between Rita's fingers, looking up at Stan. "Why'd you have to do it, honey? You knew it was all the money we had."

"Christ, you think I don't know that? I've been killin' myself all morning with the thought of havin' to ask you."

"It ain't no big thing, Laurie," Rita said. "After the first couple of times, you'll know that." Her hands again sought to take the younger girl's face, but with the withdrawal she reconsidered and let them fall to her sides. "We had us a hell of a time for the last couple months, ain' we? It's just bad luck time, that's all."

The second man, coming from the bathroom, looked at the scene for a moment, sleepy eyes trying to read the situation. He cursed mildly. "Not one beer left, goddamn it."

"Make a pot of coffee, Rita," Stan said. "This is something we got to give Laurel time to think over?" There was a faint question in the inflection.

Danny did not catch the inflection and barged on ahead. "What's to think over? Our asses are on the rack, and if we can't get that mother-lovin' greaser off our backs we've had it." He scratched his belly with both his heavy hands. "My pants are too tight—make me itch."

"If you'd lay off the beer once in a while, your pants wouldn't be so tight." The blonde girl stood at the hot plate with the coffeepot in hand. "Last of the coffee, too."

Stan's long arm tightened around Laurel's waist. "It just takes a few days, baby. You know that." He pulled her close to him.

"But those things . . . they make me feel crawly." She held his thin face with her eyes. "I never did anything with any man but you, Stan—you know that."

"I know, baby. Don't you think I know?" He pulled her tighter against him. "I even know you don't like it. You just do it to make me happy." He tilted her face back and looked directly at her. "Sometimes I want you to like it so bad, I just go crazy thinkin' I'm no good for you."

"I like it when you hold me. I really like that."

"A few days, baby. That's all it will take. We pay off the spik and get a couple hunnerd bucks together, then we scram out of here and forget it ever had to be this way."

"You won't—hate me?"

"Baby, you're mine. How could I hate you? You and Rita are doin' this for all of us."

"I don't know if I can do it." Her voice was sharp, trapped. "I just can't do it."

He thrust her from him, holding her at arm's length. His face flamed from his black hair to deep on his throat. "You ain't gonna get me killed to protect that precious snatch of yours—not without me beatin' hell out of you first!"

"Let her alone!" Rita snapped. "I'll hustle for both of us if she can't do it."

There was silence, finally broken by Laurel's mechanical voice. "Don't be mad at me, Stan. I'll—I'll try."

Laurel's voice snapped me back to the present. "They were right about one thing, Doctor Howard. It doesn't mean a goddamn thing. Not then, not now, not to anybody—but me."

I had the nagging feeling something was missing. She was looking at me, trying to read rejection.

"Everybody gets sick among strangers, doc. When you need somebody, they disappear or don't even know you."

"Then what, Laurel?"

"I came back to the Coast—joined up with dear old mom and home. What else?"

"You mean what else could you do?"

"I suppose. I came home so it could happen all over again. Whenever Laurel needed help, there just wasn't anybody in sight." She eyed the folder on the desk. "You didn't find that in the social worker's reports, did you?"

"No, I didn't. I hadn't really expected to find that sort of information there."

There had been much pertinent information in Alice Phelan's careful reporting. Referral information and items from the hospital were well documented, but the reported Texas episode was a complete blank. Regarding early sex, there was the implication of experiments while in a local junior high school, but that would have been a year after the Texas expedition. I had verified by ages, and there *was* a missing year between what would have been the eighth and ninth grades of school.

"I never told anyone that before—not drunk or sober. None of the doctors, that is. I don't know why I told you."

"You feel it's important that I know?"

She flared at me. "There you go with that damned do-it-yourself stuff again. That's why I never told Phelan or anyone else." She ground out her cigarette. During the telling of the episode she had ignored it until it had smoldered almost to her fingers. "She's just too goddamn sweet and interested and concerned with me and all that kind of phony crap."

"The question still stands, Laurel. Do you feel that it *is* important to talk about this—that it can help to get it into the open?"

"I . . . suppose it is. If nothing else, I guess I can't go on the way it has been, with my feelings burning holes in me." She sat back, subjecting me to that long stare of appraisal again. I was very used to that, having witnessed it many times in our weeks together.

After one is flooded with feelings, there is often a pause to allow the needed time to approach the subject again. Not for several sessions did Laurel mention Texas or continue with the description of her life following her return home. She used the time quite defensively, taking refuge in one of her favorite ploys of intellectualizing. She chose topics that could lead to debate, making sure that she could shift, at all times, from side to side of the question, guaranteeing much loss of time in useless conflict. When the time again came for movement, she was very anxious and tense.

She began this session by asking for medication, which, as a psychologist, I cannot prescribe. I asked if she wanted me to schedule her with one of our staff psychiatrists to have him evaluate her need for medication. I again explained that it requires an M.D. degree to prescribe medicine, a fact Laurel well knew. Then I asked the real question.

"Feelings getting hot again?"

"I guess so. I keep thinking that somebody's going to hand me a damned bus ticket and three dollars again. I don't like to think about that anymore."

"So the magic pill is supposed to make it go away?"

"It won't go away. I know that. I had a big part in the kind of life I lived from Texas on. I'm sure my own ouches were responsible for Paul, and the way I crapped on him."

"Paul?"

"He's the reason why I left school in the tenth grade. We ran away to Yuma and got married."

"You'd stayed at home? I mean with your mother until then?"

"And my stepfather. Ain't that a bitch? He came back—and she opened the door and took him in." She laughed bitterly. "How about that? She gives me a shit storm—I run away, get canned into the Hall, then come out to find they're back together as if nothing ever happened."

The laugh came again, but it caught in her throat. When she did speak, it was so soft an utterance that I had to ask her to repeat.

"I guess everybody needs somebody."

"Is that why there was Paul?"

"He was just a kid—it didn't mean a thing." She shook her head. "He was nineteen—worked in a gas station. A big, tall, awkward kid. We were only together for two weeks. Three weeks after that we got an annulment. His folks paid for it."

"Is that *why* there was a Paul? Because everybody needs somebody?"

"I don't! I goddamn well don't!"

With an outburst like that, the best confrontation is silence. It stretched to Laurel's limit, and then she spoke again without the heat she had used in her denial.

"When I got back here, and started school again, I tried to act like Texas never happened. But I guess it shows or something. I didn't say no very often. Paul was the first guy who really wanted to date me, instead of just take me somewhere and get me into a back seat.

"You know something, Doctor Howard? I was the first girl he ever made it with. I was fifteen and he was damned near twenty. He hadn't even been laid." There seemed a flicker of softness in her face, but it came and went so quickly I could not be sure. "Big, awkward goof—stumbling into something where he didn't belong." She looked at me again. "Isn't our time about up, or something?"

"You want it to be up?"

"Why not? We're not getting anywhere. I don't know why I even come here."

Again I waited, sensing a head of steam seeking release. Having by now been thoroughly exposed to Laurel, I was wary enough to avoid being scalded by that release. If I were to allow her to displace that anger from herself to me, she might have justified leaving treatment. Her earlier admission of need to ventilate her feelings was not so far away that she could have forgotten or blocked it. A target for her anger would have allowed her to bend time to fit. We both knew that.

Finally, I spoke. "You don't feel that Paul had anything to do with your problems?"

"He was one of my problems. Hell, he didn't know *anything* —not the way the world is, or people, or sex, or anything."

"You taught him?"

She looked at me for a long moment. "I was a better whore than that, doctor. I let him think he was teaching me." Her guard slipped again, for a moment. "Big clumsy kid. That big clumsy kid rang my bell. It scared hell out of me. I left him the next day. How's that for a kick? Maybe a hundred guys before him never even came close, and *he* got to me. That's why I ran out on him. See what a bitch I really am?"

"Too much of a bitch to leave some clumsy kid thinking he was in love with the town tramp?"

"You're trying to make me think I did something good."

"Only trying to understand why it ended so quickly."

"Because I felt trapped! He had family. They had money. He had a chance for something—but not with me. I'm bad news, and I sure as hell wasn't going to get hung up on him. I don't trust anybody enough to let them put me on a hook."

"Is that how it was? Feeling you couldn't trust or depend?"

"That's right, doctor. I lost my wide-eyed stare and child-like faith." Her face, cold and hard, matched her acid tone. "I've done all the talking I'm going to do today. Now, do you want to play gin rummy, or can I get the hell out of here?"

"Same time next week."

"Why not? Time's all I'm spending here." She looked around at the utilitarian furniture of the clinic. "Why the hell aren't you in practice for yourself, getting rich?"

"The questions would still be the same, Laurel. Here or in my private practice."

"Don't you ever get tired of all this crap you listen to?"

"Sure. Who wouldn't?"

"Then what?"

"I try to manage a couple of days off."

"You're a sucker, doctor. I could feed you any line of bull that I wanted to, and you'd listen. Like that *tender* bit with Paul. It didn't happen that way, you know."

"It's your story." I lighted a cigarette, stalling.

"I got bought off! Five hundred dollars to get the annulment and keep my mouth shut!"

"Fact or fiction?"

"You decide. You're the shrink."

"Probably both. I don't think that makes any real difference. If you'd felt you were in the right place, you wouldn't buy. If you didn't feel you were, you'd have left with or without money."

"Go to hell!"

"Same time next week."

The subject of trust was carefully avoided for a time. Laurel resorted to debates, and her deadly infighting gave me even more respect for her intellectual prowess. When she finally did decide to move into her feelings again, she waited till nearly the end of a session—a defensive maneuver that was quite rare for her but is often seen in others.

"You haven't asked me anything about my second marriage."

I shrugged. "Is it time?"

"To ask? Hell, I don't know. Maybe there's never a time for a thing like that. I'll tell you one thing, though—by the time it happened, I wasn't just a kid scared by having a climax in sex."

"You trusted him?"

"Yeah, like a stupid fish. The same thing happened all over again—I got crapped on. I was stupid enough to tell him everything—Texas, Rita, the whole thing. He's the only one I ever told. He used it against me. Christ! He even told the court I played on both sides of the sexual fence when he sued for divorce."

"He broadcast it?"

"You'd better believe it. I got it full blast! I never told anyone I was a lesbian—not officially—until right now. There wasn't a man in the world who knew it but him—not even Doctor Barnes or Doctor Fox. I went to Doctor Fox for more than a year and he never figured it out." She eyed the folder on the desk again. "But *you* knew I was, didn't you?"

"Is that why you're so interested in that folder, Laurel? It isn't even mentioned in there."

I had lost my moment. It would be weeks before it could come again. "No, you stupid bastard!" she flared. "I'm looking

16

for *me* in there. Can't you understand even a simple thing like that?"

She vaulted from her chair and slammed out the door.

Laurel vacated her next two appointments without notice. Like most therapists, I saw this as resistance and the communication of my failure and her anger. Yet there seemed as well to be a kind of fear in her failure to show up again. Laurel had seen fit to make a direct attack on one of the distorted circumstances of her life—her sexuality—and I had fumbled. In openly revealing herself as a lesbian, she had been exposed to the straight world. At some level, she had expected punishment, condemnation, or intercession to relieve her bruised and uncertain sexuality.

The two vacated appointments gave me a luxury unexpected in clinic service. I gained time to spend with the file of Laurel Mount. I pored over it again and again during the time being held for her. I felt confident that she would come back, if only to find out how much damage she might have done with her revelation. From her point of view, to be exposed was to be in danger. She would know an increasing anxiety until she was able to determine whether or not I was to be another "fat man" who would humiliate her.

Fat Man was the name she gave her second husband. He was poorly represented in the file. Laurel had married at the age of twenty-four, and the marriage had ended in divorce after five months. Its timing was consistent with the bankruptcy. Alice Phelan's report noted that Laurel had called the divorce "a dirty mess." The bankruptcy notice listed Raymond D. and Laurel Mount and described their assets. His occupation was bartender and she was listed as a waitress. But I had no clear picture of him for a very long time.

The day I did learn more about the Fat Man was conceived in anger and delivered in heat. Three or four of her appointments following the vacated ones were spendthrift sessions, wasted on evasions that could only allow for an appreciation of Laurel's exquisite skill in the game of parry and probe. This might have gone on for a long time except for movement that was being precipitated by something external to the therapy effort.

Laurel arrived for her appointment nearly thirty minutes

early, spending the time pacing the lobby, walking in and out to the parking lot, chain-smoking, and "crowding" our receptionist-secretary, Betty Garwood. Laurel questioned her for information on all sorts of things and interrupted with trivia designed to keep Betty from her work. While Mrs. Garwood does not make chart entries, she does report behavior she observes as patients await their appointments.

When Laurel came into my office, fury was the immediate thing to be sensed. She said nothing and did not take her customary chair. Instead, she stood at the end of my desk with muscles rigid, staring. She looked like a pirate on a quarterdeck deciding whether to eliminate me by plank or by yardarm.

She flung an envelope on the desk. "That *bastard!*" squeezed from her lips, the words dipped in lye.

"You want me to see this?"

"Hell, no. I put it there for you to wonder about, stupid!"

"You can't tell me about it?"

She shook her head. "What it boils down to is that that son of a bitch wants money from me. I owe him nothing! That's what I owe the son of a bitch, in addition to a broken neck!"

The storm raged for several minutes. Weathering the outburst let me learn that the ex-husband, Raymond, had written to ask for money, forgiveness, and acknowledgment—but primarily money.

"He even had the guts to remind me that I was always such a good manager—and that he didn't get a share of the Christmas Club. Isn't that one fine crock of shit?"

"Christmas Club?"

She had cooled slightly, and nodded. Only a man who knew her vulnerable spots could have provoked such anger. Slowly her voice seemed to soften, and the story came out. . . .

"You know, Red-on-the-Head, you're pretty good at managing the cash."

The man settled back into the deep chair, rocking his considerable weight to throw it back into lounge position. When his legs were elevated by the rising extension, he toed off his shoes, letting them drop onto the floor.

"This chair is a great thing." He held out one arm and she

18

came to him, dropping onto his lap and resting her head against his shoulder. "But how you gonna get us a bank account, too? If we could just get a few bucks ahead, I'd keep you right here and dawdle with you and all these here good things." He cupped her right breast and thumbed at the spot where the nipple should be.

"You're kinda crazy, I think." Laurel ruffled his tousled hair. "Fat old bartender trying to act like a kid."

"You think I'm not? I thought I proved that to you last night."

"All talk. Fat Man talk with forked tongue."

He squeezed the breast hard, bringing almost a gasp from her with the suddenness of the act. His other arm moved to circle her hips, the point of her pelvis in his palm and the fingers pressing into the solid buttock. "That not all Fat Man do with forked tongue." He felt the rising response in her breast, nipple location no longer in doubt.

"I thought you wanted some dinner. You keep this up and all you get is my undying appreciation—and maybe a backache." She wriggled from his arms, moving away. "I've got pot roast and all sorts of good things on the stove."

"Manage money, cook like a wizard, and heat me up across a room. That's pretty good stuff."

"I keep good house, too."

He nodded, looking at her. Then he shifted the subject. "We got any money?"

"Not much."

"What about the twenty bucks I gave you last night?"

"Pot roast, a bottle of burgundy, and a Chrismas Club—I got about three dollars left."

"Three bucks? That's all?" He paused. "What the hell do we need with a Christmas Club?"

"If we put away ten bucks every two weeks, we'll have two-fifty by the end of November. You wanted a bank account—well, this is the only kind the budget can handle right now."

"How about your tips?"

"That's what's paying for that damned chair you're sitting in. You bitched so much about that backbreaker the place came furnished with that I went ahead and bought it."

His face set, then relaxed. "Okay, Red-on-the-Head. Pour

me a glass of that wine and set out the chow." He shook his head. "I ain't never gonna lose any weight that way, though."

"I like you filled out. Figure if I fatten you up enough you'll keep all that good stuff here at home for me."

"You act like you never had it good before."

She shook her head, but he went on. "What you figure to get me for Christmas?"

"By then you'll probably need a splint, old man."

"Depends on how much homework you plan to give me."

"All you can handle—bet on that."

"That sounds jealous."

"Maybe it is." She thought about that for a moment, looking at her husband. "I guess maybe it is. Just that for the first time I think I'm beginning to feel what I want to feel about someone."

"You like me better than Alice or Joan or whatever?"

"That's a horrid thing to say!"

He sought to recover, quickly bouncing from the chair and coming to her.

"I'm sorry, Red. I just mean this is the way it's supposed to be, ain't it? A man and his woman?" He forced the conversation back around the forbidden corner of hurt and onto the main street, but it was a clumsy forcing.

"You *told* me about it—about that gal Rita in Juvenile Hall and how she broke you in to like women better. You told me about the last couple of years, the way it's gone for you. I'm just glad you found out what that cute little butt of yours is for—it was designed for a man. I didn't mean to—what you think I meant."

He pulled her up to him. "You're a woman, honey. That's all I meant."

"You sure picked a poor way to say it."

"I'm no poet. It ain't easy for me to say things right. But can't you see the way I meant it?"

Her body relaxed in his arms. He kept her locked tightly to him. "Let the past go, honey. We're workin' toward a future." He chuckled. "Even your damned Christmas Club. All that means is I don't shoot pool till payday—that's nothin'."

His hand slipped down to caress the roll of her buttocks.

"You just needed to learn how to be woman to a man—to *this* man."

She pushed him back. "Come on to the table. You can open the wine while I get the roast on. Then I'll show you how much of a straight I can be, and the loser has to do the dishes." She thought for a moment. "From here on I'll keep up the Christmas Club out of my tips so you'll have a stake to play pool."

That session opened the subject of Raymond—the Fat Man —and it stayed open. Quickly Laurel sketched in the man, and he emerged as something less than concerned about the welfare of his wife. The arguments were replayed in some detail to about the fourth month of their marriage. Then, abruptly, Laurel veered from the topic and once again refused confrontation regarding him, or any steering toward considering him again. She did not even make the occasional slighting remarks. Really to be able to proceed, I knew that I would have to find some new area in Laurel's feelings.

She had entered our clinic at a time when psychological testing was routine for all applicants. I looked over the paper-and-pencil tests from that earlier time. She was, as her conversational level had implied, of quite superior intelligence. Her IQ, both on our brief test and as reported from more extensive examinations at Dellwood Hospital, was above 130, and showed uniformly high function in a number of subunits. Our own experimentally applied test—the Capps Homographs—showed excellent ability to shift from one idea to another as well.

Personality tests bore out the impression Laurel had given in therapy since her first interview. On the Multiphasic Inventory she showed nonconformity, occasional impulsivity, and a tendency to anxiety and depression. It was, also, a highly defensive profile, but without naïveté. The femininity of her interests seemed over-accented, and oddly enough her suspiciousness of others was not an elevated score—unusual for one as wary and combative as Laurel.

From the test reports, I turned to the physical examination reports. They were not remarkable in terms of systems data, but then I noted that she had refused pelvic examination in four of five physical examinations. The narratives of the examinations were identical—"Pt. refused pelvic, stating recent exam had been made by family physician."

The single gynecologic exam reported showed no condition, infection, or distortion appropriate to her refusals to undergo examination. She denied pregnancy at any time, and was reported to have cursed the intern who had asked about pregnancies in the one examination performed.

The police report of the arson episode that had led to her arrest and commitment stated, "Suspect had argued with roommate over sharing of closet space. When roommate left house, suspect threw lighter fluid over clothing in closet and ignited same, fire spread to remainder of house. At scene, suspect's statement was 'I burned the goddamn place down because of that bitch.' Suspect arrested and booked 11:40 P.M."

Laurel did not tell me about this for some time. She stayed behind her intellectual shield, and added a new defense. For several weeks she implicitly demanded that I accept anecdotes of the condition and actions of her numerous pet animals as material for discussion. She was telling me, in no uncertain terms, that I did not understand people and that she hoped animal stories might not overstretch my limited capacities.

Laurel had owned, and changed, pets in quantity. She provided a home for stray cats, dogs of uncertain pedigree, and any animal with a history of abuse. Her concern seemed to have two functions, in addition to putting me in my place. She could hold therapy at a distance, but also, in the reporting of these animal stories, she was showing how she could foster and demand dependency from the animals and then revile them for having become a burden. She closely identified with them, symbolizing her own uncertainties and abuse in their grief and misfortunes.

How deeply she felt this took time to grasp. One day, when relating the animal stories, she was suddenly talking of herself.

"I tried to kill one of them once."

"Angry?"

"Suicidal. I was killing myself, or thought I was. I tried to take the dog with me."

"When was this?"

"After the fat bastard hung the tag of homosexual on me."

"Fat Man?"

"Yeah. I tried a couple of times before—chicken scratches on the wrist after Paul. But I never really meant it. This was my first time to try for real."

She paused, then went on. "I had some reds—Seconal. I don't know how many of the damned things I took. I put five of them into bits of hamburger and gave them to the dog. Then I took the rest of the bottle and lay down."

"A lot of them?"

"Whatever there was, twelve or fourteen in one bottle, maybe three or four in another." She lighted a cigarette. "I lay there and was getting groggy as hell. I do remember the dog gettin' sick and puking up what I'd given him. I don't remember much else for three or four days. . . ."

"Laurie! Wake up!" The hand was slapping her face. "Come on! Get up!"

Crack—a slap. *Crack, crack*—more slaps. Gradually they began to be felt through the stupor. Again they came, harder and faster in response to the vague stirring.

"Get up! Laurie, baby! Wake up! Oh, God, please make her wake up!"

Arms were under her armpits, straining to lift her to her feet. Some vague word burbled through her thickened, dried-out lips. The command came to walk, and her support fell away from her, forcing her to fall forward like an exhausted marathon dancer of the thirties. Again the command, and the near falling move into the arms again.

"Walk! Come on, honey. Walk!"

"Momma?" This time the sound was recognized. The woman redoubled her efforts and her commands.

"Walk!"

"Thirsty," came from the leather lips on the third or fourth try.

"Plenty of water in the kitchen. Walk, now! We'll get water for you. Fight it, honey! Don't go to sleep! Walk!"

"Wanna sleep. Lemme 'lone."

There was a sudden lurching pull. "Don't be an idiot! You come with me! Do you hear me?"

She collapsed forward into the mother's stocky breast. Pull and fall, pull and fall—they made it to the kitchen. Laurel felt her head being forced forward, into the sink, and then cold water gushed from the opened tap onto the back of her neck. With one hand cupped and the other arm around Laurel's waist, her mother caught some of the cascading water and brought it to Laurel's lips.

She drank, sputtered from water in her nose, drank some more. The water hit her dehydrated body like a sledge, bouncing from her belly and spewing green foam back into the sink.

"Do it again, Laurie! Take more!"

"Nothin' in there—nothin' in me."

"Take more water. You've got to get some water down you."

From the cupped hand, the girl drank. Her retching was not so shudderingly deep. The third time, some of the water managed to stay down.

"Now! Walk with me!"

Arm around waist, they kept slowly circling the kitchen table. The mother, panting from exertion, tried to pump words into the girl to wake and rouse her. "It was three days, Laurie. You didn't call me, and I came by to find out if you were sick. You'd have died if I'd waited any longer."

"Wanted die. Don' wanna live."

"I can't let you die, Laurie. I love you too much! I'm gonna get you well. I'm gonna take you home with me."

"Ev'body knows, momma. Ev'body."

"It'll be all right, honey: It will be different. Things'll be different. We can make 'em different."

The girl seemed to straighten. Her drug-slurred speech cleared for a sentence. "I'm a bastard and a queer! How's that gonna be different?" She staggered against her mother. "How you gonna fix that, momma?"

I delayed a long time before I asked any questions, waiting to be sure she had revealed all of the incident that she could report. We stayed in silence for something like five minutes.

"You didn't go to a hospital, or have medical attention?"

"Not then. The other times I've tried pills, I did. Good old mom saw to that. I've had my damned stomach pumped four times. I don't like it. It's messy, and there are entirely too many scurrying little people who do that sort of thing."

She paused, staring at me with her blue-rimmed lids firmly held open. "Ever stop to think that death shouldn't be so damned messy? Not that kind of messy. How come, Doctor Howard? How come some people won't let you die when you want to die, but sure don't give a damn whether you live or die when you're choosing to live?"

I could only shake my head.

"The dog had a hell of a hangover. I did, too. It was a week before I could walk to the bathroom alone. I either crawled or somebody helped me."

"Somebody?"

"My mother. She stayed at my place the first day, and then when she went back to work she spent all her off-duty hours with me till I could move a little. I was through resisting, so she moved me back to the other side of the duplex she owns, so that she could stop me whenever I tried it again."

"Does she stop you?"

"Sure. Somebody has to do something when you pull a *stupid*. She's a nurse, you know. She gets to me and I either get to puke out my guts or get taken to the nearest emergency room to have those damn tubes rammed down into my guts."

"Ever try to take any animal with you after that?"

"No. It was a silly thing the one time I did try it. I wish I hadn't." She paused, using time with a cigarette. "I loved that mutt. I really did. I was glad that he didn't die." She blew a long, thin stream of smoke at me and laughed bitterly. "So what happens? Within a week after I was on my feet again, he got hit by a car and killed. He was mashed flat, not just crippled, like the time I got him."

She broke the eye contact. When she looked at me again, she was staring through tears. "This is a first, Doctor Howard. You should be very proud of yourself. Nobody has seen me cry since I was about eight years old. Not even when I found out about my father or any other time."

"Eight years old? Long time to go without crying, isn't it?"
She nodded.

"You must have cried sometime during that interval."

"Sure. Just not where anyone could see me. That's something to do when you're alone—like praying. You remember what it says about praying in your closet."

I felt close to something and didn't want to risk the chance that she would shift from this tack. When she didn't speak for a time, I took the chance and reflected what I thought she had been saying. "You mean it isn't safe to let anyone know your feelings? Or maybe that you feel anything?"

"I'd think I held the track record in that event."

"Having been hurt so much?"

"It's *weak!* I don't want to be weak—that gets you nowhere. If there's one damned thing I've learned in my whole stupid life, I've sure learned that."

"So it's safer to trust nobody."

Her tears were drying as she built back the shield of anger that she presented to the world. "That's right. If you don't let anybody get close, you can't get hit."

"You can't get kissed, either."

For a moment, she recoiled. Then tears flowed again, and the angry surge dissipated. Her voice carried a note of pain, aimed at no one in particular. "Why can't they just let you live? Why do they have to make you hurt so much?"

"Like a dog with a broken hip?"

"Yes." It was a whisper, and Laurel continued to weep softly.

A moment had come, and it remained with us for a time to let itself be felt. When there finally were words, I looked at Laurel. Her face was soft behind the makeup.

"He needed me. He couldn't walk and fight his way among dogs that didn't have anything wrong with their hips. He needed me—there wasn't anybody else."

"That's why you tried to take him with you?"

She straightened in the chair, trying for some kind of composure. "Don't know why I cried like that."

"Maybe because it had been such a long time?"

"Maybe."

It was a logical and appropriate place to break the session and let the termination on this note underscore the freedom from conflict. I stood to signal that our time was up. Laurel rose, but there was a touch of helpless distress in her face.

"If you'd like a moment to put your face in order," I said, "you can stay here for a little while. Nobody is scheduled next period."

She met my eyes in what seemed to be a gesture of gratitude at my recognizing her need to gird herself to leave. I felt it essential to head off any direct expression of her thanks, so I thanked her.

"For what?"

"For trusting me enough to cry in front of me, I guess."

For a time, work with Laurel went smoothly in this new alliance. We centered on her feelings toward her brothers and sister. A direct parallel showed in her treatment of her animals and the concern she showed for the brothers—Tom and Allen. Both were in their teens, with Tom being sixteen and Allen fourteen. She was hostile, resentful, and savagely protective toward them.

"Would you talk with Tommy if I can get him to come?" she asked me.

"He needs help?"

"He's on the scene—pot, pills, and huffing glue."

"Hung up?"

"I don't really know how bad. He got busted last week. I think he'll draw probation, but I don't know."

"Does he want to see me?"

"I want him to. Somebody's got to straighten that kid out."

"Does *he* want any help?"

"What the hell does he know? He's just a kid with his finger up his nose. He *needs* help." She picked at the nail polish on her fingers, rolling up a scrap of orange silver film. Finally she spoke further. "I think I can get him to come. Then you can decide."

"It's only worthwhile if he wants help, Laurel. You know that. What have you tried with him?"

"Everything but beating his ass off."

"Am I supposed to do that?"

She went on as if she hadn't heard. "I get so goddamn mad

at him I could strangle him. He's smart, but he's so damned dumb! Wants to drop out of school because some idiot can get him a job where he'll make three bucks an hour. He wants a car and instant money."

"That's unusual?"

"No, I guess not. But what the hell will that leave him with when the job runs out? A guy who can clean pickle barrels, for Christ's sake!" She shook her head, sat for a moment, then came back to my question. "No, I don't want you to beat his ass off—unless you think that's the way. I just want him to find one guy in the know who tells it straight—dope, school, the fuzz. I don't want him all screwed up like I am."

"What does the dope mean to him? How long and how hard a run?"

"I'm not sure. I just found out about it a couple of weeks ago, when he came to my side of the duplex instead of going home one night. It was about eleven thirty. . . ."

The boy was tall. He shambled rather than walked into the living room. Laurel looked up from the couch to see the boy toss his head, laying the unruly brown hair back across his ears and approximately onto the back of his neck.

"Ever hear about that stuff called knocking?" she asked. Her voice was edgy, but not angry, and she seemed more startled than upset.

"Oh, yeah. I'm sorry. Jus' wanned to see you a minute." The boy lumbered on into the room and folded uncertainly into a chair. His face was pale and his eyes red rimmed. "Ain' nothin' wrong with wantin' to see my sister, is there? I like you, you know."

"Sure as hell I know it. Specially if I've got a couple of bucks."

"Naw, sis. I really do like you—really do. Jus' wanna talk and maybe pet your cats and dogs and tell 'em I like them, too." He giggled, voice going a shade too sharp. "Ev'body oughta tell the people they like that they like 'em . . . you know that?"

"You been diggin' into the old man's wine again?"

"Whass the crime in tellin' people you like 'em?"

It hit Laurel then. She came across the room to the boy's chair and tipped his head back so that the faint light permitted her to see his eyes.

"Oh, for Christ's sake! You're stoned! You stupid little freak. What the hell are you on?"

"Ain' no way to talk. I come in here to tell my sister I think she's somethin' good, and right away you gotta 'cuse me of bein' a big doper."

"Accuse, hell! I know! What are you on?"

"Nothin' but a damned little bit of weed. How's that grab yuh?"

"You're talkin' like a swamp bird. You got more than grass behind that." She yanked back the sleeve of his shirt, rolling his arm to look for marks. "What is it? Pills? Speed?" She rolled his head back toward the light. The pupils weren't reacting. "Weed would make you drift and slow down. You're high on an upper."

"Awright . . . I had a couple of pills, that's all. I ain't stoned. Just didn't want to go home and find I ought to sleep and can't. Wanted to talk to my sister—that some damned crime? I take some pills once in a while, or blow some weed. You ain't gonna try to tell me that you never did."

She slapped him, hard. His face went white with the sudden shock. He struggled up out of the chair, off-balance from the tangling of his feet. He took a lurching step toward her. She caught him and pulled him close to her to keep him from falling. "You stupid little jerk! Don't you know what that crap can do to you? You think I can just stand by and let it happen?"

"What you gonna do? Finger me for the Man?"

He pulled, as if to get away from her, and for a moment she tightened her grip. Then she let him go, and he stood facing her for a moment. Time froze for both of them, and it did not thaw easily.

"Laurel?" His voice was questioning, almost pleading. "I didn't mean that. I'm a real pain in the ass to you, I know. But I —I really did come in here to tell you I like you."

She sat on the arm of the chair he had vacated and looked up at the tall boy. "I know, Tommy. It's just that I know where that road leads. Pretty soon you'll be all strung out, and to stay that way you'll deal to some of your friends, then pretty soon you get busted, and even if you don't, you'll blow school and any chance you've got to get the hell out of this kind of rat race."

Some of the protective feelings Laurel had toward Tommy and Allen were worked through in this session, as well as the hostile and ambivalent ones. She found her way to the realization that her true feelings for her brothers were one thing, and her need to be in a role of punishing protector to them was another. She reached the realization that she used them as an escape from her own loneliness, but also that her own escape failures should become successes for them—that they had to profit from her distress in some miraculous fashion.

"I don't want them unsure of themselves like I am of myself," was one of the statements she made, and "I guess I need them to make it into being something because I never did," was another.

She also was able to see the competitive use of her brothers, to demonstrate to all of the family members that she could meet the boys' needs in some fashion, as her mother had never succeeded in doing with respect to her needs. It was Laurel who tied in the mothering response toward hurt animals and strays. Yet she couldn't reach the level of saying, "I mother them." Instead it came out as "Somebody's got to take care of animals and kids."

Tom did not come for treatment at Laurel's urging. When he did come, it was much later and in a situation quite different from my work with Laurel. At this time, he made no effort to obtain help, and Laurel's forecast came true. He was arrested for possession of dangerous drugs and placed on probation. No pressure from the court toward professional help was part of the probation, nor was any demand made that he stay in school. He left school and took the factory job. After that, Laurel ceased to mention him in sessions.

She again focused on animals and their meaning. Where she had previously used them defensively, to keep me at bay, she now used them in challenging herself to know about her need to give of herself. What she had learned of this, almost in passing as she concentrated on Tommy, came to fruition in a single session.

A lesbian friend had given her a new dog, complete with a proud history, several blue ribbons, and a lineage of unblemished champions. At the time she received the gift, Laurel had been lavish in her praise. Several weeks later, she had something quite different to say.

"I sold that dog. Got a hundred dollars for him."

"Was that enough? He was quite a dog, from what you told me about him. Didn't he lack just about one or two ribbons to be a champion?"

"I needed money."

"Oh?"

"Besides, he didn't get along with Lochinvar." She named one of her later mongrels. "So I sold him." She paused for her defensive cigarette lighting. "I was in a bar last week, and a guy said that he wanted to find a Great Dane. So I sold him." She drew on the cigarette. "I guess if I'd advertised him, I might have gotten more. Marty told me she was offered six hundred."

"But you didn't look for a buyer at that kind of money?"

She shook her head.

"I thought you needed money."

"I always need money. What's so significant about that?"

"Five hundred dollars' difference seems pretty significant."

She exploded in the fashion of the earlier Laurel. "All right! I didn't like the goddamn mutt. He was snooty!"

"He didn't need you like Lochinvar does?"

"I needed money, and needed it in a hurry. The guy offered cash and the whole deal was over in ten minutes."

"You're ducking."

She tried to hold the anger, but could not manage it. Her face twisted into a wry smile. "Okay. I like mutts. They need somebody. A dog like that stupid Dane doesn't need anyone."

"Which are you, Laurel?"

The sound of a storm came and fell. I had seen many a storm in Laurel when a confrontation was placed. It took a moment to subside, then was replaced with a small smile. "It hurts when you call me on a thing like that."

"I know. You probably wanted to slug me."

"A few weeks ago I would have. Suppose I'm getting soft?"

"No. You wouldn't let *that* happen. But you do need to be needed."

She broke from my gaze. "Yeah. I'm a mutt, too. The Mad Russian. Russians are supposed to have a thing about tragedy, aren't they?"

"Maybe everybody does."

"Everybody's supposed to have a thing about his mother or father, too."

"They can find ways past it."

I knew that Laurel had read almost as much psychoanalytic literature as most practicing clinicians. She might not have been able to extract all the qualifications and the finest shadings of meaning, but she had intelligence and a real capacity to store, process, and use what she could learn from reading. Whether or not she might ever admit it or feel it true, Laurel Mount was a student.

"So what do you do when you've never even known who your father was? Who are you supposed to beat mother's time with then?" Her voice was rising to stridency. "I've seen some of the things she went for, and I wouldn't touch them with a fork!" She looked at me with a flamelike intensity. "That's where it comes apart, Doctor Howard. How do you make your nice clean theory fit for us on the gay side of the walk?"

"You tell me, Laurel. You've thought enough about it."

"It doesn't work. Not at all. If I wanted a man—even a man like dear old daddy—I could just go out and get one."

"Could you?"

"You're damned right. I did! I really felt something for the Fat Man."

"Sexually, too?"

"Sure. I can climax with a man. I enjoy both sides of the street, remember? Because it's good on both sides of the street!" Laurel paused, and for a long moment there was silence, broken only when she spoke again. "Stop staring at me! Doctor Fox always stared. I don't like it! I'm not some damned bug under a microscope."

"Quick easy out—get angry?"

"And don't read something into everything I do. Once in a

while it might occur to you idiots that some people do some things for no damn reason at all!"

"I'm sorry if I stare and bother you, but I won't let you duck without calling you."

"So you called me! Now shut up!"

It was not a long wait.

"If you really want to know what's wrong with men, it's that they're clumsy and ugly. They've got no softness to them."

"You mean *no breasts*. Is that why you're femme instead of butch, Laurel? To be able to have something sort of masculine that can still be soft and comforting?"

Her look was glazed destruction, ready to burst through its thin coat of glass. I knew I could lose her if I didn't press through this before our time was expended. Once lost, the moment might never come again.

"That's why you call him Fat Man instead of Raymond or Ray, isn't it?"

The confrontation felt right, but I wondered about it the moment I set it up. In this sort of emotional infighting, Laurel could counterpunch with deadly effect. She was a fighter. She had to be an infighter to have survived the twilight kind of world in which she chose to hide. She had skirted this area a number of times, being drawn to the fringe of it, but never without a prepared line of retreat. I wanted Laurel openly to consider her feelings about heterosexuality, to have some measure of the extent to which she saw homosexuality as a contradiction within her own feelings. I wondered if this driving confrontation had not taken me too far.

When she did speak, it was as if she were talking to herself. "I tried so hard. So very hard. I spent hours on that apartment—planning meals, sewing drapes and curtains, and scrubbing it like it was a hospital room. I tried so hard to be right with it." Tears stood in her eyes for the second time in the five months we had worked together.

"It was working. I was making it work! I kept the best and cleanest house on the block. I made do with pennies where other women throw away dollars. I know I was good in bed. Why didn't it work?"

She sat. Her next words came in a whisper I couldn't hear. When she noticed that I was in the room with her, it was as if she had never really seen me before.

"Was *he* good in bed, Laurel? Was he *enough?*"

"He could have been. If only he hadn't been such a bastard. Why do people have to be cruel? Do they get a thrill out of making other people hurt? Couldn't he forget Rita and the way I'd gone before? Didn't he know that it was different? Did he have to throw me right back on the dung heap?"

"What happened?"

"*Who* happened. A succession of bosomy tramps—blonde, brunette, redheaded floozies—even some gray-haired babes with money enough to buy him. That's *who* happened. When I tried to tell him—tried to show him what was missing—he mashed me with what I'd told him about Texas, and about Rita's teaching me that a woman's tongue's got more than a man's—" She broke off and started again. "He called me good only to hustle for him and give him the money."

"And you weren't a whore anymore. Not for sale."

"Oh, yeah, I was. That's one business where you can't turn amateur, doctor—not once you've been a pro."

"You really think you don't have anything to say about who and what you are?"

"I don't, Doctor Howard. Not a hell of a lot."

The hour had taken a different turn from what I had expected. I had been sure that the connections Laurel made would be toward her need to be maternal. I felt she would make use of her need to love and give love to the small and helpless.

She taught me, in the way my work frequently teaches something not underscored in textbooks, that there is a chronology for each person. Everyone has a time scale fitted to his accumulating knowledge of himself. Laurel would first have to show herself to herself as a female. If she could accomplish this, then she could come to view herself as a woman, and then become aware of herself as a feminine woman. Only if this could be achieved, and she could grow firm in these convictions, could she consider herself as a mate and show her instinctual reaching toward being a mother.

Laurel retreated behind her barricades. For a number of sessions I could find only lance points thrusting through any breach I tried to force. Whenever I came close to the subject of Fat Man, she evaded, exploded, or punished me with silence for my effrontery.

She did use the interim, however, to treat me to an education in the actions of the homosexual colony in which she traveled. She taught me the language, the mores, and the expectancies. She herself often seemed estranged and unfulfilled in this society just as in her attempts to be straight. She described the bickering, the frantic and petty jealousies, and the wild imaginings often translated into public brawls. Drunkenness, drug experimentation, and the constant thrust at the limits of laughingly regarded law and customs of the straight community were also topics. Her own malaise showed in her attempts to be at peace in the lesbian community.

"They're idiotic. The things they do are sickening. How they can be so stupid as to hug and kiss each other in bars. Me, I'll dance with them, but to pet in some back booth is nauseating." She grinned, almost openly, for the first time since the savage session. "About all I'll do in public is fight," she said wryly.

I took the moment to ask her feelings about male homosexuals. She met this with nearly complete disgust and her body showed a tremor of revulsion.

"I don't know where I get off feeling nauseated by it. Some of the women are the same way. I suppose when I'm being the quarrelsome bitch, some of the things I do must nauseate some of them."

At one point she told me of a lesbian "wedding" being planned for some weeks later. Actual engraved invitations had been printed and sent, and the "bride" was being treated to the usual showers by her friends. Laurel showed considerable disgust with this arrangement.

"Hell!" she snorted. "I'm not going up to some girl friend of mine and ask her to rent a tuxedo to take me, even though I did get an invitation. The whole thing makes me ill. They've got a woman minister from some crackpot church. There'll be one man there, playing the organ—and he's a queen who'll come in drag."

She shook her head. "I'm homosexual. But those people—*they're queer.*"

Laurel had been at the clinic for some time. I was pleased with what I saw as her gains, but, as in all cases, a constant element of the work of the psychologist is the need to determine the goals of treatment. Not only are there the realities of waiting lists, but, even without work pressure, there is the internal demand to know what it is feasible to do, rather than to hope for some unattainably perfect solution to all problems. In Laurel's case, there were other agencies to consider, as well.

In nearly constant financial need, Laurel was dodging and scraping by with money from unemployment compensation or welfare aid. For a time, after two brief hospitalizations in the local general hospital, her income had come from disability insurance. When she found her eligibility for any of these exhausted, she would supplement her income by brief jobs as a waitress.

She usually lasted two or three weeks on such jobs. Then she would test her employers, much as she tested everyone. She would fail to report for work, or demand some change of hours or pay. Once she drank on the job. Always she was fired. With a formal education ending in her sophomore year of high school, she had no marketable skills.

With some difficulty, she was able to convince herself that independence and escape from her mother's side depended on a steady job, the recovery of credit, and the slow accumulation of an "escape fund." She had always given lip service to such goals, but the need to make the straight world pay for its past transgressions against her had also made her avoid any emotionally complete acceptance of these realities. When she was able, tortuously, to bring herself through to this realization, she applied to the Vocational Rehabilitation Service, which accepted her for training.

The agency arranged schooling in electronics assembly. Putting her good intelligence and rapid learning ability to the task, Laurel led her training class. Consistently, she was several weeks ahead of the others in assembly problems, schematic diagram reading, precision inspection, and the increasingly complex training tasks. She finished all of the projects of the course almost three weeks ahead of the scheduled thirteen weeks.

School success built confidence in her, too. She could begin to see herself as a worker, if not yet as a person. For a time, it was as if she had suspended her other problems in the interest of getting herself set in a job.

What she drew, however, were rejections. They came rapidly, and each was more bitter for her than the last. She had many interviews, but the electronics and aerospace firms did not see Laurel Mount as an asset to their work forces. Her necessary truthfulness on application blanks led to evasions or outright refusals to hire. Less able classmates, with no stigma of a onetime mental hospital commitment, were hired by the very firms that had rejected her.

Her anger came off the shelf, to be used in a fashion that was different for her. It came in self-hating surges of depression. Impulsive and uncontrolled actions became more and more commonplace, and her drinking increased. She began a round of promiscuity in the lesbian community that led her to scorn herself.

"I never had it so good. I'm not depressed anymore, or killing myself with housework or anything. I've got the answer, doctor. It's just good old sex!"

"Oh? We're talking about sex?"

"We're talking about me and sex. I've had five episodes in three days with five different girls, doctor. If I can find another new one when I leave here that'll establish me as playing a doubleheader every day. How's that for a new track record?"

"You've gone cruising?"

"Hell, no! You know what I think of cruisers. I just stopped saying, 'some other time, honey,' to the ones who're after me." She met my gaze with a bitter grin. "Never was so much done for so few, that is, for one, by so many."

"Okay, Churchill. How do you square that with what you told me about the float-easy being a quick way to have nobody at all?"

"It is—but—"

"You that desperate to know that somebody wants you?"

"I don't ask for anything. They come to me."

"Did you advertise that you and Fran had split up? Or did you just want to see if you could play wide open in your own league? You testing them, too?"

"Who the hell appointed you my conscience?"

"You did, I guess. I'm just trying to figure out how it could switch from something you couldn't stand in other people a couple of weeks ago, and be your bag now."

Laurel's reaction was the best cue to the distance our relationship had come. She did not explode. I took a moment to point that out to her. "You at least seem able to look at these confrontations now."

"Maybe. But the way I'm going, it could be that I'm just too armored for anything to touch me. It's a good way to be."

"Is it?"

"You're damned right. If you've got good enough armor, you never get touched. You can play any way you want, and never get a scratch."

"You get tired of carrying heavy armor around?"

"I suppose. It seems to get heavier. I was sick of the whole bunch of them by today. I get like that sometimes."

"Sick of people?"

"Maybe it's that I'm sick of myself." She broke away from that direction, changing her mind. "So I decide what I'm going to be for that moment, and then be that thing. Like putting on another mask."

"Enjoy playing roles?"

"Your education has been neglected, doctor. Everybody plays roles, all the time. Nobody's for real. You know, like that 'Will the *real* Laurel Mount please stand up?' I guess she would if there was any real Laurel Mount."

"What do you do with your feelings while you're keeping up the mask?"

"I'm having a blast, doctor—a real blast!"

"Better practice that role a little more, Laurel. You didn't read that line very well."

"What's better? 'To thine own self be true' or some of that bullshit?"

"What's better for you? What happens to your friends, Laurel? To what people think of you?"

She laughed—a high, derisive sharpness spilling from her mouth like broken glass. "Don't you know by this time that I haven't any friends? The last bar job I had—a friend owned the place. One night some guy was trying to hustle me. My *boss and friend* touted him off in a voice you could have heard in Pomona.

'Don't waste your time on Laurel. She's just a lesbian we keep around to entertain hard-up broads.' The *bastard!*"

She was trembling. Her cigarette dropped from her fingers onto the rug. She averted her face and bent to pick it up. "That's what people think of me, doctor. I'm through kidding myself about that. I'm through fighting over stupid women like the last one who left me. *I'm gonna take!* I'm through bein' a nobody who doesn't fit on either side of the line."

"You against the world."

"You got the picture."

Laurel held that picture for the world to see for weeks. She lashed at the lesbian world, the straight one, herself, and treatment. Attendance became an erratic thing for her. When she did keep an appointment, she usually came late, demanded to leave early, or cursed me for not being able to accomplish favors or answer unanswerable questions.

She chose a badge of defiance, wearing it flagrantly. Her current butch was a black woman. One of the reasons for this was obvious. When Laurel was angry, she sought to court trouble wherever she could. With a black lover, she could invite criticism by others—her friends, straights, or any others she could provoke. In fact, she proudly recited her accomplishments: the restaurant that asked them to leave, where she could make a scene and did; the pitting of the black girl in a hair-pulling match against a jilted white butch from her past; a denunciation of them by a little old lady in an art gallery.

Laurel found conflict a kind of personal stimulant and provoked it whenever possible. She demanded to test the world as well as the black girl. Of me, she demanded proof that I was not prejudiced in race matters. It seemed significant that this was one of the few times when her anger raced ahead of her intelligence. She telegraphed this trap, making it easier to avoid. Laurel wanted to force me to reject her so that she would be free to reject treatment—and me.

The final massive blow she struck to secure rejection was a violent scene in the clinic itself. The black woman brought her there in an excited condition and seemed to be trying hard to calm her. Laurel was alternately cursing and weeping hysterically. She seemed to be approaching a state of collapse. The two secretaries, along with the lesbian friend, managed to get her into an office that was not currently being used. The screaming protests and wailing in the hallway disturbed the sessions of all the therapists who were working with patients.

A nearly unheard-of event took place when my interoffice phone rang during a therapy period and I heard Betty Garwood's voice.

"It's Laurel, doctor. She tried to kill herself. Can you come? We need help!"

I excused myself, breaking in on my patient of that period to ask her to wait until we could continue.

It was perhaps forty feet to the office where Laurel had been taken. I had the time it takes to walk forty feet to make my decision. If I met Laurel with softness, I felt she would have the wedge she could use to destroy any hope of my helping her. She needed to be able to trust my strength as well as my acceptance.

I entered the room. Laurel was huddled in a chair, weeping and sobbing with exaggerated volume. The black girl, Elizabeth, stood beside the chair, her hand softly stroking the red hair while she tried to placate Laurel. Her voice was soft and smooth, as if it had been strained through a fine mesh. She was small, with ironed hair cropped close and skin a deep, smooth brown, somewhere between Egyptian and mahogany.

Laurel looked up as I slammed the door behind me. "I can't stand it, Doctor Howard. I just want to die. Nobody'll let me. You've got to do something!"

"Who the hell do you think you are? Deciding a thing like that? You talk about wanting people to stop hurting you—what are you doing? Right now? Right here? Not one time did you ever have a session of yours interrupted in all the months we've been working together. If you want respect from me to you, you'll pay for it with respect from you to me!"

The crying stopped with a slight, gurgling choke. "I don't want to live. Don't you understand? Not this way. I need help, and you don't give me any!"

I turned away from Laurel to the black woman. "How much did she take?"

"I don' know, doctuh." The patois was there, even in her

excitement about Laurel. She was a black, and she was going to shine me on like Topsy. "She took somethin' before I got theah. I ain' let her have nothin' since dat."

"And she's been drinking for how long?"

"She don' drink much, doctuh."

"Bullshit!" Laurel yelled. "I've been bombed since Friday."

I kept my face on the girl, not looking at Laurel. "You want something done. I do, too. Take her to the hospital and admit her from the emergency service. Do it right now. I'll call and tell them that you're coming. Whenever she's sober and free of drugs, she can come back here."

"I don' wan' take her to no hospital. I jus' take her home." I kin take care of her awright theah. She be all fine, doctuh."

"That's not your decision. Laurel made it this way for herself when she swallowed those pills."

"I don' wan' take her to no hospital. I jus' take her home." She turned to Laurel. "We jus' go home, honey. Lochinvah an' the kitties is theah."

"Lochinvar's dead! He got hit by a damned car and crushed. I wish it had been me!"

"Lochinvah numbuh two, he theah."

"Laurel's not going home," I said coldly. "Now are you going to take her to the hospital, or do I call a police ambulance to do it?"

"I ain' gonna take her to no hospital!"

"I'll have the secretary call for an ambulance." I reached for the phone on the desk.

"Do I have to go?" Laurel's voice was free of histrionics, and there was a plea in it.

"Yes, Laurel, you do. You know that."

The girl, Elizabeth, stared at me. "Don' call no police. If she got to go, I'll take her." Tears filmed in her eyes suddenly like steam condensing on a dark brown plate. "I don't want to have the police take her there." The patois was gone from her voice, and its softness was now applied to a cultured accent. "May I call you about her, doctor, or go to see her there?"

I turned to Laurel. "Do I have your permission to talk with Elizabeth?"

"Whatever you think is all right, Doctor Howard."

I made an estimate. Laurel did not seem hard hit by the drugs, even with alcohol. She did not look unsteady, and her eyes were clear. She had straightened in the chair and was alert enough to suggest that she was not in instant danger.

"All right, Laurel. I want you to take time for a cup of coffee, then turn yourself in at the General Hospital Emergency Room."

"The stomach pump again?"

"That'll be up to the admitting physician." I looked at her for a long moment. "Now, I'm going back to work."

The episode had taken less than ten minutes, yet it was perhaps the most valuable ten minutes I had had with Laurel. I ran late for the remainder of the day, unwilling to penalize other patients for the time I had given Laurel. Strangely, being late was not the usual irritation. I knew that I had passed the trial by ordeal and that Laurel could accept my anger and the drawing of firm limits.

She had learned that a therapist is not an all-forgiving accepter. The demand for accordance of rights to patient and to therapist is an integral part of treatment. When met and accepted by the patient, it marks a significant step. In accepting a responsibility to protect the rights of others, a patient comes to be aware of his own entitlements. This allows new focus on relationships, setting up a signpost in the unexplored and frightening territory of resentments and affection that cannot be fully known or expressed.

Elizabeth sought an appointment the following day, but only after she learned that I would not discuss Laurel with her by telephone. It was apparent that the black girl was concerned, but she did not relish what she felt I might possibly ask of her in a face-to-face meeting. She was on time for the session, well-groomed and showing her anxiety only by the catlike movements of her eyes.

I had barely closed the door behind us when she threw her first question. Her speech was a bit slurred, though it was not as much the Mississippi patois as she had shown the day before.

"Have they tol' you anything about Laurel, doctuh?"

"She's going to be all right—at least this trip."

"She done this other times?"

"Yes. This time it seems to have been done mostly to scare people, but any action like this is serious." I looked at the girl, noting her good grooming, the calculated selection of unobtrusive clothing, and her wary manner. "Did she scare you?"

"Yessuh. I ain' never been in on nothin' like this."

"How long have you been with Laurel?"

"Mus' be five or six weeks."

"You shine her on, too?"

She looked sharply at me, and I went on. "Your speech. Is it really necessary to make me think that you're not bright or educated?"

I offered her a cigarette to break the impact of my question. She took it, lighting it from the match I held, then raised her eyes.

"It's easier than explaining," she said.

I nodded. "A few times, when this has happened, Laurel was making a genuine move to kill herself. Most of the time, it's a part of the package that makes her jab at people—or at the world."

"She's like she's on fire, all right." Elizabeth's speech was cleared of the patois, her voice soft and expressive. "But she is just *so much people* when she's right."

"So where does that lead you? Either of you?"

"Her, I don't know. Me, I'd rather not say." She looked closely at me. "You have trouble with lesbians, don't you, doctor?"

"What do you mean?"

"Getting on the inside—knowing what it feels like."

"They seem to be able to hide pretty well."

"And you don't always know how to help?"

I took the chance. "Seems to me you're saying something else, Elizabeth."

"I'm good at hiding from everyone—including myself. But be assured of one thing, doctor. I do care what happens to Laurel. I love her in a very special sort of way—even knowing that she's just using me."

"Using you?"

"Is it really necessary to make me think that you're not bright or educated?"

I grinned at her confrontation of me. "You mean she hits people over the head with the fact that you're black?"

"That's only part of it. She wears me like a badge or label, sure. But I don't resent that. The good part is that she just can't help giving something of herself to everyone. That's the part I need, I suppose. She loves, in her way, for whatever time there is. That's good for me."

"Sex?"

"Sure. That's it—sex." Her voice had gone flat and colorless.

"Malarkey! She's as much a shield for you as you are for her."

"Ouch."

"You have the same need to belong that she does. She can keep you away from straight whites and screwed-up blacks—all at once."

"You hit hard." She paused and drew on the cigarette. When the smoke came back, it was in a long and seemingly unending stream. "All right. It is a place to hide without having to bury myself somewhere. I give some of that to Laurel, she to me— it's not all one way."

"How could it be, when it costs you both so much? Maybe it's even better for you than any other affair. Neither of you has to presume that it should last forever or that it will end in a big flap. You can be safe for the time being."

"I came in here to try and find out how to help her, not to unload things about myself."

"She's going to have to help herself. If you want to assist, find some way to get her to put that angry steam into building something solid for herself."

"You mean with me out of her life?"

For the first time, I had to confront myself with the big question of Laurel—whether or not she could choose to forgo lesbian relationships in favor of heterosexual ones. I took a long moment to think. Elizabeth's face was no longer a mask, and I could feel her stiffen, waiting for my answer. I decided the best thing would be to think out loud, so that she would not be braced against my answer.

"Laurel almost made it straight one time—but I don't think she could stand to fail again. She'll probably not try to make it in the straight set again. The question becomes, how much can she

44

do for herself and you for her and still be on the gay side. I don't know—do you?"

"She's not stupid. She's got a great deal to work with."

"If she wants to use it. She needs somebody as smart as she is to help her want to go with what she's got. You could be that somebody—but it sure won't be easy for you."

"Doctor Howard, I'm a black dike—a butch at that. Now just what in the hell would ever come easy for me?"

She stood up and offered me her hand. "You really want to help Laurel? Teach her to fight when it's time to fight, and not to fight when there's nothing out there to swing at."

I held onto her hand. "If you want to help Laurel—give her a few stable weeks to try to turn that corner with me."

"I'se suah gwine do dat, doctuh!" She parodied her own defensive patois of speech, meeting my grin with one of her own.

Laurel was held in the hospital for seventy-two hours and then released to outpatient care. She was haggard and pale when I saw her, and the extreme eye makeup was even more startling. Alcohol and drugs had been leached from her. She was holding herself tightly and took a long moment to bring herself to speak.

"What the hell are you going to do with me, Doctor Howard?"

"Why should I do anything with you?" I lighted a cigarette. "Isn't it about time you did something for yourself?"

"Like what?"

"Like making up your mind what you're going to do about work and home and all the other things that create problems for you."

"It's not that simple. I'm sick and tired of trying."

"Try getting sick and tired of being sick and tired! Then you'll do something."

"I've tried every damned place I was sent. I had eight interviews before my electronics class even graduated. Eight! Not a prayer! They never get past the application blank that says I was in Dellwood State Hospital. It doesn't matter a damn what the school tells them about me. Mr. Davis from Rehab even set up an interview personally. I had letters of recommendation—good ones." She bit her lip to keep it from trembling. "Nobody wants to hire a *lesbian nut*. What good is all the training if you can't find anyone willing to let you use it? Who'll let you even show what you can do?"

"I don't know—but you can knock off playing that old accordion. The question still is what you're going to do about you."

"I could go back to being a waitress, I guess. Guy at the bar down the street asked me if I wanted to work there."

She shook her head. "I could go back to being a carhop. I used to be a good one—on roller skates, yet. It was the gimmick— everybody waiting to see one of us fall on her ass with a tray full of somebody else's malts and burgers. I was on skates there for eleven months. I never gave anybody that pleasure."

"That won't work for you, Laurel—not anymore."

"I know," she said sadly. "Somebody would make a crack about lesbians, or some guy would get turned down on a proposition, and that'd be it."

"What else?"

"I could draw another eight weeks of disability, having been in the hospital again."

"You're stalling. That feeds you two months. Then what? Back to welfare?"

She shuddered. The pride that had forced her to lead her class might have been squelched, but it was far from dead. She no longer felt that public agencies were to make up for Texas. I had hoped to see her in this moment, when she rejected being dependent on them.

"You need work—the kind you hack out with the lunch pail crowd—forty hours in the daytime. It should be in a place where it's production that matters, not how you get along with people."

"Great. Where do I find this?"

I handed her the city telephone directory, turning to the Yellow Pages. "You had eight interviews. But there are two pages of listings under electronics—that's a hell of a lot more than eight places. Not all of them can pay three bucks an hour for assemblers, but if you work a solid year for one of them, you've put the patch on that missing year at Dellwood."

"Just start with 'A,' is that it?"

"No. Start with a city map. If you have to go to work for one of the little firms that can't pay top money, you need to make back whatever you can on gas and wear on your old car. If you work close to home, you can take at least ten or twelve bucks a week less than if you drive across the city."

"What if they say the same as the big guys?"

"Spread it out—go to 'B' or 'C' or 'Q' if you have to."

"And when I get to 'Z' and still have nothing?"

"Start all over again."

"I'm not that tough."

"The hell you aren't. You couldn't have survived this long in your life if you weren't able to get back on your feet any time you got knocked down."

She nodded. Her mouth twisted into a sardonic grin, then she let the smile soften. She put the final touch on the rightness of my setting limits on her in our last meeting.

"I was a big noisy mess the last time I was here. I should have had my butt kicked."

"I thought it was kicked."

She loosed the strings at the corners of her smile, letting it spread into an open, natural grin. "Quite substantially. I guess I have to raise hell, sometimes, for reasons I don't even know."

"You know."

"To see how far I can push?"

"Mmmm."

"I've got to get this one myself, huh?"

I nodded. She took a deep breath, then continued.

"All right. I've got to keep pushing—pushing a lot harder than I should—to see if somebody gives a sufficient damn to stop me. I have to know that somebody cares what happens to me."

I confirmed this for her. Her own interpretation was firm and realistic. For the remainder of the session, Laurel began the task of setting herself for a round of rejections. She showed good anticipation of realities, but equally good use of herself in preparing sound rebuttal to show her drive and her willingness to work.

She got rejections—five weeks of them. When Laurel did find a job, she did not tell me until she had worked a full pay period and was satisfied with her performance and her outlook for holding the job.

"I've got a paycheck coming tomorrow," she said one Thursday.

"You're working?"

"I'm a pattern tracer for a plastics outfit. Funny as hell, isn't it? I work my tail off to become a good electronics assembler, then find a job using carbon paper to trace simple patterns onto sheets of plastic and cut it out on the lines I've traced."

She laughed with genuine amusement. "I went on the night shift, so that I can keep my appointments. I've got more than ninety bucks coming tomorrow. They like my work."

Laurel and I were coming to the end of our journey, but I spent a considerable amount of time in thinking through the whole action. As always, I faced the constant question of how much might yet be accomplished. I reviewed the gains and turned again to the case folder, trying to find an answer I knew was not there.

The blind spots that remained seemed to boil down to three: her difficulties in meeting the straight society; her maladaptation to the homosexual world as she was living in it; and the kind of fear that led her to run from her own basic, primitive needs. These are, of course, closely intertwined in anyone, but for Laurel they were the three areas in which she was seeking an identity for herself.

I felt far from certain that there were any major gains to be secured in her gut-level acceptance of herself. Social conformity in either the straight or the lesbian community depended on a stability within herself that Laurel could manage only briefly. If she could gain more peace within herself, she might manage it with less conflict in whichever world she would choose. For a psychologist, this can be viewed in terms of conditioning—the reinforcement of positive moves, the extinction of her unthinking responses. Laurel would have to learn to play a role more adeptly than she had ever done before—when she could retreat to hostile attacking. On the level of self-realization, I reluctantly admitted that her scars were too deep and encrusted for any major gain.

I was furious with myself for being unable to help her debride her scars and undo the damage done to her in the life she had lived.

It was the self-anger that led me to make one more massive attempt against the distortion that limited her life to the things within her immediate capabilities and left her potential untapped.

I also faced the fact that in therapy, as in chess or boxing, I've always considered a draw as something of a defeat. A friend once observed that a tie "is like kissing your sister."

I consulted with other staff members who had in any way been involved with Laurel—Alice Phelan, M.S.W., who had done the intake report; Dr. Barnes, who had transferred her case to me; my current "team chief," Les Daimler, M.D. Gradually, I was forced to be realistic in my expectancies for Laurel.

The case file, in which Laurel had put faith that she might find herself, did provide cues for another attempt. I searched my memories of the sessions, which had stretched for almost two years, hoping for a way to move into the still unexplored regions of Laurel Mount's hidden self. I discarded dozens of possibilities, always with the nagging feeling that I was missing something— some vital point of entry.

The fashion in which she related to younger children, particularly her brothers, and her attachment to hurt animals could not be ignored. It was a kind of attempt at undoing damage, or perhaps making up. I decided to press hard against this barrier, waiting for my chance.

The opening came relatively soon. She had been telling me about her dogs and cats, this time in friendly conversation, rather than as a demonstration of my stupidities.

"They're a bunch of mixed-up characters."

"And they all need you."

"I suppose so. We're a bunch of misfits in that house— all of us."

"Tommy and Allen, too?" I named the younger brothers. "It seems like you're always trying to keep them out of some kind of grief."

"Somebody has to keep them out of it." She tensed in the old familiar pattern, then covered the tightening movements of her muscles with exaggerated stretching and relaxing, sprawling back into the chair and letting her legs extend. Her back was pulled away from the leather, making her body a straight line supported by heels, buttocks, and shoulders. "That stupid Allen is talking about doing what Tom did—leaving school to pump gas in some filling station."

"You don't favor that."

"God, no. I know what it did to me not to have finished high school. I should have, or else I should have gone back and done it, even a couple of years ago. That diploma can be important in getting a decent job. You get nowhere without it."

"What does your mother have to say about it?"

"I live in one side of her duplex. That way I can keep an eye on the boys."

"With Elizabeth?"

"I don't have my butches live with me—at least not often. Usually I stay with them for a few days at a time and then come home."

"Why is that? So mother doesn't know?"

"Hell, she knows. I just don't want to rub it at the boys."

"No static from mother?"

"I wonder if she even cares, one way or the other. As long as I'm there for her to take care of, and for me to take care of her and keep her from being lonely by being her darling Laurel, she couldn't care less what happens to the boys. It makes me sick."

"Mothers who don't care make you sick?"

"She cares, I guess. But she's mostly caring what happens to her—not the rest of us. I don't know about other mothers. I'm sure there have got to be some of them who can do the job, somewhere. I just haven't met any like that."

"What is the job?"

"You mean what does it take to be a mother? More than most people have got." She tightened almost imperceptibly, shoulders tensing and drawing in her belly muscles under the tight sweater. Her breasts leaped, and she caught herself and broke from the straight-line position.

"More than you have?"

"I don't want to talk about that."

"I think it's important."

"Not to me, it isn't."

"You duck that topic every time. Yet I'm sure you've had a lot of thoughts on that subject."

"They're my thoughts, doctor. Not for sharing."

"Am I supposed to let you duck?"

"I don't give a particular damn what you're supposed to do. I just don't intend to talk about that."

"All right. But once in a while I wonder why mother makes you sick, why most people don't have what it takes to be a mother, why it's sickening to see girls paw each other publicly, why a hurt animal of uncertain pedigree is the one thing that gets through to you." I braced her with a direct question. "Why don't you take that subject and move into it? You can do something with it."

"I don't choose to. Isn't that clear?" She sat back, mute for several minutes.

Finally she broke her silence. "Isn't it about time we got somewhere with these damned sessions? I've been coming to this clinic for almost two years. Isn't that enough?"

"You tell me."

"What is it you *want* of me?"

"What is it you want of yourself?"

"I don't want to be a mother, if that's what you're implying. Hell, any moronic bitch who can lie on her back long enough to get screwed can become a mother. That doesn't fit them for the job."

"What does fit them for the job?"

"They've got to *care*. That's what it takes. If they're to be mothers at all, they ought to be able to care enough to see that nobody gets hurt. That's why I don't ever want to be a mother. I don't care. I don't give a damn when somebody gets hurt, just so long as it isn't me, or I don't have to feel it."

"Like those biological mothers who just lie back and get properly screwed?"

She glared at me in silence for a time. I waited a moment, then went on with it. "No, Laurel. It is precisely because you do care that you find the idea so difficult and so painful. It isn't the sex act, or the responsibility of caring what happens to another person. You've shown that with your brothers, with Elizabeth, even with your animals. It's the idea that you would or might fail at the job. That would make you like those other mothers—that's what stops you, isn't it?"

"Everybody fails at something, doctor." Her voice was shattered ice. "That's why they put erasers on pencils, bumpers on cars, and girdles on women."

"Flipping your way out of it?"

51

She set her jaw. "I suppose so." Tears began to gather in her eyes. "I either get flip about it or blow my cork—I don't want to do that."

"That's something of a change."

"You play rough sometimes."

"Yes. You've had a lifetime of experience in getting rough right back. It's almost a reflex with you. That's what's kept you going."

"I get tired of fighting all the time."

"So why keep punching? Not *everyone* is fighting with you."

"No. Not everyone. You're not. That's one thing I've found out in the past two years. How the hell have you put up with me for that long? How can you take all of my bitchiness and not rap me in the mouth?"

"That wasn't the way. You'd have known how to handle that, and you wouldn't have had to hunt for a better way."

"I guess not. Even when I was asking for it, I didn't ever want you to do it."

"The subject is still motherhood."

"You are a bastard." She smiled at me. "You know that, don't you? When I want to duck, you tell me I'm ducking."

"I try to. Sometimes you fool me—lead me away."

"You don't stay conned. That's another thing I've learned. People just don't stay fooled." She drew a long breath. "I just can't talk about it. You're right about my not wanting to be responsible for somebody winding up as screwed up in this world as I am. That's a part of it—a big part, I think."

"And refusing to take pelvic examinations when they were requested in your physical exams?"

"There's nothing wrong with the baby factory, if that's what you're getting at. I just don't like even being reminded that it's there."

"There, and not being used."

Tears welled in her eyes again. "That's right. I'm not capable of operating it—not any more than the stupid bitches who want to be one-woman population explosions. You've got to be cleaner than I've been to make babies and give them a decent chance in life."

"So how do you get clean?" I nearly held my breath against her answer.

"Some of us can't, Doctor Howard. All the fresh-scrubbed antiseptic young interns in the world could put me in the stirrups and tell me I'm a biological wonder of cleanliness and capacity. It wouldn't matter a damned bit. They can't make me feel it."

"And the frantic seizures of housecleaning and painting and floor scrubbing? They don't do it for you either, do they?"

Her head went into her hands. The words came out in a gasp, strained between fingers as if she were trying to grapple them and force them back into herself. "God! How many ways I've tried to find out how to feel clean—to convince myself I could be clean again. Even to know that the filth wouldn't rub off on anyone else. I thought, with Fat Man"—she corrected herself quickly —"with Raymond, that I was going to be able to make it. Wanting doesn't do it, working like a slave doesn't do it. That's why I won't have a pelvic unless there's no way to get out of it." She raised her head and looked at me. "What's happened to me has just had to leave its mark."

"Russians, with a thing about tragedy—and mothers?"

"If I don't have a baby, then I can't be like her—not all like her, anyhow. I wouldn't have to fail in that, too."

"Whoever told you you had to be like her?"

The look spreading across her face was like the slow, formless ebbing of spilled oil. For a long time, it could not be defined as an expression. Slowly it settled into a pattern of bemused puzzlement.

"I don't know that anyone ever did. I know that she didn't—she always told me I could be better than anybody. I guess . . ." Her voice trailed into wonder. "I guess I set that up for myself."

"With her the imaginary mother you wanted her to be? With what the little girl in you *wanted* her to be?"

"Sure as hell it isn't with what she *is*."

"What *is* she, Laurel? Did you ever find out?"

"My mother?"

"With the suicide gestures you made? With the demands that she do something to stop you? With some kind of constant plea for her to intervene? With screams that demanded to be stopped? With running away? *Did you ever find out?*"

"I guess I never did find out."

"Yet she *did* stop you. She did intervene. She did make you puke out pills, or swallow tubes and get your stomach washed."

"She had to. She's a nurse."

I let it hang in the air for a long moment, watching the strangely gelatinous face mold itself through half a dozen fleeting formations as she wrestled with her feelings.

"She's . . . a mother. She had to care, somehow. She had to try to make up for what she did."

"So she could feel clean? Doing what she could to make up for failings she knew damned well she had?"

It came in a whisper. "She did what she could. She did it her own way, but she gave what she could give."

"Gave what *she* had to give? Failing where she either didn't have enough to give or didn't know what to do?"

"Yes."

"Like all of us do? Erasers on pencils, bumpers on cars, girdles on women?"

She nodded. We sat for a long time without words. Laurel used that time putting together her feelings. I could almost see her weigh and set the parts to build a new pattern in those feelings. She still could hate, but she could let herself love.

In the ten minutes left to us, no word was passed. Yet we communicated more without words than we had ever done with them.

About ten days later, I saw Laurel again. She was neither light nor serious, angry nor distressed, harsh nor happy. She wore a dress for one of the few times in the entire two years we had been meeting in my office. It was plain cotton, suitable for the night shift at a plastics factory. Yet her hair was done simply and attractively, and while she still had accent lines on her eyes, they were neither so heavy nor so startling as they had always been.

Midway in the session, Laurel marked the changes in her behavior. "I'm not playing loose anymore—no five or six girls on the string, no setting up humiliating situations for Elizabeth."

"Are you still with Elizabeth?"

"No. We've graduated from that. We're not lovers anymore. I put her through so much crap I'm ashamed. She's a good person, and for the first time somebody I was involved with has become my friend." She smiled in a puzzled fashion. "Always before, when I'd break up with a girl, it was some kind of battle. It isn't that way with Elizabeth. She's a special sort of person."

"If you and Elizabeth are through, have you got a new butch?"

"Not really. I don't suppose I'll ever be much different on that score. I'll probably plant myself firmly in midair, just like I've always done—straight sometimes but more often gay. But I'm just tired of trouble all the time. So I take it as it comes. I just don't want any more brawls or being bent out of shape."

"Sounds like you're telling me we've reached some kind of an end."

"I don't think there is any end for me. I'll probably just go on with my private brand of misery. But I don't think I'll be burned anymore."

"Or burning anymore?" I said. "Or burning others?"

"I had that coming, I guess. I used to swing out at anything that might hurt me, or even that I thought might hurt me. I was pretty much of a bum—to myself as well as everybody. Maybe, if I can be a little less of a louse to other people, I might be feeling a little less like a bum to myself."

"And maybe feel a little . . . *cleaner?*"

She nodded.

In stories of suspense, from Arabian Nights' tales to the current Mystery Writers of America anthology, there are occasionally those frustrating stories where the reader has to form his own ending. The classic of these, "The Lady or the Tiger?" leaves the young warrior at the point of having to choose between two doors. Behind one of the doors, the Princess is waiting to be his, and behind the other the tiger is waiting to destroy him. We must leave Laurel in the same enigma.

She has not returned to my office. I do have three facts to report. She has left the city and is no longer battling with family or with lesbian associates. She has upgraded herself from factory work to office work, putting her intelligence into becoming an accountant with a large firm in another city. She went to the city and to the new job on her own initiative, and not in flight.

For me to draw conclusions, even having known Laurel for nearly two years in the unvarnished, naked intimacy of therapy, would be to speculate and assume. She does not seem so defeated as in her runaway episodes. This time, the medicine she took with her is the pharmacy of her own emotional capacities. I think it will be enough.

I have only one thing to support even this much of a presumption. A five-word note came about three weeks after she left:

"I'll be in touch. Thanks."

*

Laurel had a unique language. In working with her, I had tried to translate and understand the argot of the lesbian world. It was in this world that she had clung to a safe sort of misery. Yet, in her internal struggle, she had been misunderstood in that world as frequently as among the straights. Perhaps, even in such a society, those who do not conform must continually find themselves misunderstood.

All of us seem emotionally tongue-tied at times. When we feel something that defies expression, our trials in speech or action rarely satisfy us. Remember asking or being asked for that first very special date? Confronting the boss to seek a raise? Acknowledging an unexpected honor? Similarly, when what we want to express is anger, but we are fearful of the aftermath, our sputtering and stuttering speech may well be a defense against a sensed danger. These things we can usually acknowledge without severe problems, for our workable defenses restore our feelings of worth. Generally, the stronger the feeling, the more probable the failing of our expression of it.

At best, our feelings spatter our speech. At worst, they can shatter it and lead us to be locked tightly in a struggle to express and not to express feelings. Stuttering patterns and other speech failures frequently have their beginnings in this struggle.

So it was with David. . . .

PART TWO

* DAVID *

Play Melancholy, Baby

HE STILL HADN'T SPOKEN. WE HAD COME FROM THE LOBBY TO MY office, seated ourselves, and waited for what seemed a long time. He had nodded in response to my greeting, risen from his chair, and come to take another seat beyond the closed door. It appeared that he did not plan to speak at all.

I utilized the silent moments to appraise him, instinctively liking what I saw. His face was well tanned and framed by brown hair with iron gray flecks. The planes of his face were sharp, the cheekbones high, and a square jawline led to a slightly pointed chin. His eyes were well-set, widely spaced, and were fastened on my face with a kind of green intensity that was wary but not antagonistic.

He took the cigarette I offered, then spoke his first word.

"Thanks."

"What do you like to be called? Mr. Curtis sounds a little formal with every question."

His face erupted, suddenly losing its pleasing mien. His right cheek bulged, pushed outward by a thrust of his tongue. He set his jaw as if to hold it back, but could not restrain the sliding globe of muscle. The tongue exploded from between his hard-set lips, lashing forward into the air like a wet whip.

No typescript can reproduce the sound that came from him. He intended only a single syllable, but it emerged encrusted with wet, burbling noise.

"Dave."

I suddenly remembered having discussed this case with the local physician who was seeking to refer him to our clinic. When no action followed the referral, I had forgotten about the discussion that had occurred during a luncheon meeting three months previously.

"Dr. Jarrad sent you, didn't he?"

"Yes." The tongue did not lash. I remembered the strange fact that speech-handicapped persons often experience great difficulty in saying their own names.

"That was quite a while ago. I didn't connect your name with the man he was telling me about."

"He couldn't find anything wrong with my tongue." The symptom was displayed in massive fashion, meat exploding and lashing at the air. He blocked at least five times on those eight words. "He says it's"—burble—"motional."

"And sent you to a psychologist."

He nodded, lapsing into safe silence. His eyes still locked with mine, as if he were gripping them in clenched fists.

"You don't think much of that idea."

For the first time, there was a trace of relaxation in his face. He grinned faintly, then closed it off. "No, I don't. I don't know if there's anything in it."

While David showed problems in this sentence, it seemed to come much easier than his shorter speech of a moment before. He burbled only two or three times. With the clearing of his speech, I had a chance to appraise the quality of his voice. Inflection, tone, timbre—all were quite good. Pitch was mid-baritone.

"But you *did* come."

"I'll try anything!" The symptom was back in full heat. "Can you help?"

"I don't know. Dr. Jarrad said there wasn't any physical damage. If he's right, and the problem is emotional, then maybe we can."

"How long will it take?"

"I can't answer that. How long did it take to get locked into the pattern like this?"

" 'Bout seven years—got worse all the time." The sentence was so raggedly distorted that I had to ask him to repeat. The second attempt was almost identical, but hearing it again let me manage it.

"What do you think it is?"

"I hurt my tongue, playing saxophone."

"You blow sax? Professional?"

"Not much work anymore—bands are all shot down."

I wanted to hold him on himself as the topic. "You say you hurt your tongue, but Dr. Jarrad says there's nothing wrong with it."

"Look at the damned thing! It's disgusting!" His body tensed, and I had the feeling David Curtis was ready to leap from the chair and bolt from my office. There had been no distortion in his angry outburst. The words had come through loud and clear.

"You can really talk when you get mad, can't you, Dave?"

His lean face darkened with the blush of sudden awareness of his outburst and its clarity. I took a stab at focusing him on the feeling level underlying the symptom.

"You have trouble getting angry out loud don't you, Dave?"

"Sometimes I can talk pretty good, and cuss some. When I just want to say somethin', then it hits me."

"It's not there all the time." I waited a few seconds, then went on. "That makes this pretty damned selective. If it was an actual injury of tongue muscles or nerves, you'd block all the time."

His reply was a long time coming, and when it arrived his voice was very soft, showing no loss of speech control. "I guess so."

The loss of volume seemed to be genuine embarrassment. I honored that discomfort, choosing not to push further at the moment. A too-early press often entails the risk of forcing latent defenses to become active, and one loses a working contact for the sake of a small gain. Accordingly, I shifted the direction to give David a moment.

"What were you doing when the problem first manifested itself?"

"Working at Space-Tek." He blocked severely.

"What were you doing there?"

"Kid stuff!" He wrinkled his lip, disgust showing clearly. "They called it scheduling. Stupid!"

"Kid stuff? Stupid?"

"That's the way the bastards treated everybody. Any moron could do the job they had me on—writin' down the dimensions of pieces of tubing and piping that go into a missile. Hell, it was already on the blueprints, but I was supposed to make a list of it."

"That's all you did? Make lists of items?"

He nodded again. " 'N' check other lists against 'em. I did that for six years." He stubbed out his cigarette. "Then I got laid off." I managed to decipher his message from within the twisted sounds that spattered from his mouth. "Hell, guys who'd been there since during the war got laid off."

"What kind of work do you do now?" I asked.

He grimaced. "Gardening work—mowing lawns, cutting hedges, that sort of thing. Couldn't find anything else." He reached for and lighted a cigarette of his own, took a nervous puff. "I'm just a goddamn loser, that's all."

"Loser?"

"Just get screwed out of one thing after another."

It was too early to pursue this. I simply nodded and gave him another direction in which to go, not knowing that it would somehow be the same direction. "You married, Dave?"

He nodded, not using words.

I went on. "Any kids?"

"Wife had a boy—my stepson. We . . . didn't have kids." He blocked with savagery on this short report. A hunch grew inside me.

I had decided, since this was a first interview, to play it very calm and cool. However, I couldn't hold to the decision. The logical question slipped from my lips. "By choice or because of something else?"

He exploded from his symptom into clear speech and anger for the second time. "Not from any goddamn choice! Some son of a bitch of a clap doctor made sure of that!"

"You had gonorrhea?"

"When I was a green kid. That son of a bitch just wanted my money—kept me comin' back for almost two years. When I got smart and went to a good doctor, I was all right in six weeks."

"Six weeks? That would have been before penicillin."

The anger that had cleared David's speech gave way to wariness. He looked at me intently. "What we say here is private, ain't it?"

"Yes."

"Does anyone have to know I'm comin' here?"

"Nobody gets any information on a patient without the patient's written consent."

He thought that over for a moment, then seemed to relax, visibly. When he spoke again, his words were only slightly slurred. "Do you think you can help me with this?"

"I think so. How much help and how quickly, I can't tell at this point. I'll promise you one thing, however. If I ever come to the conclusion that there's nothing I can do to help, I'll tell you immediately."

He nodded, then licked his lips. "I'll try anything! I gotta get over this." The tone was desperate, but there was only one example of the blockage.

"Even if it really is psychological?"

"I gotta be honest with you, doc. I still think it's something they just couldn't find. I ain't crazy."

"Who said you were?"

"I'm in a psychiatric clinic, talking to a psychologist. Bein' crazy is what gets you sent to one of them, isn't it?"

"Problems are what get you sent to a psychiatrist or a psychologist. With that speech, you've got a problem." I looked at him for a long moment. "If this place had to depend on the kind of people you'd call crazy, it would only need to remain open about one afternoon a week."

There was a long delay. "What do you do about something like this?"

"First we try to find out what hung you up with a twitch in your tongue—or probably what combination of events did." Now it was my turn to pause. I used the time to light a cigarette and frame the words I wanted to use. "It isn't easy. We must learn to talk in a language that doesn't have any words. What you're feeling inside now, and have felt in the past, is not words.

"The easy way would be if I could climb inside of you and see with your eyes, feel with your guts, sweat with your glands, and react with your muscles. I can't. You've got to tell me about these things—translate them into English, since that's the only language we share. I'm going to have to translate your words into my feelings. We are both going to lose something in translation. But if we're lucky and stick with it, we will get closer to understanding each other."

"What good does that do?"

"If I can know your particular situation the way you do, then perhaps we can determine the causes and the way to handle it."

"What causes it is I'm a goddamn *loser.*" He snorted. "Hangin' on, tryin' to make it in the big people's league, and always bein' screwed out like a kid." He looked at me for a long moment, as if appraising what effect his burbling confession had made on me. "What comes next?"

"I'll see you every week. I'll have you consult one of our psychiatrists, too, and he'll consider medication for you. Dr. Jarrad gave you some tranquilizers, didn't he?"

"Yeah. They helped a little."

"When we get better acquainted, I'll collect a history and write an intake report. Then Dr. Daimler will have an independent look so that he becomes familiar with your situation, too. You'll be having appointments with me while that's happening."

I rose and extended my hand. "Let's step out to the desk now, and we'll set up your appointment for next week."

I thought about David through that week, as time permitted. He was obviously so ashamed of seeking help in a psychiatric clinic that there was a real question in my mind as to whether he would keep the second appointment. I did believe we had set up as a team in the first appointment, but I had no assurance that his view of the value of that first session would be enough to motivate him to stay with treatment. With an ingrained, unconscious mechanism like his distorted speech, it might well be difficult to lead him to do the very hard work of therapy. He was ashamed and despairing, coming to us only because he had been told to do so. He might well run from treatment.

Yet there was another element that could not be denied. When feelings and unconscious attitudes "create a monster" in the form of a tic or visible mannerism that is itself embarrassing, this does not reduce the anxiety that led to its formation in anything like the measure of a "hidden symptom" such as ulcer or migraine. The residual anxiety, along with the apprehension one feels about the symptom, can provide motivation to change. If David could be shown some improvement soon, he might well continue.

For us to work, it was going to be necessary for David to speak. He was going to have to endure the anger and shame he felt in his distorted speech. If we could ease the symptom, he would continue. If not, he would quickly withdraw from treatment, rationalizing that we could not help him and perhaps cursing us for our failure.

This was the thinking that led me to make a direct attack on the symptom. I hoped that some of the things I had learned under Dr. Joseph Sheehan during my internship at the UCLA speech therapy clinic might fit with this unique speech problem. Dr. Sheehan, primarily known for his treatment of stutterers, believes that the psychological "payoff" for having a speech blockage is the relief of anxiety that withdrawing from the speaking situation gives. He feels the problem speaker has fear that grows as he comes closer to the act of speaking, and that this fear is reduced by escaping from speaking. To speak well, or not to block or stutter, either the fear intensity must be lowered or the pressure to speak must increase. It is an "approach-avoidance" conflict.

I sidetracked history taking, moving into an attack on the symptom in the second session. I felt that David needed the encouragement of some gain in his tongue, and that I needed to function as a speech correctionist before I could help him get at the emotional basis of his speech problems.

By the end of the session, I was sure that David's speech problem was entirely rooted in his feelings. I had a personal confirmation of Dr. Jarrad's conclusion.

The session had been devoted to corrective speech exercises remembered from my earlier training. I promised myself the task of digging through my old notes and books to come up with more in the way of techniques for our next session.

"This relearning stuff can help, Dave. We'll add some of these speech exercises to our talks, a few minutes each session. The most important thing you can learn to do at first is to think of your voice as an instrument and play it *largo* and *lentamente*."

"You a musician, doc?"

"No. I just like music, that's all."

He thought for a moment. "I do try to slow down, most of the time. It's when I'm tired or pressed—that's when I hit clinkers."

"What's pressing you right now? Anything you want to talk about?"

The denial came quickly. He claimed fatigue from a day of clipping hedges. I asked a few questions about his work and his quite apparent dislike of it.

"I got good customers, mostly. But I don't like being a yard boy much." His voice trailed off toward the end of the sentence.

"You mean not at fifty years of age."

He nodded. "The old lady whose hedge I trimmed really gets to me. Nothin' ever suits her."

"Old women who complain bother you?"

"When they treat you like some kid who doesn't know anything."

"Can you get someone else in her place? Let her go?"

"She bitches a lot, but she pays forty dollars a month. It isn't a hard place to do. I got to keep her." He paused, and when he spoke again the burble had come back and the tongue lashed. "She's just old . . . and used to having things her way."

"Do that last sentence again. After all, she's only a customer." I paused a moment, waiting. "Use the tricks you've been practicing."

He said the line again. This time he relaxed and opened his mouth wide. The blockage was far less.

I did not press, for our time was about up. The last few moments were devoted to reviewing a "yawning" exercise I had introduced to try to break through his speech blockage. David did fairly well and seemed encouraged. We set a third appointment.

Before David came to the clinic for his next session, I had a talk with my colleagues—Dr. Jeff Dillon, the clinic's medical director, and Dr. Les Daimler, our part-time psychiatrist. I was convinced I had discovered something with the speech exercises but, while I had reached him with one thing he would use, I still feared I might lose David before he really began to move against his internal conflicts. It was going to take something more dramatic in the way of a gain to motivate him strongly enough. We had a rapport of sorts, but not the kind of close contact that could induce David to make an all-out effort.

"What have you in mind, Jim?" Dr. Daimler asked.

"Some way to knock out the symptom—at least temporarily. I was thinking of using hypnosis."

The medical director rubbed his cheek with a forefinger. "A lot of patients ask you for hypnosis. I don't think the magic pill can take things out of existence."

"You know I don't regard it as any magic pill."

"Don't ruffle your feathers, Jim," Les Daimler said easily. "Tell us what you've got in mind."

"If I don't knock out that damned symptom, I think he'll quit. He can be helped. I'm sure of that."

"A lot of people become too dependent. What makes you think he wouldn't?"

"I know. They want somebody else to take the responsibility for uncovering their hot spots, just like an alcoholic can blame the booze. But I don't think that's the case with Dave Curtis."

Jeff Dillon sat back, a slight frown on his face. He didn't verbalize his opinion, but I could tell he wasn't sold on the idea.

"We'd been together about ten minutes when he challenged me to 'look at the damned thing.' He's got plenty of hostile steam, and one of my hunches is that the speech defect is a screen to keep him from letting out that steam. There's enough independence in him to go with, I think." I looked at the medical director. "I can handle it."

"I'm not doubting your ability," Dr. Dillon responded. "I've seen you work and do some interesting things in those teaching demonstrations for the staff. I just wonder about choosing this technique for this kind of situation. When is it that you think of using hypnosis in a case?"

"I think of it as a rifle, not a shotgun or a fishing pole. When there's a clearly defined target and an open field of fire, then I pull the trigger. I think this kind of situation pertains here. May I at least discuss it with the patient?"

"If it looks all right to you, go ahead. Do you agree, Les?"

Dr. Daimler grinned and nodded. "Having worked with this maverick for three years, I'm surprised he didn't ask for permission about six months after he had started."

The staff discussion turned to other topics. I had my permission to move as I saw fit. In fact, I learned only what I had known for a long time—a clinic team is really a collection of decision-making individuals, not an authoritarian structure.

The momentum generated by the speech exercises had made David eager to continue. I presented the possibility of hypnosis to him at the start of our third session.

"How's that gonna help?" The threat of this procedure moved the tic up to the fore, and his tongue lashed out at me.

"Those muscles of yours that don't want to work right. If we can help you relax them, then the exercises can go easier, and maybe even better."

"I don't know." His face was set, showing both curiosity and resistance to the idea. I knew that we must make very sure of his understanding. I led with a question.

"What do you know about hypnosis?"

"You go to sleep, I guess. I don't know much about it at all."

"But what do you feel about it? Tell me anything you've thought about it or felt about it—whatever you can remember."

"I'm willin' to try anything. I told you that."

"But you don't believe there's anything to it—is that it?"

David was silent for a moment. "I guess there's something to it, all right. A band I was with one time was backing a stage show that had a hypnotist. He made people do some crazy things."

"I couldn't care less about tricks. This isn't a stage show. All I'll be trying to do is help you learn to relax and pay attention to the sensations of your own body. You're fighting your tongue so hard that you probably don't even feel it anymore."

"When I wake up, will you tell me what went on?"

"I won't have to. Hypnosis isn't sleep. We don't *have* to block your ability to remember what happened. If you want to remember, we can make sure that you do. For what we'll be trying to accomplish here—deep relaxation and muscle control—we probably won't have to go any deeper than a point where you can let your guard down. We'll probably be more effective if we don't attempt to reach deeper hypnotic states and amnesia."

"What's gonna happen? What will it feel like?"

"Like being very relaxed, where you aren't much concerned about arguing with yourself. You concentrate your attention on your own body sensations and let me talk to you—direct your attention."

"I don't think you can hypnotize me."

"Maybe I can't. Whether you become hypnotized or not is more up to you than me. But I'll bet there have been a good many times when you have hypnotized yourself in the past."

"What the hell does that mean?"

"You're a musician. You mean to tell me you never got into something and just went on blowing what you felt?"

"You mean improvise? Sure. That isn't hypnosis."

"Were you paying any attention to how long a chorus you took?"

"Hell, no. I was just tryin' to make it sound right."

"And you didn't let go that part of it till you'd been with it and actually brought your attention back to the rest of the band or the audience or whatever?"

"It was usually in some after-hours session—when we were just noodlin' . . . or when I'm just workin' alone to try somethin'."

"It's very much like that—like getting so lost in a good situation that you forget all about being hungry or that you need to go to the john or something."

His speech defect had risen when we first began to discuss this possible technique. Now that it was less a threat to him, the defect was receding. The blocks were less frequent, and I did not have to ask him to repeat.

"Okay, doc. I'm willing to try. What do I do?"

"All we'll try for today is to get you to learn how to relax your body. I may suggest moving your arm or something like that, but it will only be to see how relaxed you are."

I took a deep breath, paused, then spoke toward the objective of easing him.

"Put yourself in the most comfortable position you can find in that chair. I want you to relax, and let that good stout chair support your weight. You've told me you work pretty hard, so it shouldn't be difficult to let your body rest. I'm going to start calling your attention to your muscles and how to relax them. We'll just let it come as you're ready for it."

I began an induction, working slowly and easily. As his breathing slowed, I took my cues from the posture and the easing of the set muscles of his face and brow. I worked for about five or six minutes before I could really be sure I was witnessing enough softening for him to be approachable.

"Just stay relaxed and easy, Dave. I'm going to talk with you, ask some questions, but just let the words slide out without doing any work with those nice relaxed muscles. With this much relaxation, you can ease the words out. Pay attention to how easy the throat and jaw feel when you talk."

"All right."

"The questions will just be some history. If you don't have an answer right away, don't try to force it. Just stay relaxed and comfortable."

There were added relaxation instructions, and then I posed some simple questions and collected some history. There was no distortion of his speech, and his deep, gentle voice emerged easily and with the normal flow of air as he exhaled each breath.

David was the youngest of four children, having two older brothers and a sister. His father was known to him only by the report of his mother, who told him that the father had deserted when he was about three years old and the roaring twenties were beginning. They lived on the outskirts of Houston, Texas, and his mother eked out a living for them by dressmaking and selling home-canned vegetables and the milk and butter she could produce with one milch cow. He described in some detail the old house and the room he shared with his brothers. The boys supplemented the family income by working whenever they could.

I saw my patient trying to rouse himself as he told me about this, and I reinforced the relaxation suggestions, holding him in the somewhat torpid state. There was almost no disruption of his speech throughout the rather extended narrative.

"What kind of a childhood did you have, Dave?"

"Lousy. Worked all the time, and mostly for nothin'—just to stay alive."

"Were you interested in music then?"

"My mother wanted me to play the piano. I didn't like that, but I liked music. She traded butter to the music teacher for me to take lessons from the time I was five. I never did like piano."

"What did you like?"

The reply was a long time coming. When it did come, the

familiar lashing of the tongue, as if roused from the inside of him, appeared with it. He stirred in the chair. "Trombone," he finally managed to say.

I took a moment to reassure him and deepen the relaxation again. When the upsurge of tension had relaxed and his muscles were softening again, I asked the next question.

"Tell me about the trombone. How old were you then? . . ."

"What about the other men, David? Are you going to quit working for them, too?"

The boy was uncomfortable, facing the paunchy man in the white pharmacist's coat. He looked directly at him, trying to keep his young face from showing anguish.

"Yes, sir, Mr. Adams," he said. His voice implied a readiness to crack from its uncertain baritone to a pubescent soprano. "I'm sorry, but it's like I told you. I won't have time to clean all eight stores before school in the morning anymore. Not if I'm gonna learn enough to be with the orchestra next year." A flush of pride filled the subsurface reservoirs of his gaunt cheeks and showed them as two red spots. "I told you I would only work until I got enough money put by to get my instrument."

"How old are you, David?"

"Twelve now, Mr. Adams. I'll be thirteen in August."

"Thirteen years old, and you intend to be trombonist with the Houston Symphony." The older man spoke the words in something of wondering approval. "You aim high, boy."

David's cheek spots spread to become great rouged splashes. "Mebbe so, Mr. Adams. All I know is it's what I want."

"You studyin' trombone in school?"

"No sir. All the trombones were taken when I got permission to take music. I had to take a saxophone. That's why I came here to work last spring—so's I could buy my own instrument."

"I'll bet you've got a beauty picked out." The old man took a cigar from the inside of his white jacket, lifting the tiny sliding ring cutter from the watch chain across his ample paunch. An elk's tooth and some other fraternal charm bounced against his stained vest when he dropped the chain back. "You gonna buy that instrument at Mr. Hawkin's store?"

The boy was on familiar ground now. His pride was obvious,

and he could forget himself in his explanation of the miracle that was to be. "Yes sir. It's a genuine Conn—full bell and twenty-two-karat plate throughout. A real beauty. Gonna take me a hunnerd 'n' forty-two dollars to pick it up."

The boy's face was so much alight that the man became uncomfortable with the memories of his own childhood excitements welling up inside himself. He suddenly tried to remember the last time he had been genuinely excited about anything.

"Then mebbe I better pay you more'n ten cents for sweeping and a quarter on the day you mop and wash the windows."

"That's all I charge any of the gentlemen—eighty-five cents a week. That makes almost seven dollars a week toward my trombone."

"Don't you try to help your momma any, Dave? She's got a hard life."

The boy was furious. "Of course I do! She gets every cent I make after school and on Saturdays. I carry two paper routes and do yard work and cut firewood and stuff. I make as high as nine dollars a week to give her!" His temper was subsiding, and he remembered he was talking to an elder. "It's never less than eight dollars, Mr. Adams. The morning work is for me—night work is for the family."

"Lot of grown men workin' for less than fifteen dollars a week, David. Lot of 'em ain't even able to find work since the crash." The paunchy man took a long pull on the cigar. " 'Course, it's better now than it was last year." He looked at the boy with some pride. "You guys who are willin' to really get out and dig can do all right. I reckon you're gonna get whatever you want out of your life."

The older man had embarrassed himself, as well as the boy. Like many another person, he covered his embarrassment with unconscious cruelty. "You really ought to work another day or two and get a new pair of knickerbockers. The way you're stretchin' out, you look like Ichabod Crane with one stocking down in those things."

The boy's face went cold. "I put the mop and the bucket back in the basement, Mr. Adams. Now I've got to get on to school."

Suddenly ashamed, the man reached over the low counter and punched the No Sale key of the cash register. He extracted a dollar bill, extending it toward the boy. "Call this a bonus, since it's your last day."

"Men don't get no bonus, Mr. Adams." He dug into his pocket and brought out coins, picking through them to find a dime and a nickel. He held them out to the man. "Your pay has always been fair. But I thank you very much, anyhow."

The man took the extended money. "Good luck, David."

The boy nodded, then turned to bolt from the store. On the early-morning sidewalk, he ran the five blocks to the music store. Mr. Hawkin was rolling down the awning, surveying the sidewalk David had swept two hours before.

"Morning, David," he said quietly. "Come back for another look?"

"No, sir. I've got somethin' different in mind." The boy plunged on, amazed at his own boldness. "I was thinkin'. I'm gonna be needing trombone books and symphony scores, too. I would like to keep on workin' for you mornings, so that I can earn them. If you'll let me go on keepin' your store swept out—if I could keep the store key—I could come here just like always, clean up the store and have a place to practice for a couple of hours before I had to go to school, and before you came to open up."

"We might be able to work out something like that."

"If I was to mop free, and polish the instruments you have on display once a week, you'd be gettin' the same service for sixty cents that you pay eighty-five for now. If polishin' the horns is worth forty cents a week, then I could trade you for a dollar's worth of books and scores, couldn't I?"

"Well, now, I don't know." The man's pride was obvious.

"You'd be havin' your profit on the things I traded for, too. That would maybe make it stay at eighty-five cents of actual cost to you, and you'd get the instruments polished, too."

"You got a pretty good head, David. I reckon when you get a little older I'll have a job for you in this music emporium. I'd like to have one salesman as excited about music as you are." He grinned at the boy. "Now, do you want to see that Conn Band-master with the fourteen-inch bell again?"

"No, sir. I want to give you somethin' on it and come in with the rest of the money this very afternoon. I want it all to be businesslike and proper." The boy's face was flushed and triumphant with having found a way to get his music as well as his instrument.

"You're my first customer today, David. I better treat you real good."

The pair walked into the store, past the counter top through whose well-polished glass the Jew's harps and harmonicas could be seen. The boy turned out his pocket, letting the change and the one crumpled bill spill onto the glass. Reverently, he counted it out, then pocketed one nickel.

"That's six seventy-five, Mr. Hawkin. I got the other hundred and thirty-five at home. I'll bring it in this afternoon when I come to pick up the trombone. That'll probably be about five thirty, when I've finished carryin' my papers."

"I'll be here, David. We're open till six." The thin man busied himself with writing a receipt describing the terms of the sale. When he handed it to the boy, David read it carefully, folded it, and put it into the pocket of his shirt.

It was that folded piece of paper that sustained him through the longest of days. He would open it, as tenderly as he would later have opened a love letter, look at it, then refold it gently. It often covered the printed text of his American history book, and the scene from *A Midsummer Night's Dream*, the assignment designed to ready seventh-year students for the appearance of full-scale Shakespearean plays in the years to come.

The hours seemed to drag. But for the resurgent glow with which he looked at the receipt, the whole day would have taken David a dozen years to endure.

With the final bell, he was gone from the classroom, dashing over the oiled wood floors, down the stairs, and across the playground. He forced-marched the suddenly beautiful streets of Houston, aimed like a one-boy infantry attack on the weatherbeaten five-room frame house that held his treasure.

He saw the men on the roof, and the bundles of shingles. The ring of their hammers kept time with his hurrying pace. The thing they were doing was helping him hurry, he thought.

He exploded into the house, past the dressmaker forms his mother used in plying her underpaid craft, making for the bedroom he shared with his two brothers. He yanked open his drawer of the old bureau, extracting the one-pound tin can with the tight-fitting lid.

Lightning flashed behind his eyes, and the heavy hammer mashed at his entrails. The can was light—terribly light. He reeled back onto the edge of his single bed.

He didn't look at his mother, nor at the tobacco can. She stood framed in the doorway, the light behind her. He remembered being glad that he could not see her face.

"I took the money, Davey. We have to fix the roof and put food on the table."

"But, momma—"

"But, nothing. Last week when it rained, your brothers' bed got soaked, and the water seeped downstairs and ruined ten pounds of flour in the bin in the kitchen." She looked at the shattered boy. "We've all got to live, Davey. What we want and what we can have are two different things."

He looked at her, feelings rioting within and through his body. Shock was first, but quickly gave way to rage.

"It's not *fair!* It isn't fair at all!" Tears flooded into his eyes. David felt ashamed of them. Ashamed that he could not maintain control. *"You stole my money!"*

"Stop that!" Her voice cut like a whip. She crossed toward him to stand at the edge of the bed. He lunged away, standing at a distance, but her tone forced him to look at her.

She was lean, and her weathered face was a mask of pain, so hard-set that the muscles along her sharp jaw vibrated like guitar strings. It looked as if the skin of her drawn face was flickering with flashing lights under its surface.

"You think I *wanted* to take it? Don't you think I realize what it meant to you? How hard you'd worked?"

He plunged ahead in fury, fighting with everything he had, unreasoning of any cost, sealed against any rational argument. "What about my word? I gave Mr. Hawkin my *word* that I'd buy that trombone!" His voice dropped low and slashing. "You shamed me, momma. You made me out a *liar!"*

She sank onto the edge of the bed. "Go ahead, Davey. I did what I had to do, but you've got a right to yell at me." Tears exuded from the broken iron of her own eyes. "I'll try to explain to Mr. Hawkin, but you'll never feel the same about me again, I know." A tear coursed down her right cheek. "I can't even lie to you. Can't even say there's a way I can make it up to you. But it had to be done. We're a family—me and my boys. That's all that counts with me."

He spit the words at her. "You and your boys? You don't even count Marilyn? She's your daughter, ain't she? Or is it only Paul and Clarence and me that can work and give you things?

"We get out and bust our asses with paper routes and lawn jobs or whatever we can do to give you money. Some weeks you get as much as fifteen dollars from us. You leave Marilyn out 'cause she's only a girl and can't make no money? Ain't we entitled to somethin' for ourselves? You gotta cut our guts out, too?" His uncertain voice broke into soprano, adding to his fury.

He reached for the final insult. "No wonder dad ran away from you!"

He broke off, beyond rage, beyond speech, beyond awareness.

Her congealed face collapsed. David had to watch it as it dissolved into a formless thing. She stared at the boy as if she had never seen him before, arms folded across her chest, gnarled fingers clutching at her emaciated breasts. The stare was long, wordless, indescribable. When she could stand it no longer, she turned, falling, burying her face in the bed.

David's rage could not endure. The fire of his anger died in a torrent of remorse. He moved toward her, throwing himself onto the bed beside her, arms grappling for her heaving shoulders.

"I'm sorry, momma. I'm sorry. I didn't . . ."

He clutched at her shoulders, trying to hold her together.

"I love you, momma. Don't hate me for what I said. Don't hate me for being mad. I didn't mean it. Momma—I'm sorry."

The session was nearly over. In fact, it was five minutes into the next period. I knew it would take at least another five minutes to ease the musician back up through the mild drowsiness that follows a hypnotic state. I had many questions to ask, but would have to defer them. There was one I would have to ask, however.

"Did you ever play a trombone, Dave?"

"I went on with the sax. Never did anything with a 'bone.

I got interested in dance music. I was makin' ten dollars a night, playin' locals during that summer."

"Locals?"

"Little band jobs—dances and pavilion stuff—around the Houston area."

"You were thirteen?"

"Yeah."

"All right, David. Next time we'll talk some more like this. Right now I want you to feel the deeply relaxed state you are in, then begin coming back up out of it, like you were climbing a flight of stairs. Let your muscles firm up and be ready to wake up. For a few moments you may be a little drowsy, but that will pass, and you'll awake to be yourself in every way, feeling rested and completely awake."

I roused him, taking a few moments to be sure he was ready to relinquish the hypnotic state before I counted him awake.

"How do you feel, Dave?"

"Good," he yawned. "You ought to bottle this stuff."

"You liked the feeling?"

"Yeah."

"Good. That will make it easier next time, so that you can just drift right down into that deep easy feeling you experienced a moment ago."

We set the next appointment before David left the office. I was still later with my next appointment, taking a moment to think through the scene he had relived in this first hypnotic session. Perhaps I was remembering my own boyhood and a project I had wanted as badly as David had wanted his trombone. It is difficult to shrug off the memory of the first real goal one has sacrificed to obtain.

A week later, when I saw him, he wanted to concentrate on speech exercises. "My wife says I'm talking better," he said. "I want some more of whatever that can do." Fewer than the usual number of blockages were in the first sentence.

"All right. We can do both the speech exercises and the deep relaxation. If we can focus your attention on the tiny bit of time when you feel a block coming on, you could perhaps find a way to ease yourself around it."

We worked through an induction, using about the same amount of time as in the first session. When David was deeply relaxed, I went ahead.

"You say your wife is noticing an improvement?"

"Yeah."

"You've been married since when?"

"Since thirty-eight when I was nineteen."

"Is she a musician, too?"

"No. She liked to dance, and likes music. Used to come to the ballroom when I was with a house band. We got acquainted there." He paused a moment. "That was the closest to a steady job I ever had in the band business. We had seven months of Friday, Saturday, and Sunday nights, and two weeks of a marathon dance contest. We worked every night and afternoon, then— twelve hours."

"You'd alternate with another band?"

"No. They played records from 2 A.M. till 2 P.M., then we came on."

"How'd you like that?"

"I liked the money." He sat for a moment, and his face twisted with the memory. "But I sure don't like seeing people used up like whipped animals, just so some bastard can make money."

"Your wife didn't enter the marathon, did she?"

"Hell, no!" He accented the denial. "She thought it was silly —like most of us. But it was a job, and in 1937 jobs didn't come easy for anybody."

"How long did you two go together?"

"Two years—maybe a little over."

"Lean years, thirty-seven and thirty-eight, weren't they?"

"One hell of a lot of good musicians were out of work." He tried the next sentence and the tongue lashed. "Better'n me. I was lucky to be able to hold on to what I had."

I could not help noticing that when David talked of being bested by another musician, there was an intense pressure on him. I deepened the relaxation with some reinforcing suggestions, urging him to put himself at ease and to use the speech tricks we had been practicing. He twisted his body in the chair, easing legs and hips.

"When you got married, Dave, were you still supporting your mother?"

"Some. I had to stay with her for almost four months after Stell and I were married." There was another marked explosive movement of the tongue.

I deepened the state still further, using more time than before. When he had finally eased and was approaching the depth he had achieved in our first session, I went on with the questions.

"You took your bride home to mother?"

"In a pig's ass! My mother wouldn't even let me bring her so that they could meet! Stell had to live with her folks and I stayed with my mother till I could get enough money to rent a place of our own."

"Your mother wouldn't *meet* your wife?"

"She *never* did." The plug was pulled, and words flowed from David in a torrent of uncluttered and rapid speech. "It was always that way. Paul, my brother, tried to bring his girl home when he was nineteen. Mother just ran into the bedroom crying. She never would come out, and she didn't talk to Paul for almost three months.

"She wouldn't even talk about our dating or having homes of our own—hated to even hear anything like that. She wouldn't even let us go talk to anybody. I got a dose of clap when I wasn't quite seventeen because I didn't know a goddamn thing!"

He stirred in his chair, and it took quite a while to slow his breathing and return him to the relaxed state. The flush in his gaunt cheeks was a long time in receding. When it finally disappeared, he went on, in a voice that was flat and dispassionate.

"Mother died in fifty-eight. Stell and I had been married for twenty years, and in all that time they had never once talked to each other. She never talked to Paul's wife, either. Clarence never married, and Marilyn killed herself when she was twenty-six. That's the way things were with my family."

"Did you ever face your mother about meeting your wife?"

"Yeah. She just wouldn't listen. Then she'd run away to the bedroom cryin', and I'd have to leave feelin' like a son of a bitch."

"Her not meeting Stell must have made you mad as hell."

"I got used to it, I guess. The night she died, I went out on the patio. I cried for a while, then found myself cussing a blue streak. I didn't even know what I was doing. I busted up a picnic table."

It was coming too fast, and too soon. I deepened the hypnotic state, using most of the remaining time to lever him down into a quiescent state where I could hope for the amnesia I had so confidently told him we probably would not need.

He was far from a fully trained subject. I did not know to what extent he was going to have to react to the early disclosure. The sister's suicide, the estrangement by the mother's punishing exclusion—these were deep scars. When he was in a fairly deep state, I suggested that his memory for the session would be fuzzy and that he would quickly forget by thinking of the progress we had made with his speech flow. He slid into a highly torpid state, and I brought him up slowly and easily.

When next we met, there was a marked regression in David's speech. The blockages were nearly as severe as when we had first met. His jaw muscles were tight and the tongue lashed with almost the savage frequency of his initial session. He had been rubbed on long-painful sores, and was punishing me in the only way he could accept—by showing me that our progress was reversible.

I did not use or suggest hypnosis in this session. In fact, the next two sessions were spent in reviewing the articulation exercises and calling his conscious attention to the sensations in his tongue and jaw muscles. The fact that he wanted the improvement he had thrown back into my face was apparent by the end of the second of these sessions, when he had regained the fairly good level of speech we had developed through the first hypnotic session. Apparently David had integrated the insights, however vague, of the explosive session, and had gone back to work again.

To make sure we didn't press too far and too fast again, I decided to stay with his musical development, letting him put articulation practice to work in giving me more details of his history.

"You traveled with some of the big bands, didn't you, Dave?"

"A few. None of the real big ones, like Dorsey or Miller or Shaw. Biggest one I was with was Mel."

"Mel Miner and His Music in a Major Key?"

He grinned. "Ain't that a silly damned title? Yeah. I was with him in thirty-nine and forty."

"Did Stell travel with you?"

"Most of the long tours. I didn't take her on short swings or one-nighters. She had to stay home with the kid, anyhow."

"You two had a child?"

"No. She'd been married before, when she was eighteen. It lasted a couple of months, and the guy took off when she became pregnant. By the time we got married, she had a two-year-old boy." The block came on the next sentence. "We never had kids —that's another thing that quack of a clap dotor fixed for me. I'm sterile."

"How do you and the boy get along?"

His reply was slow. "Okay, I guess. We're closer now that he's a man than when he was little."

"What do you mean?"

"Stell never let me correct him on anything. He got to be pretty spoiled—between her and her mother. Her mother would keep him when Stell was on the road with me."

"Did he ever travel with you?"

"Maybe one or two trips in the summers, when the money was long enough that Stell could manage it. Of course, he had to be in school during the rest of the year, anyhow, so he was with Agnes—Stell's mother."

"How did you and Agnes get along?"

"Pretty good. I get along with her a hell of a lot better'n I did with my own mother. At least, she'll talk with you." He stiffened in his chair. "How about some more exercises?"

The remainder of the session was used in practice on words and phrases that were "Jonahs" and could trigger the blockage.

I resumed combination tactics in the next several sessions with David. Hypnosis and speech exercises were reducing the symptom from a constant feature to an occasionally troublesome distortion. The gains we were able to make were improving the trust David was developing in my ability to handle and help the problem.

I still steered him away from the topic of his mother, holding him in the present situation whenever I could. He had a present need, however, to reminisce about the band business. I learned in one of these sessions how much value he placed on his ability to perform well.

It was in a moderately deep state of hypnosis, where there was only rare cluttering of his speech. We had been discussing one of the bands in which he had worked.

"What outfit did you like best?"

"From what standpoint? Mel Miner had the best musicians, but he kept his men in a box. I took care of the arrangements, but he would only let me do canned ones. He paid extra for scoring and arranging the stuff, but it all had to come out the same —sort of bush-league Garber. I liked a little outfit you probably never heard of—Johnny Heller."

"Johnny Heller and the Imps?"

"I'll be damned! You do know."

"He was in El Paso when I got leave one weekend. Playing the ballroom at the Bowie Hotel. That's where I remember him."

"When was that?"

"Forty-two. I was at Pecos Army Air Base then."

"I was there," David said. "It was the last gig I worked before I went into the army."

"You guys really got things movin' that night. Nobody wanted to go home."

"With Heller, that could have been almost any night. That's why I liked being with him so much. The guys would go on as long as there was anyone around to listen, or maybe just make it for themselves." He smiled in remembrance, tiny wrinkles snapping themselves around his closed eyes, lips easing into a grin. "With the amount of stuff in those horn cases, it's a wonder we're not still there."

"Stuff?"

"Marijuana, mostly. Some benzedrine once in a while. Hell, a lot of guys on the band circuit were using. It was no big thing."

"Ever use anything hard?"

"No. Damned few musicians did in those days. Bennies and marijuana weren't anything like today. Now every kid on the block is takin' whatever he can get his hands on. Then, it just was a sometimes thing—not a crutch like it is now."

"How'd you get it?"

"Some guy on the outgoing band would set up somebody comin' in—some local contact. No big business, just 'a guy knows a guy' stuff."

"How come you used it? Prop you up some?"

"Nothin' like that. Just a way to relax after fourteen hours on a bus, or maybe a way to stay awake on the bandstand." David thought a moment. "Maybe that's not all. It smooths out my delivery, I think. I can play better."

"You really believe that? Do you really think somebody who loves music like you needs anything except a good arrangement and a feel?"

"I didn't used to need anything. Now, I'm old. With a bean or two, I don't tire out so quick, and I have more confidence."

"You're still using, then?"

"I don't mess around with pot. It's too dangerous if you get caught with it. In the thirties and forties, nobody made anything out of it. Kids didn't even know what it looked like. Hell, somebody even took the word out of the song, 'La Cucaracha,' that's how scared the world is now."

"You can get your ass busted for pills, too," I reminded him.

"Not under prescription. Mine are."

"Marijuana was legal till 1937, anyhow—not even defined under the law."

"Sure, make somethin' illegal and everybody wants some."

"You said benzedrine gave you confidence. Hell, Dave, you're a pro with lots of experience—even in arranging. How come you feel you need that crap to make it better?"

"I'm all right without anything—till some guy who can really chew his way through a reed bites into somethin' I can't match." He lighted a cigarette. "That's hell—a note or a phrase I can't match. Then I don't feel I make it worth a shit."

"You feel he's out to cut you down?"

"Naw. He just wants to make music. I just don't like to think somebody's better." His face set. He struggled against the hypnoidal state. His speech block had come again, fairly severely.

"Just stay right there, Dave. Nice and relaxed. Stay in that drowsy state and let it all smooth out. Let your breathing go back, slow and natural."

"I froze up completely once. Got up to play a goddamn solo and couldn't blow a note. Had the spotlight on me and every goddamn thing. I went blank, doc. Absolutely blank!" He rolled in the chair, and I thought he was going to lift himself right out of his light state of hypnosis. I was going to deepen the state when he went on. "Then, a couple of years later, my tone slipped from what I wanted it to be. That's when I started really using any boost that I could get.

"Till that happened to me, I usually had enough juice to just keep going without bein' too tired. I suppose the couple of bennies I use just helped me over a rough spot. I've used one or two every time I've worked since then."

"Ever freeze again?"

"No. I think I came close one time, when the same reed man was in the house. He sat in with us. Maybe you've heard of him —Gary Thompson? I really bitched up some solos that night. He's got a real come-get-it tone."

"Good reed man, all right. Used to be with Al Harner, didn't he?"

Dave nodded. "He had a tone, like Matt Morgan did on trumpet. Ever hear Matt go?"

"Yeah. I liked what I heard, too."

"We worked together for almost four years with Miner. He's here in town. I see him once in a while."

"He's here in town?"

"When he isn't doing records or studio band jobs. And you're right, doc. He places right up there with James, Hackett, and Berigan."

"Were you cut down by Gary sitting in?"

"He didn't intend it to be that way. But he's just that good. I—I guess I like to think I'm somethin' and it hurts to get reminded that I'm not." His voice dropped lower. I had to strain to hear the next sentence. "I just wish I could have done my own job that night. Maybe I'd have felt like I had some balls."

I worked him up gently from the hypnotic state. Our time was nearly up, and I wanted to get in a few questions to check his reaction without the slightest fog hypnosis might leave in his memory. He came out and stretched, lolling in the chair.

84

"I don't get that much rest in bed. Feels good. I talk better, too, don't I?"

"Considerably." I offered him a cigarette, lighting one for myself. Then I posed the first question. "What would you think about my using a tape recorder, so that you could hear the difference in your speech in and out of hypnosis?"

"All right with me, doc. I got a tape of myself from before I had any problem with this damned tongue. It ain't too bad, if you like to hear drunks talk. I can bring that for you to hear, if you want."

"Fine. Sometime, if there's a chance, I'd like to hear you play, too."

"Here?" His voice was incredulous.

"No. I mean sometime when you're playing some local job."

His nose wrinkled. "I work with some pretty crummy outfits —little combos—most weekends. Let me give you a call sometime when I know who's gonna be with me on a date. Right now, everybody wants guitars and amplifiers—and most of the kids who claim to handle the box are pretty lousy musicians."

"You like classical music?" I dropped the question lightly, almost as an afterthought.

"Most all of it. I studied symphony scores from the time I was about eleven. The only composer who sounds phony to me is Beethoven."

"Phony?"

"Forced, I guess. Not genuine—like Bach, Schumann, Mozart. They said things you could feel."

When David was speaking of music, there was a marked difference in the amount of blocking. The closer the topic came to himself or his family, the more severe the symptom became. From the time I had roused him, his jaw had locked and his tongue exploded only two or three times. Some of his sounds were slurs, but the grimace and the full-scale distortion had not occurred.

"Any music a man can feel is good music," he concluded.

My strongest ally in dealing with David was that part of himself which was aware of the tremendous cost of his symptom.

He was like a man who has painted himself into a corner and is faced with the prospect of either getting his feet sticky or spending the remainder of his life on a tiny, separated space that will allow him no freedom of movement or open contact with others. His lashing tongue whipped back those who might try to reach him, insuring his lonely isolation.

Yet arrayed against us was the cost he would have to pay to forgo the symptom. Good speech would carry no guarantee of any improvement in his home, personal, occupational, or performance life. His most fluent language would not let him express his pain, especially his anger, in the way that he could express it by forcing people to shun contact with him. The few who did remain for him—his wife and the trumpet player, Matt Morgan—were too valuable for him to risk. What feeling he could express to them with the instrument of his voice was a heavily muted sound—a scream reduced to a whisper.

I got the chance to meet Matt Morgan, but not through David. Without the signed consent of a patient, no contact is made with friends or relatives, no matter how valuable that contact would be.

My opportunity to meet his friend came later, through an entirely unexpected channel. The coincidence occurred when my friend Tommy Andrews, a horn man of the big-band days now teaching music in a local high school, invited me over. Tommy had been second trumpet to Matt Morgan with a dozen name bands before a wife and three fine youngsters made him give up his place in the bus. It was he who introduced me to the man who knew my patient, on one of those fine evenings when a jazz and swing buff who cannot read music gets a chance to hear of the "good old days."

Jean Andrews is an exceedingly perceptive woman who knows her husband well. Seemingly she can smell the first wisp of nostalgia for the "gig" in Tommy whenever the drain of teaching music courses has flattened his natural enthusiasm. When that occurs, she dispenses beer, pretzels, and people. The reminiscences about the old days make her home a place where youth can again be tasted. For me, such evenings are a rare treat and a high point in my own relaxation. On one of them, I met Matt Morgan.

"Whaddyuh blow, man?" he inquired after the necessary introductions.

"Usually my top. I just spin the discs and let you guys blow up the sounds."

"You a deejay?"

"Not for years. When I was in college in the late forties I worked some radio stations. You had the chair with Billie Benson then. You guys cut some great stuff."

"If it was me. A lot of stuff was taken by terrible Tom, here."

"Not the real good stuff," Tommy inserted. "I could have broken your lip for what you did with that four-track cut of 'Runnin' Wild.' That was somethin' else."

"I must have been drunk or something else interestin'." The lean man's face lighted, and he broke a grin against the hard ring muscle of the trumpet man's upper lip.

"I got that disc," Tommy said. "Why don't we let doc decide?"

"I think the earlier stuff is a better showcase for Matt," I said. "He did a cut with Mel Miner in about thirty-eight that says more to me. No double-recording tricks, just good brass on 'Joseph, Joseph.' He had a hell of a lot more band behind him."

"Christ!" Morgan said, his grin spreading even more. "I'd have thought nobody would even remember that one. Mel folded up that band and went into the RCAF in 1939. That was one of the last things we ever cut in a studio." His face softened. "The flip side on it ain't too bad, either."

"I think I got that one," Tom said. "Why don't I put on 'Running Wild' and look for the other one? Then we can have a damned good argument."

"Why not?" I asked. "The women aren't really listening to what's spinning, anyhow. At least, I don't think they are. They're in the kitchen arguing about something else, or else hoarding the beer."

"Oh, hell!" Tommy exploded. "I'm a hell of a host. Jim, will you do something about beer for me while I dig out the records?"

Taking my cue, I played waiter long enough to seize five beers and to break up a political argument between Paul Davis, a sometimes reed man and full-time engineer, and Gary Neal, a history teacher in Tommy's school who had been a piano man in the forties.

"Tom's got some of Matt's early discs," I told them. "Why don't you guys knock off the bull and help us settle an argument?"

For all of the technical recording problems of the earlier day, the two discs held up well. So there was a good basis for an argument. Tommy and the piano man, Gary, held out for the early try at multiple recording, while Davis and I plugged for the Mel Miner disc of the minor jump tune of the thirties. As in all such arguments, it was the performer himself who finally cast the deciding ballot.

"I think I've got to go with the doc," Matt Morgan said. "I was eight years younger, and the stuff they did with the dials, it's not really me." He looked at Tommy for a moment. "The band had to blow it all and not bitch it up in those days. Turn that disc over and play the other side. I can show you what I mean."

When the record was turned, Morgan's trumpet came through in a beautiful, clear-water tone. Coming up under the brass was an alto sax, enclosing that clear water in a mountain pool.

"That's Dave Curtis. Pay attention and learn somethin'."

The reed throbbed, grew husky, grew light, gave shading and dimension to the horn. After sixty-four bars, the two reversed lead, and the muted horn lay under the brightening saxophone. The reed solo was compatible, but all too short.

"What'd you think of that?" Morgan asked.

"Good sideman, all right, but Coleman Hawkins he ain't," was Davis's opinion.

"Who the hell said he was? Only thing is that he was, and is, a musician. The Hawk was a specialist, not a sideman. All I'm tryin' to point out is that in those days a band had to have real workmen. That's a guy who loves music—even if he didn't want to play reeds."

"Didn't want to play reeds?" Neal asked.

I was glad the question had been raised. I couldn't have brought it up, or at least I didn't want to. I was glad when Davis, the reed man present, put the rest of the question together for us all. "How do you know that?"

Morgan took a long draft of his beer, preparing for storytelling time. A rime of foam clung to the ring muscle in his upper lip. He licked it away.

"I've known Dave a long time. He lives a few miles from here. I see him once or twice a month. We're old friends."

I knew that I could not enter this conversation with anything that Dave had ever told me. But I could be what I was, —a big-band buff who could ask conventional questions, and a psychologist who could listen. None of the people there knew that I was trying to treat Dave Curtis, and it had to stay that way.

"We got mashed together one time," Morgan said. "We were doing a stand in Houston—that was his hometown—and when he got drunk, he did a lot of talking. He'd wanted to be symphony man—trombone. How do you like that? He started playin' sax in school and never did get onto horns. Played gigs when he wasn't even fifteen years old." He took another swallow of his beer. "By the way, that arrangement is his, too."

Neal jumped in. "It's a damned good arrangement."

"One of the few that Mel didn't screw around with. He was hooked on one style, and he didn't let Dave have much elbowroom most of the time—but that one was too good to change." Morgan glanced toward the kitchen where the women were still engrossed in their own conversation, then lowered his voice. "Dave hated those arrangements. Said it was like getting hooked on the local whore—you know everybody can lay her and you're just another faceless john."

"Sounds like he was lookin' to be loved for himself," Neal put in, "and wound up without his balls."

"Somethin' like that, I guess. Anyhow, when he was a kid and from then on, he never touched a 'bone in his life. He stuck with reeds. I never knew why. He said he didn't like mouthin' a wet reed, but he never really worked on any other instrument except bangin' big vibes." He nodded in silent agreement with himself. "He sometimes worked out his arrangements on the vibes, and was good enough to double on them."

"Does he do anything with music now?" Davis asked.

"Weekends he blows a little sax and vibes with pickup out-fits around town. Gets a little walkin'-around money that way." Matt's face was flattened with remembrance. "If you want a real kick in the ass, he went into an aircraft factory and became some kind of a clerk. Hated every damned minute of it, but stuck with it for years, till he got caught in the thing he's in now. The bastards let him go."

"What's he in now?" Tom asked.

"He messed up some nerves in his tongue or somethin'—can't hardly talk. Now he's scrapin' the bottom—mowing lawns—just to keep eatin'."

The entry of the wives, Jean Andrews in the lead and flanked by four ignored women, ended all reminiscing for the moment. To be more accurate, the conversation switched to the labors and favorite anecdotes of band wives, which all except Pat Davis and my wife had been. I took a moment to think of the information I had gained about David, then reveled in a hilarious tale of a put-down. Jean was talking about an orchestra wife known as "the dowager" and her insistence on identifying her husband's horn on a radio broadcast, when Tommy was playing the solo and the supposedly great musician husband was racked out in the local jail on a drunk charge.

The warm evening was filled with many more tales, but none of them gave me any further insight into David Curtis.

It was a few days later when David kept his scheduled appointment. He was holding his own, not yet becoming restive under the absence of further gain. We chatted for a time, and then I commented on this.

"Seems sort of like you're on a plateau, Dave. Is there anything you can think of that's holding up progress?"

He parried the question too quickly. "I brought in that tape of me before I had the goddamn trouble. Want to hear it?"

"When did you make it?"

"At Christmas, fifty-six, I think." He lighted a cigarette. "Yeah, it was fifty-six. I'd gotten the recorder for a present, and tried it."

"All by yourself?"

"We were around the tree, all of us—Stell and Robert, the boy, and his wife. My brother Paul and his wife were there, too."

"I thought you told me your brother didn't marry."

"That was Clarence—he got so damned gun-shy that he

wouldn't even let mother know he had a woman anywhere. Paul married; his wife's name is Edna."

"Clarence must have had a hell of a crimp in his social life."

David's nose wrinkled, and his tongue lashed on the next sentence, the first real block of the session. "It put a hell of a crimp in everybody's social life. Mother wouldn't even come to the house for Christmas or at any time." At least four blockages punctuated the sentence.

"Did you go to her house?"

"Not then. Usually I'd go by every damned Christmas when I was in town to drop off a present. I mailed them when I was on the road." He stubbed out the cigarette with a sharp motion. "I didn't go that year. Figured it was time to say, 'To hell with it.'" He paused for a long moment. "Then she got sick and died in May." The tongue was lashing as badly as I had ever seen it, his speech becoming almost totally cluttered. The facial contortion was back, a thing we had managed to eliminate almost entirely.

"Let's use light hypnosis so that we can talk about this, Dave."

He shook his head. "I've always had trouble talking about my mother."

I took a shot that I had been considering using for a very long time. "Because you're so furious with her?"

"She's dead. How can you be angry at somebody who's dead?"

"Isn't that the way it really is, Dave? You block more when talking about your mother than any other time. Seems like you block especially hard when you try to tell about her treatment of Stella."

"What's my being mad got to do with my tongue not working?"

"A hell of a lot. Remember challenging me to 'look at the damned thing' the first time you were mad at me? You were so angry at the idea that I'd tell you it was an emotional rather than a physical problem."

David's face set hard. He did not speak. I pressed confrontation at him. "One thing most people forget about speech defects is the fact that the speaker can punish his listeners with the defect itself. He can force them to see, hear, and accept it."

His silence stretched so long that I feared I had pressed too hard at him. Had I been mistaken in reading his growing ability to tolerate looking at himself? I was committed to the action, whether I had overestimated him or not. I simply waited, lighting a cigarette for myself and keeping watch on his face. It took a long time for his frozen expression to melt. When it broke, his face showed fleeting impressions of feeling I could not read. He tried to speak, but the blockage was so severe that only fractions of wet sounds keened from his throat. He glanced at me mutely for help.

Using a hand signal to which he had been trained, I induced hypnosis. He slipped into a deep state almost instantly, eager to water down the impact of his emotions. I didn't have to pose a question. Narrative came from his inner depths in massive flow, erupting like the pus of a lanced boil, with the hard core being thrown from the center of a long-contained infection. His voice was disembodied. Critical scenes unfolded, blending one into another, though they had happened years apart.

His block-free voice cast us back well beyond twenty years. . . .

The train clattered onto a siding, barely sidestepping the main line in time to avoid being run down by the heavy freight that hammered along the rails. Car after car pounded by, laden with great green machines of war—tanks, amtracs, heavy guns—soon to become rusting junk on the coral reef of Tarawa atoll.

"God, look at all that stuff, Stell." David's voice was wonder-filled.

The full-bodied girl brushed imaginary lint from her collar, raising her hand on upward to smooth the pageboy roll of her hair. A war more immediate than in the Pacific islands occupied her thoughts.

"I look all right, Davey?"

"Fine, Stell. Just fine."

"I still wish you'd told her I was coming with you."

"It's gotta be settled. After five years there's got to be a change." He used time checking his own clothing, straightening his uniform blouse, brushing at the fresh single stripe on his sleeve, then trimming his garrison cap. "Five years is too damn long for this to have gone on without being settled."

"It's not going to be any different, Dave. She won't admit I exist, or that we're married."

"Then she'd better have a damned good reason. I won't take this kind of crap any longer." David looked at his wife, delighted she had chosen the beige wool suit that cut down the full appearance of her breasts. "I'm twenty-four next month. I'm my own man!"

"I know that, honey. But she's not going to welcome me. No woman can have any of her boys," Stella insisted. "I don't think I should even get off the train."

"You belong with me." He said it with an air of finality.

He's such a little boy, Stella thought. She stayed silent, wondering how David could still hope for a change in something that had been so very plain to her years before. *He clutches at straws —like when he thought it was because I am three years older than he.*

The passenger train started moving again, easing out onto the main line. Some of the standing people grumbled about the roughness of the start, casting withering looks at those who had been seated for so much of the journey west. David was singled out for a look by an older woman whose face was lined with fatigue. He found himself uncomfortable under the stare.

"It's only another fifteen minutes," he said. "I'll stand."

"Honey, you stood up all last night so that pregnant girl could have a seat. You need rest, too."

"I'm okay, Stell—honest." He nodded to the older woman.

She made her way to the seat, dropping rawboned bigness onto the worn plush. She mumbled something, partly in thanks, partly in complaint.

The train ground through the clear morning sunshine of southern California, rocking over the flowing plain between San Bernardino and Pasadena. David was glad his mother now lived near Pasadena, so they would not be lost in the mass exodus at the Union Station in Los Angeles.

The station was called. David wrestled their two suitcases from the overhead rack, then broke trail through the mass of still standing passengers. They dropped onto the long brick platform with some two dozen others. Stella then took the light bag, linked her arm through David's, and began walking. The other passengers flowed around them like waters parting around a slower moving vessel.

David's mother stood near the parking lot, waiting. He saw her first, straight and thin as the semaphore tower behind her. Her concession had been in dress. It was Thursday, yet she was dressed as if for Sunday services, a flower pinned to her navy blue jacket.

Then she saw him coming, a tall man in uniform, his arm linked through that of the woman in the beige suit. David saw the momentary flash of expression—as if she had been slapped. They were still forty yards apart. The older woman wheeled about, walking quickly the few steps to the parking lot and the waiting car.

Had he reacted instantly on seeing the expression, David might have been able to force the issue. It was his stunned moment of inaction that lost him the chance. She was gone by the time he reached the edge of the lot.

Stella, left behind when he began to run toward the car, came hesitantly up to him. David sank onto one of the short posts that kept cars from the brick platform of the station. His face was chalky, lined with a hopeless fatigue that previewed how he would look when he was twice his age of twenty-four.

She put a hand on his shoulder. "Don't say anything, Davey. It's all right."

"It's not all right! There's a hell of a lot that's got to be said! She's got no right to treat me—treat us—the way she does."

He turned toward her. Stella's hand slid from his shoulder around to the back of his neck, pulling his face toward her breasts. "Don't talk about it, Davey. We'll find a place to stay, get something to eat, some drinks, and have our own homecoming. . . ."

"I went to have it out with my mother the next day. She wouldn't even talk to me, doctor." He was perspiring on the upper lip, and his tongue came forth and licked at the dampness. It had not protruded or lashed anywhere in the narrative.

"Did she ever say anything about Stella? Anything at all?" I inquired.

"Not directly. All she ever said was that she'd lost the only four men she ever loved . . . that we'd all run away from her. That she couldn't ever share us with anyone. Then she broke out cryin' and ran into her bedroom and closed the door. I waited almost an hour, trying to talk to her through the door, but she never came out."

"Stella never met her?"

"The closest was on that train platform—until mother died. Even when she was in the hospital, she wouldn't let Stella visit or do anything. She knew she might die, but she still wouldn't set it straight."

"Did she die in a hospital?"

"No. She was home. She'd had two heart attacks, but the doctor had sent her home after a couple of weeks. It happened there. . . ."

"I wish I could tell you it was goin' to be different than the other times."

Stella Curtis tried to hold her plump face in the expression of concern. She managed it rather well, since she had much concern for what David was feeling—enough to set aside the old hurts in her own feelings. Yet she remembered them acutely—the slights, the denial of her existence by her mother-in-law. She also remembered the oft-taken task of consoling David when his mother had rejected them, and the discomfort of seeing her man hurt and powerless.

"I know. It doesn't matter about me. You should go."

She reached across the back of the car seat and patted his shoulder.

He flashed a grateful glance to her, feeling relieved that her expression was a concerned one, yet also sensing the hidden resentments in his wife. For a moment he could almost see the brown-haired, full-breasted girl he had married within the corseted matron on the seat opposite him. He took his left hand from the wheel, laying it atop her hand on his right shoulder, squeezing for a moment.

"You're a good woman, Stell. I—"

She cut him off. "I'll just wait in the car. If she . . . if there's anything . . ." Stella broke off the sentence, uncertain as to how it might be finished without saying something either hurtful or angry. She had had to break in to cut off what she felt he would say—something about being able to depend on her. She had given up on another score, also. Stella was resigned to taking care of David, too often being maternal to welcome admission of her value or his love for her.

Silence hung in the moving automobile.

Both of them knew that there would be no move of conciliation on the mother's part. David changed the subject quickly.

"The doctor said she'll probably make it."

"It'll be all right, Davey."

He winced for a moment with the name, then slammed the car into the access ramp that dropped onto the freeway. "I don't know. This is her third attack in four months. Paul thinks it will be the last one."

Stella didn't know whether to pray for or against Paul's prediction. *At least it would be all over,* she thought. *It wouldn't be cutting you up every time you see her.*

"Paul said that about the second one."

They were silent, and the car meshed into the late afternoon traffic. David knew that her reassurance was a gift. Her appreciation of his need touched him, and it made him feel uncomfortable. He tried to escape the discomfort, pushing the old Ford out into the fast lanes and finding his escape in anger.

"Stupid bastard!" he cursed at another driver. Even as he let loose the invective, he wondered if the curse was for the other driver, his brother Paul, or perhaps himself.

"Our getting into a wreck won't help her," Stella said sharply, sucking in her breath.

He could feel his rage shifting, whiplike, toward his wife, but stifled the angry reply in his throat with the internal admission that she was right. The lane ahead cleared. He fed more gasoline to the old car, forcing it.

"I won't take Magnolia—it's too crowded at this time of day. I'll get off at Collingwood and double back."

They rode in silence. The plump woman eased slightly in her seat as he seemed to cool. No words were spoken until he was off the freeway, moving into the tract of late-forties housing units. They looked like tiny two-bedroom cages built to trap the newly established GI mortgage money of those days. After a few blocks of doubling on his tracks, David steered the Ford into a driveway, placing it behind Paul's Oldsmobile on the narrow slab of concrete. Then he turned to his wife.

"You'll be all right?"

She pressed his hand and nodded. "Go ahead, Dave. It'll be all right. I'll just wait here till you come back and tell me."

He squeezed back on her hand, having no words. For a long moment he looked at her. He left the car, making his way around it and across the postage-stamp-size front lawn onto the concrete slab that formed a front porch.

Stella sat, wrapped in thought, for a long time. The car radio droned on, but was ignored. The light was dimming in the sky of the May evening when she became aware that someone was standing outside her car door, speaking to her through the lowered window. She turned to see Paul talking to her. The cord on the right side of his throat jumped under the surface of his skin. He was shorter than David, stockier, and considerably better dressed.

"It's all over, Stella. She died about fifteen minutes ago."

"I . . . I'm sorry, Paul." The words came easily, rising from her genuine liking for the businessman brother-in-law.

"Davey is pretty upset, I think. Maybe you'd better go in."

"Are you coming?"

"It isn't me he needs. Let me move your car so I can get out. I'll bring the keys to you. Then I'll go home and tell Edna and the kids. I've got a call in for Clarence—haven't been able to locate him since mother had this attack. He's supposed to be in Des Moines."

"How is Dave taking it?"

The twitch in the man's throat was nearly constant. He hesitated for a moment, and their eyes met. "When a man harbors so much hate for someone he loves, it can't be easy." He opened the door for the chubby woman. "Go on in. I'll bring your keys."

Hesitatingly, she moved from the driveway to the concrete porch. She paused a moment, squared her shoulders, and opened the door to the forbidden territory. There was no sound to guide her, but she instinctively turned across the living room and into the narrow hallway. Beyond the bath the door stood open on a softly lighted room.

Stella Curtis stood in the doorway, looking at the woman whom she had never met. The face of the corpse was a dissolved thing, hard worn and seemingly without significant features in the relaxation of death. Gray hair spilled onto the pillows under the head and shoulders. The hands were atop the quilted cover—gripping folds into it. Eyes glazed and open, the corpse, elevated by the stack of pillows, dominated the room. No one else was in the room.

Stella moved across the room. Using her hand, she gently closed the dead woman's eyes. She kneaded the fingers open and folded the worn hands together. For a long moment she stood beside the bed, as if uncertain what she had done. Then she turned to look for her husband.

She walked quietly through the house, glancing into all the rooms with closed doors as well as the open area of dining, living, and kitchen continuum. From the kitchen she saw David sitting outside on the nearly darkened patio. He was at the picnic table, his elbows propped to support the face he held in his hands. She eased the kitchen door open and stepped down onto the patio surface, moving toward him hesitantly.

His head bobbed a bit, and his shoulders heaved as a low sobbing began and muffled itself in his throat. A hand touched Stella's shoulder. She turned to see Paul, his free hand extending her keys. She took them and he nodded, tightening the touch on her shoulder. Then the stocky man turned silently and strode back through the house.

Stella went to her husband, reaching across the back of his neck with her arm. He reacted like a stupefied animal, turning his face toward her. It was wet. Tears streamed down his cheek furrows like rivulets. He tried to fight back his sobs, and from deep within them a flow of curses started.

"Goddamn it! Goddamn the bitches all to hell! Dirty, miserable sons of bitches. Goddamn!" It went on like a litany, being repeated over and over again. At times it was punctuated, "Dirty, selfish bitch! Goddamn the dirty, selfish bitch!"

Stella brought her other hand to his shoulder and turned him further, pulling him until his face was buried in the soft fold of stomach under her breasts.

"It's all right, Davey. It's going to be all right!"

He relaxed for a moment. She could feel him moving into her softness, responding to his need for tender comfort. She made her honest mistake then.

"Davey, Davey . . . all right. All right now. I know . . . I know."

His shoulders tensed, and he jerked away from her.

"The hell you do! Nobody knows! Nobody knows enough not to treat you like anything but a kid!" He struggled away from her, lurching to his feet. The bench of the picnic table turned over from the narrowness of its sawbuck support, crashing down onto the cement floor of the patio.

He seized the upended legs of the bench, raised it high in the air, and smashed it down onto the table. "Goddamn her! Why couldn't she just once have treated me like a *man!* Now she never will!" He smashed the bench onto the table again and again. Redwood splintered and tore. "It's not fair! Goddamn it all to hell! It's not fair! I ain't no goddamn kid!" He turned toward his wife. "Do you hear? I ain't no goddamn kid!"

"Then straighten up and stop acting like one!" Her voice was harsh, and it stopped him like a sudden blow. "Whatever she was, she's dead! Just stop your filthy tongue!"

David was deep in hypnosis. This was the point at which I had aimed the hypnotic sessions—the dam was broken and his accumulated pains were gushing forth. In anticipation of its happening, I had put David on the schedule near the end of the day and asked Betty Garwood, our clinic secretary, to hold the time open for me unless there was a genuine crisis for some other patient. I soothed David with suggested relaxation for a few moments before we went on, then stepped out to check with the schedule and bring back the tape recorder. I cursed myself for not having recorded the accounting of his reaction to his mother's death.

Fortunately, the periods for the remainder of the day were still open. I had to find out where David's volcanic eruption of anger would lead. Certainly there was no lack of traumatic material to choose from in attempts to explain his current situation. As always, it would not be any choice of mine that would have meaning. What had to be learned was how the multiple insults that life affords to all of us had crystallized into David's particular and unique reaction.

I returned to the office, setting the cassette recorder on the corner of the desk. David was soporific, as if he had been drugged. He waited placidly.

"That's it, Dave. Stay relaxed and comfortable. I'm using a recorder now, so you'll be able to hear yourself. Just stay in that dreamy frame of mind while I ask some questions."

I punched the button on the recorder. "You told me that you felt your mother treated you like a kid. Who else treated you like a kid?"

"Who didn't? At work I was doing things an eighth grader could have done."

"Tell me."

"All I did was take blueprints and list the tubing dimensions the draftsman had put down—make a goddamn list of sizes and lengths without even having to say it was to be formed or bent. Nothing but just the length and type of tube. Hell, we only had nine types."

"Sounds simple enough."

"Yeah."

"Easy way to make a living."

"Hell! Six out of every eight hours I was stretching it just to keep lookin' busy. I could have done my whole job in two hours."

"No chance to get on any other job?"

"Only if you were willing to suck ass. That's like all them damned places. But the thing I hated most was the way they tried to make you do things—just like you'd try with a kid. They'd put memos on the board about 'have a pleasing telephone personality' or 'please don't steal the paper clips.' " He snorted, even in the depth of his lethargy. "I hated it."

"For seven years?"

"I had to have the money. I could double up on my mortgage and get way ahead on my house payments—especially with band jobs on weekends. If I could get together another four hundred bucks right now, the place would be mine. That's one damned thing I can say for Space-Tek—I had seven years of bein' able to make double payments."

"And you only need a little more? A couple more months to knock off that mortgage?"

"That's still a hell of a lot of lawns to cut—and cuttin' lawns is kid stuff, too."

"Tried for any other jobs?"

"Sure, but who'd hire me? The way I talk?"

"Lots of jobs don't depend on talking, Dave."

"You still have to talk to somebody to get them to hire you."

"We're getting away from the idea of being treated like a kid."

"All my life. Mel Miner made me write arrangements like a kid—same thing over and over. The army treated me like a kid, just like it does everybody. Then when I lost my tone, I felt like I really was a kid."

"When did that happen?"

"It all happened at about the same time. My job was goin' to hell—we all knew we were gonna get hit with a big layoff at Space-Tek. The available band jobs weren't much good. Everything went to hell in June."

"Right after your mother died in May?"

"I had a job to play the biggest hotel in town—Junior League ball. I was lousy! Couldn't hit a goddamn note!" Even in the deep hypnotic state, his speech showed a blockage. "I didn't have any tone—couldn't even read my score right. I'd made the arrangements and couldn't even follow my own things."

"Were you on anything? Any pills?"

"I'd taken a couple of diet pills. They didn't help that time."

"You couldn't express anything?"

"That's it. I couldn't get anything but the damnedest flat sound you could imagine. Mechanical and lousy, no feeling at all."

"What do you mean?"

"All night long it was like we hadn't even warmed up or ever played any of it. Some bitchy girl on the dance floor put it right on the nose."

"What?"

"She and this guy were dancing right in front of the stand. She was bitching about the music, loud enough to make sure all of us could hear. She said, 'A bunch of never-make-it fruity kids and over-the-hill has-beens.'" He grimaced again. I thought for a moment David would lose the thread of his narrative, the pause was so long. "The hell of it was, she was right. Nobody on that whole bandstand had the least sign of having any balls. I . . . I haven't had my old tone since."

"You still work jobs, though, don't you?"

"Sure. But I'm a lousy thief. I get by on what I know— not what I do. I just blow the notes that are there, or hammer 'em out on the vibes. I don't feel it—not like I should. Once in a great while, I think maybe I'm getting something goin' again—but the next job, it's gone again."

"You still want to say something with your music."

"Every musician wants to say something with his music. He wants to say that it's really him—say it so clear that everybody's got to listen."

"Who stopped listening, Dave?"

The room was suddenly as quiet as if it had been filled with shredded cork from floor to ceiling. It was as if no penetration of the quiet would ever again be possible. The silence lay so heavy that I had to glance out of the window toward moving traffic on the highway to prove that the world had not stopped and frozen. That it was only me who waited on David to speak.

When he did let his voice come, at last, it was again the flat, faraway sound of deep hypnosis. With no suggestion or coaching, David had dropped himself into a depth like the one of twenty minutes before, when he had reexperienced his enraged reaction to his mother's death. I was tense in my chair, leaning forward to enter the past with him. I was sure that I would see the man live over another wounding. . . .

"Marmon called. I forgot to tell you." Stella sat on the end of the old couch, pinning up her hair. "Wants you to work the job in San Bernardino Saturday night. I told him you would."

David shifted his attention from the television commercial. "Okay, I guess." His voice was dubious. "Did he say he'd pay anything for transportation?"

"I didn't ask."

"Why the hell not? It's nearly a hundred miles. When you take that out of thirty bucks, there ain't a hell of a lot left."

"We need the money."

"What else is new?" He poured wine into his glass from the bottle on the floor beside his chair. "No goddamn money and gettin' nothin' for what you do." He added the last in a mutter.

"Don't be mad at me. I told you tonight, so you could get your yard work done through the week. That money will help make this month's payment. If we can make five more without missing, it'll finally be all our house."

"I'm sorry, Stell. It's just that . . . I get damned tired of bein' damned tired. That's all."

"You don't eat right."

He felt the words, more than heard them. They grated along his spine. For a moment, he felt that he'd heard those words all his life, and he resented them. "I get enough. I don't want to be fat."

"You couldn't get fat if you wanted to. But it's true. You start on a glass of wine when you get home in the afternoon, and by suppertime you couldn't care less about eating right." She stuffed hairpins into her mouth, but couldn't stifle her request for some acknowledgment from him. "I try to give you good meals, and it isn't easy, working all day and then coming home and having to prepare dinner."

"I know, Stell. You do your share and most of mine, it seems like. I'm not much good anymore."

Stella paused in her hair pinning and looked at him. "You really *are* in a mood of some kind. What's the trouble?"

"I ran into Matt Morgan—in the liquor store." He drained the red wine from the tumbler, then set the glass on the stand beside his chair.

"How is Matt?"

"He looks good—ten years younger than I do. He's makin' a lot of records and doin' studio jobs. He works ten, maybe fifteen dates a month in Hollywood. He's livin' out here in the Valley— over on Lenham."

"That much work." Her voice was calculating. "Can he get anything for you?"

"I didn't ask. Hell! I couldn't hardly talk." He filled his glass again. "He said he'll be comin' over to see us sometime."

"That's good. You two always got along well. You need someone to talk to—somebody besides me."

David looked at the shabby furnishings that had been overused through the years when all extra money had been poured into trying to pay off the mortgage. "I don't want him to come." He said it softly.

She watched his eyes sweeping across the old belongings, understanding what he was feeling. She removed the last hairpin from her mouth, catching the final curl with it and lacing it tight to her head. She tied the scarf around her head before she replied.

"He won't even notice the place—it's you he's interested in seeing."

"Like going to a freak show?"

"Quit feeling sorry for yourself. You're a man who's got an injury—not a freak."

"I haven't even got an injury. The psychologist showed me it couldn't be an injury when he hypnotized me and made it disappear." He shook his head. "It's my way of bein' nuts."

"Don't say that!" She rose from the couch and moved to a position behind his chair. "You get tired and nervous and upset with things not going right." She put her hands on his shoulders, kneading his muscles, rubbing the shoulders and nape of his neck. "You should have asked Matt if he could use a sideman or arranger."

"I don't want charity. I haven't got it anymore. I know it."

"How do you know? With the kind of kids and arrangements you have to work with these days? Is there a single one of them who gives you any of the lift you need?" She rubbed harder on the suddenly tightening muscles in the back of his neck. "You need to work with some good musicians—that's all." She kneaded the knots of muscle for a moment in silence. "That feel better?"

He reached up to touch her hand. "You know it does."

"Did Matt say when he might come over?"

"No. I don't want you askin' him for help if he does."

"I wouldn't. I'd just like to see him. Does he know where we live?"

"I told him we were in the book. He said he'd call, but I know he won't. All the good things are in the past, anyhow."

"You *really* are in a mood. Wine isn't going to help that. Why don't you put the cork in the bottle, take a hot shower, and go to bed?"

She left off kneading his neck, stepped to the side of the chair, bent quickly, and pecked a kiss onto his forehead. As she leaned forward, the old housecoat opened, showing the smooth plumpness of chest and shoulders above her nightgown. David raised his hands to her shoulders and pulled her back down toward him, burying his face in the hollow at the base of her neck. He could feel her stiffen and pull away from him.

"Relax, for Chrissake. We're married."

"I—I'm sorry." She bent toward him again. "That—well—your beard is scratchy."

He recognized the lie, and the apology it was intended to convey. "Thanks for rubbing my neck." He let her go, then rose from his chair, crossing the room to the television set and watching for a moment before he turned it off. The slim blonde was lathering her throat and shoulders under a shower, and the husky feminine voice was asking, "Don't you wish everybody did?"

He snapped the set off, watching the picture dissolve to a tiny white spot in the middle of the screen. He came back and took the bottle from the floor, returning it to the kitchen with a wry notice of the scant two inches of red liquid remaining. Then he moved toward the bedroom, stripping off his shirt as he went.

He was in the shower for as little time as it took to soap and rinse. At the sink he scraped his whiskers, brushed his teeth, splashed on some astringent, sprayed deodorant, and freshened his mouth with a rinse. Then, a towel around his lean waist and twisted over his left hip, he walked from the bath across the dimly lighted bedroom to let himself down onto the top of the covers. His shoulders and neck lay across her chest, his face nuzzling into her neck.

"That a clean enough shave?"

"Take off that stupid towel and come to bed."

He nuzzled her further, tongue tip tracing patterns under her jaw and below her ear. "When you take off that stupid nightie." He bit lightly on her earlobe. The edge of the scarf in which her hair was bound was nudged upward by his nose. Through the blankets his hand traced the outline of her hip.

"Dave. I'm—I'm more than fifty years old. Don't try to make me into something that I'm not."

He continued to explore her body with his hand through the

blankets, and did not lift his face from the side of her neck. "Are you sure you're that old?"

"I'm sure."

He lifted himself and slipped the towel from his waist. With his other hand, he took the top edge of the blankets and hurled them over the foot of the bed. Then he leaped onto the bed beside her. His arms went around her and he pulled her close to him, pressing her ample breasts against his chest. He could feel the soft fullness of them against his lean chest. His upper hand slid down her back, fingers spread and hard on her buttocks. He slid his body down until his face was between her breasts.

"I want to help you feel young again. I want to caress you till you forget about that—so it's like it used to be."

She drew away from him, sat up, and with difficulty peeled the cotton nightgown up and over her head. She stared at him for a moment, then lowered herself stiffly onto the bed, lying quietly on her back.

He moved toward her, lips and hands moving over her. The hand stroked her thighs, belly, the points of her padded hips, coming to concentrated pressure on the fork of her body. He slid back up the bed to kiss her, pressing his lips hard against hers and slipping his tongue toward her strangely set lips. She still had not moved. He lifted his head from her face, looking at her. Her eyes were closed.

"What the hell is the matter?"

Her jaw was set. "I'm not some damned high school kid in the back seat of a Model A. I don't want all this buildup when it can't lead anywhere. Just go ahead. Get it over with."

He drew back from her. "To hell with it! That's like—like—jacking off."

"Dave, I'm sorry. I really am. I know what you want—I just don't have it to give. Not anymore."

"Not really for five or six years, you mean." His voice was hard and cold. "You won't even see a doctor about it."

"No. Why don't you find somebody else for sex? I love you and like you, Dave. You're a good person. If you need sex, then go find it somewhere. Just don't tell me about it. . . ."

The voice that recited the narrative was quite mechanical.

106

"I just said, 'Piss on it,' and rolled over and went to sleep." He lay quietly in the chair.

"That was five years ago?"

"No. A couple of years ago. Her not bein' able to respond—that was quite a while before that."

"How often did you have sex before—during that five years before the night you told me about?"

"Two or three times a month."

"Have you ever approached Stella since that night?"

"No."

"Did you find a girl friend?"

"No. I tried once, but I—I'm too old, too."

"What do you mean, exactly?"

"What do you think? I couldn't hold my hard on. I just lay there and dribbled on the sheets. I never tried again."

I had no further questions. The massive outflow of pain and compromise had been complete. David's concept of himself as a man had been in doubt at a deep level of his feelings from his early years, and the chain of circumstances had faced him with impotence in career, in financial success, in a hated job, in his music, his fatherhood, and in his sex life.

I prepared to rouse him from the deep torpor, ready to use all of the techniques I knew to insure that he would not remember what we had done in the session that had stretched nearly two and a half hours. I leaned toward him, but there was one question I had posed which David chose this moment to answer.

"Who stopped listening, doc? *Everybody.*"

The session had been long. The amount of thinking it generated in me was much greater. I could not shake David from my thoughts that night. His feeling of complete impotence was so pervasive as to touch every aspect of his life. I reflected, pondering all of the fine shadings that could be given to these many aspects. Each of my reflections led me to another conjecture, like streets among subdivisions in my mind.

I prowled the subdivisions like a ragpicker, searching among the discards for overlooked values. I had brought home the tape of the session. I played it over and over, adding from my memory the portion I had not had sufficient foresight to record.

The goals were clear. David would have to alter the things that could be made to yield, to accept those that would not change. His work situation, for one, was a situation where stable employment would help him to feel that he was a functioning man. His drinking would lessen to the extent that he could credit himself for doing something for himself. The situation with his stepson probably would not alter, since he had been shut out of the role of a father from very early in his marriage. His wife's lack of responsiveness did not seem capable of significant change, yet he might reevaluate it to be less castrating in his feelings about himself. He did not seem likely to risk another sexual failure with a woman, yet it would undoubtedly be his sexuality that could be sublimated to revitalize his music.

I knew that not all of the hypnotic amnesia would hold. Some of the things David had brought out of his tortured past would find their way into his conscious recollection. My hope was that the confrontations he would give himself, and those I could later add, would be softened enough by a hypnotic barrier to allow them to be handled in some manageable fashion.

A considerable number of them had worked to the surface by the next time I saw David. Even more surprising was the equanimity with which he was meeting them. His awkward manner of speech was far less marked than it had been. He was slowed neither in his articulation nor in the tricks we had practiced. Fairly extended sentences emerged without the familiar blockage.

We chatted for a few moments, then I opened the subject of employment.

"This lawn work you're doing, Dave. Do you do anything that would be considered real gardening? Flowers, shrubs—that sort of thing?"

"On my own place."

"You don't like factory work. In fact, you chose to do lawn work rather than pump gasoline or something else after you were laid off. You must have had some reason."

"I like being outdoors. It's better than being tied to a desk."

"Do you do any landscaping?"

"My place is pretty good. I've got terraces, bend-board lay-outs, and shrubs. I even put in some stone planter boxes."

"You like that better than just cutting grass and trimming—that seems clear."

He thought about it for a moment. "You're right. I do like that kind of work—but people just want their lawns mowed. They won't pay for much fancy stuff."

"Ever think about doing something with that?"

"Like what?"

"Parks, schools, golf courses—someplace where you'd have a regular job with a steady paycheck?"

"A regular paycheck I could sure use."

"There's a city exam for gardeners going on all the time. Starts at four hundred and ninety dollars a month, higher for landscape gardeners."

"What about my speech?" He burbled slightly, but the tongue did not extrude.

"What about it? You really need that to hide behind?"

His face flamed, suffused with anger, but he said nothing.

"That stuck you, didn't it?"

He started to explode his tongue. I cut him off.

"Don't block at me! I've seen it! I know that you *can* speak. Now show me that you can let your anger out, too."

"You—" He bit back the word.

"Bastard." I finished the curse for him. "Sure I am. The world has a plentiful share of us. Every goddamn one of us bastards has about thirty feet of intestine—but what it takes is guts."

"You tryin' to make me mad?"

"You've been mad since you were a kid. I'm trying to force you to let it out. You've got the right to holler when you're hurt."

"I haven't let myself get mad since—"

"Since your mother died and you blew up. You kept yourself bottled up at Space-Tek, too. You try to do what you think other people want you to do—and look what it's cost you. The only way you could let it go was to whip at people with your tongue."

"That's dirty!"

"You want that mortgage in your hand to burn. You put in fourteen years, paid off twenty-four of twenty-five. Are you going to go along without finishing that?"

"I'll pay it off, somehow."

"Take the damned exam—or else go tackle somebody for a job so you can do it in a hurry. Get your butt in gear. Go after your own piece of territory."

"What the hell do you think I've been doing?" David's voice was strained, but emerged clear and hard. "I've wanted a place free and clear all my life. A place—"

"Where nobody could tell you what to do. That's right, Dave. That's what that place means to you—the chance to be your own man."

It took a moment to sink through his anger. Then he smiled. "You're right, doc. All along I've wanted to feel I could do something my way, instead of somebody else's."

"That was the real bitch at Space-Tek, too. Wasn't it? 'Have a pleasing telephone personality' had to mean to use a speech disorder to tell other people to go to hell."

"Is that why I did it?"

"That's only part of the answer. It all fits together. We'll be working for a while to fit in all the pieces."

"You're still a bastard," he said, smiling.

"I'm too ugly to be a love child." I returned his smile. "Next week, I want to hear what you've done about a job."

It took less than a month for David's action to result in his qualifying as a gardener for the Parks and Recreation Department. He missed the landscape gardener appointment, but his score was high enough to let him start at a pay grade above the base as a gardener.

"It's hard work, doc, but I'm enjoying it."

"How many men in the crew?"

"Five of us, plus the boss. We get along, and he likes my work. Gotta admit I have to stretch to hold up my end."

"Maybe that feels good, too? Having to stretch."

"Yeah. It does. Makes me know I can put it out."

"Doin' anything else?"

"I . . . did some arrangements. Made eighty bucks. Matt Morgan tipped it my way."

"I thought you weren't going to ask Matt for anything."

"I didn't. He came to me. Brought over a tune and asked

me to take a crack at it. Funny thing—it fell right in place like I'd never been away. He took it back and they recorded it. It'll be released next month."

"Going to lead to maybe some more?"

"I don't know. Doesn't matter if it don't. Least I know I can still do the job." He paused for a moment, looking at me. "I been thinkin' about taking on some students—kids who couldn't pay much but want to play. I got a rec room at the end of the garage. With a little soundproofin' I could take students there. Might make a couple of bucks."

"Playing any better yourself?"

"I like to think so."

"I like to thing so, too." I matched his pause. "What about Stella?"

"She's a good old gal, doc. She's put up with a lot of crap from me." He slipped into a pensive mood, and his voice reflected it, as if he were talking to himself. "I guess there's not gonna be anything to make it like it was before—but what the hell? Does that really matter so much, at my age?"

*

David faced an indifferent world, impersonal in the way it ground away his hopes. There was no designed malice arrayed against him, no active enemies forcing him to barricade himself behind a tongue running wild, no confrontation with his own emasculation. He did not truly face destructive adversaries set to punish him.

Yet, in a world where lives interweave, goals unique to one person sometimes conflict with the needs of others. Then, should the opponents hold the power to punish, they become adversaries and the battle lines are drawn. That malice can exist is too often discounted as the paranoidal interpretation of the patient . . . a rationalization offered to escape personal failings.

Families have been known to "elect a sick member," runs a psychiatric cliché. On this member, blame, abuse, and rationalizations are dumped in wholesale lots: "We couldn't make your party because Eloise had one of her headaches"; "If only he didn't drink"; "You know you're not very strong, dear, so—" The list continues ad infinitum. *All of us are familiar with examples.*

It is when the elected member becomes a threat to the group that hostilities commence. The planning that follows reveals the probable illness of the others, yet they are not within the scope of the work the therapist is attempting with the "patient."

This kind of patient, irrespective of internal problems, is

113

also the reflector of the illness of others, and needs to be able to see their motives, as well as his own. The therapist gets terrifying glimpses of the human condition as the patient struggles for a view of himself.

Such a case was Karen. . . .

PART THREE

* KAREN *

Hostages to Fortune

"I WENT OVER ALL OF THAT WITH THE POLICE." THE WOMAN'S voice was something set in coarse plaster, her irritation not quite concealing the smooth evenness of her inflection.

"I know. I'm only trying to understand what went on, Mrs. Dant. When a fourteen-year-old boy uses dynamite, I can't help but be curious about the action."

"I came here to find out what you had learned about my boy."

"Of course. I'll be glad to tell you anything I can." I paused a moment. "I had hoped to see the boy's father here for this conference."

"We are . . . separated. I think he is in Montgomery with his cousins. I haven't heard from him in several months."

"I'm sorry."

"What can you tell me about Lee?"

I looked down at the test protocols and my report to the court that had ordered our clinic to examine the boy. "He is a very angry boy."

"Is he . . . *sick?*" She put an accent on the word that made it sound unclean.

I peered closely at the woman. The extreme tension that gripped her was betrayed by her rigid posture in the chair. My glance was a reward in itself. Karen Dant was holding her late thirties in a fashion for which many women would sacrifice a great deal. Her grooming and posture were impeccable. Her clothing, while not new, was of good quality and artlessly complimentary. The features were even and harmonious, the hands graceful and smooth, the figure, the simple hairstyle, the wary brightness of her deep brown eyes all combined to make Karen Dant an exceptionally attractive woman. She was five feet tall, yet gave the appearance of standing head and shoulders above the level of the well-kept southern genteel women of the small town where our clinic was located. Her voice was cultured, free of regionalisms of accent usually found in the area.

"Lee is very angry," I repeated. "He's upset, perhaps disturbed. But I find no real evidence that he is mentally ill."

"Then it was deliberate." Her tone was that of a woman resigning herself to torture.

"There was a precipitating cause. You said 'deliberate' as if it were a curse."

A bitter laugh tore itself from her. "It will be, Doctor Howard." She did not elaborate.

"I realize this is very difficult. You seem shaken by it yourself."

"My son could go to jail, doctor. I consider that sufficient reason to be upset."

"No matter what provocation he had?"

"Anger is no excuse for vandalism."

"Not an excuse, Mrs. Dant. Probably only the steam behind the act." I studied her set face. "Can you help us to understand why he chose to blow the dike from his grandfather's fishing pond? Why not ruin someone else's pond?"

"Why do you ask me questions? You're supposed to review your test findings on my son with me. That was the court order."

The conflict was there, and I was its target. We faced each other for a long moment, then I nodded. "Your son is bright— well above average. There is no evidence of brain damage or defect that would make him incapable of being responsible for his actions. He has some emotional problems, according to the projective tests—mostly centered around temper control and a tendency to act impulsively. The tests further indicate immaturity, confusion, and hostility.

"He has a great deal of tender regard for you, and appreciably shows feelings of protectiveness toward his younger sisters. He very much wants, but resists wanting, an identification with some strong man. In short, Mrs. Dant, Lee is pushing to learn what the limits really are. He seems to be testing to determine when someone will love him enough to stop him."

The silence stretched. Her dark eyes burned at me like two polished, darting chips of obsidian.

"Is that all?"

"No. That is only the beginning. We're reasonably sure that we can work with Lee in this clinic. We want to help him to know himself and his own motives."

"Will the court allow that?"

"We're recommending treatment for him in our report, rather than punishment. It will be up to the court to decide."

"How long would you need to help him?"

"I don't know. That would be up to the two of you."

"The two of us? What do you mean?"

"When we work with a juvenile, we also try to work with one or both of the parents during the course of treatment." I paused a moment. "Since his father isn't with his family, I'd like to be working with you."

"My problems aren't for public consumption, doctor." Her voice was icy.

"Neither are those of anyone else. Our records are confidential." I looked at her for a moment and felt my voice soften. "This current situation *is* a problem, Mrs. Dant. Why should you expect to carry it all alone?"

Her shoulders quivered for a moment, but except for a momentary, flickering agreement she did not respond. Instead she changed the topic, but to one that indicated some acceptance.

"What possessed him to do that?"

I hazarded a guess. "To take something away from his grandfather?"

"To kill the fish? To ruin the pond? He'd worked all winter to help build it—after school and on weekends. He was as proud of the wages he earned as any man on the crew. He even went fishing there, right after it was stocked. We all went."

"To admire R. B. Dant's latest trophy?"

She flashed me a surprised glance, waited a moment, then went on in a pained voice. "I suppose so. If you know R. B. Dant, you know why this is such a monstrous thing. No one destroys his things without a great deal of trouble."

117

"Or without some kind of retaliation?"

She snapped her head around, dark eyes lancing into my face. "What do you mean by that?"

"He is the richest man in Seminole County, yet when his grandson is arrested the court asks a public clinic to evaluate him without fee."

"Why should *he* pay? It was his property Lee dynamited. It was even his dynamite, stolen from one of his own sheds."

"Why didn't Lee's father take the bill?"

She stiffened her already rigid posture. "Roy Dant has only the money he obtains from his mother. R. B. Dant keeps his family entirely dependent." She glanced about her, as if she felt she was saying too much.

I took the opportunity she was presenting. "Wouldn't you like to talk about these feelings?"

"I—I'm not sure. Would it help?"

"It can help, Mrs. Dant." I glanced at my schedule sheet. "Could you come in on Tuesdays at four thirty? We can give Lee his appointment with Mr. Carson at that time, so he doesn't miss school. I could see you at the same hour."

"I suppose that would be all right."

I rose and offered my hand. The hand she placed in it was trembling.

"I came in to talk about Lee," she murmured. "I don't know if I am ready to face my own troubles."

"That's as may be, Mrs. Dant. It seems to me it's all part of the same package."

"I've failed him, doctor. Somehow I've failed my own son without even knowing I was doing it. He's always been such a dependable, quiet boy. Now he's a—" She broke off, trying to withdraw her trembling hand.

I firmed my grip for a moment before I released her. "He's all the boy he ever was. That he did a rash or stupid thing doesn't change that—or what you feel for him."

She slowly withdrew her hand from my relaxing grip. "Must I talk about everything?"

"When you feel ready to do so."

"I can't pay a fee. Not until I can find work. Then I'll pay as I can."

"We'll speak of that later, also. I won't make a fee assessment for the time being."

"Thank you." The tone held no deference or stress on feeling. Her acknowledgment was as tastefully simple as her clothing.

I was relatively new in this area of the Deep South. Many years before I had taught in an Alabama university, but had been somewhat encapsulated in faculty routines that shielded me from the realities of life in a small southern town. I had much to learn—much homework to do.

I began with a review of the case material, with special attention to the interview material gathered by Martin Fells, an old pro among social workers. He had taken the original referral and had set up the evaluation from the court's request by interviewing the boy and his mother. He had been the one who suggested Fred Carson, M.S.W. (Master of Social Work), as therapist for the son and asked if I would see the mother. If the father could be involved, he had agreed to undertake that part of the treatment problem. Therapeutically, of course, we were all responsible to our medical director, Derek Welton, M.D.

In reviewing the material, I could again appreciate what Marty Fells had been able to accomplish in a single interview. He had gentled the boy, preparing him to accept us as something besides the court's punishers. He had drawn history material from the mother adroitly, tuning her gently to describe the offense, the conflict in the boy, and the situation within the family.

At Seminole Mental Health Center, each day started with a staff conference. We sat around a battered kitchen table in what had been the special-diet kitchen of the former Danton Community Hospital. The old fifteen-room brick mansion had a faint reek of iodoform, reminding us of what had occupied its space while the new, modern hospital was being built on the next block. The clinic had taken over the building the year before I had become a member of the staff.

The coffee cups filled from the ever present urn, each of the four therapists (which included myself) set our case folders on the kitchen table, exchanged good-mornings, and went to work. We discussed the events of the preceding twenty-four hours and plans for the day ahead. Since two, possibly all, of us would be involved with the Dant situation, it occupied much of the time of the next morning's conference.

"You think she'll come with Lee?" Fred Carson asked.

"It seemed pretty firm," I replied. "But the situation may get pretty damned sticky. She was so tied up she was trembling—even at the end of the hour."

"I shouldn't wonder," Marty Fells said, straining the words around the butt of his first cigar of the day. He removed the cigar and his voice cleared a little. "She's between a rock and a hard place. Nobody knows that better than the lady herself."

"R. B. Dant?"

"He's got, and uses, a lot of leverage on everybody."

"I guessed that when she said he kept his family totally dependent on him. What about the husband?"

"Roy Dant? He's about forty, I think. Drinks beyond the level of a southern gentleman—so much so that he's been having grand mal seizures for the past six or eight years. That's something nobody admits and everybody knows. I guess he's never really grown up. As long as he has that Continental to drive and clothes to wear, he feels he doesn't have to." The cigar went back into Fell's heavy jaw. He puffed furiously.

Dr. Welton's voice was smooth, almost too soft. "What kind of trouble are you expecting, Jim?"

"I haven't much to hang it on, Derek. But I have the feeling that I've got a woman who's hanging on by her fingernails."

"A psychotic break?"

It was a question that took some reflection. I put my nose into my coffee cup for a moment, withdrawing it quickly when I found the black fluid too hot for my lips.

"No," I concluded finally. "I don't get that kind of feeling. I think it's more likely she'd break down physically—possibly even suicide."

"What's going *against* suicide?" Fred Carson asked. "Judging the information I was able to obtain from the boy, I'd say she's pretty much bound up in him and the two sisters."

"That's why I feel uneasy, I guess. She's got everything set on her children. If she lost control of them, or couldn't protect them, she might take drastic action. All I can say is, I get a hunch she's pretty close to the edge of something."

120

"Massive conversion reaction, maybe?" Fells suggested.

"Hey, Marty—that's kind of an old-fashioned diagnosis, isn't it?"

"So's CPI—constitutional psychopathic inferior—but it still fits some situations better than Inadequate Personality or some of the other new classification labels." He puffed the cigar several more times, loosing a cloud of blue gray smoke with each breath. "You haven't been in this red clay country long enough, Jim. A lot of the things the textbooks say about rare situations since people got to read Freud for themselves are still in the woodwork around here. The only book out here is scripture, with mental illness being *God's punishment for sin.*"

"There's a much more realistic reason for this woman to be hanging on," Derek Welton observed mildly. "Those three children are the only grandchildren of R. B. Dant. That probably means a million dollars or more per child."

"How long has she been married to Roy Dant?" I asked.

"Sixteen years. Before that, she worked for R. B."

"Worked for R. B.?"

"Confidential secretary for four years. She probably knows more about R. B. Dant's business than anybody other than the old man himself."

"Did she tell you about that?"

Fells grinned. "That's one of the advantages of bein' an old clay stomper. I grew up in Georgia—worked my way through school in R. B.'s Valdosta mills every summer. I saw her with him every month, when he came up there to give somebody hell."

"Anything between them?" Carson asked.

"Nothing. R. B. doesn't mix business with his pleasures. He has a taste for women who aren't quite so ladylike, anyhow." The heavy jowls disappeared behind another cloud of smoke. "If I was to be a bettin' man, I'd lay three to one the old man played matchmaker, just for insurance."

"Insurance?" Welton inquired.

"Sure. He trusted Karen McCullough like he trusted himself. He's always known that Roy couldn't pour piss out of a boot with the directions printed on the heel. If anything happened to R. B., he'd want to make sure somebody was left to run the businesses Roy would inherit."

"So when Roy is a bastard, and she leaves him and comes to R. B. looking for help—?" I left the sentence hanging in the air.

"He'd cut her down. Having made up his mind he wanted her to keep the Dant power alive, he wouldn't be likely to have anyone change that for as little reason as being fed up or loathing someone."

"He'd try to cut her down. If she knows him that well, she must have some leverage of her own."

"Providing she's got the guts to use it."

"Right now this is all speculation," Derek Welton interjected mildly. "Whatever she can or will do—what the situation really is with R. B. Dant. What she has or doesn't have in feelings for Roy Dant—the whole thing."

"And the son, Lee?" Carson asked. "If the old man has been bailing his son out of jams all his life, why does he let the law step in on his grandson? He sure wouldn't have to do that."

"He wouldn't, unless that seemed more to his advantage."

"All right," Welton said. "That part of it could fit with the idea of the old man using leverage on the mother of the boy. I can accept that, if it holds up. What I'm trying to make sure is that you three mavericks don't go into this with your minds already made up as to what is what. You might just have to backtrack in a touchy situation. I'm recommending a 'crash program of intensive listening' for all three of you. When you are really sure of the route to follow, then go ahead. I just don't want this clinic or any member of the staff prejudging people."

Coming in those terms, from the director, there could be only agreement. Our discussion shifted to the next case, and the staff meeting continued until the time for our first daily patient appointments.

Karen Dant used the first of several sessions politely, but there was very little movement toward her inner feelings. Her tension level was unabated, but there was no indication of any tangible nature as to what underlay that tension. She was guarded, poised, and chose her words carefully. She did not evade direct inquiry, but tried always to shift attention to the relationships with her son, Lee, and his younger sisters, Beth and Sandra. She quite adroitly sidestepped any attempt to shift the focus of attention to Roy Dant, or to his father, R. B. Dant.

During the fourth session, however, springs began to uncoil a bit. She seemed to find the innocuous talk and the polite parrying too heavy a burden to be supported. After a few moments, she braced me for a new facet in her problem.

"Roy will probably be calling you, doctor."

"He's back?"

The fingers of the hand resting on the arm of the deep chair clenched, but there was no other indication of adding pressure. "Yes. He's at his mother's house. He came to the farm Saturday evening, when he arrived from Montgomery."

"Farm?"

"We're living in one of his father's tenant places—the children and I." She paused momentarily, looked at me, then took the first step. "He seemed to expect to move right in there with us."

"How did you feel about that?"

The carefully set expression dissolved. For the first time her face truly mirrored her feelings. It showed disgust. "At first, I just couldn't believe it. He seems to completely ignore anything he doesn't want to believe—that anything happened. Then, very quickly, I was furious with him. We've been apart for five months. In that time he didn't seem to consider whether we were going to live or die. Then he shows up with big talk and presents for the children as if he had never been gone."

"Big talk?"

"As always—how much money he's got, all the money he's going to have, the things he's going to do. As if nothing were changed."

"What had changed, Karen?"

"Everything. It's just that it's all part of the bait."

"Bait?"

"How well we could be living if I'd give up this foolishness and forgive and forget."

"How *are* you living?"

"Like four hungry animals!" She looked at me for a long moment, pain wringing itself from her face. "I said we were living on one of R. B.'s tenant farms. That's too dignified. We're in the worst shack any sharecropper ever thought of inhabiting. When the fall rains come, it will be complete isolation—eighteen miles from town on a road that turns into a swamp with the first hard rain."

"Couldn't you find a place in town for yourself?"

"I have a grand total of eight dollars, Doctor Howard. Eight dollars, three children, and no job."

"Tell me about this, Karen."

She took a deep breath, shuddering with it. Her voice, when it came, was firm, but without the rigid control of her earlier speech.

"Things became impossible with Roy about eight months ago. We were in Jackson, Mississippi, then. We were operating a farm implement business for his father. It was failing. I knew that I'd have to take the children out of there. Roy was . . . back at his drinking."

Her voice dwindled away. She shuddered again with remembrance. The pause was long. As she talked, I found myself visualizing the scene of bitterness she was describing. . . .

"And how was your day, my dear?"

"Why not ask of my evening and my night? It's after one."

"My, aren't we cold."

"No levity, Roy. I just couldn't bear that, tonight."

"Why not tonight? Isn't it a beautiful night?"

"We lost the sale to Davidson, Roy. All our beautiful nights in Jackson are used up. All used up—our last chance."

"What do you mean, used up?"

"I mean we're through, and I'm leaving. The business is lost. There's not enough in the bank to pay the mechanic after this week. That order was for *eighty-five thousand dollars*, Roy! Even at the ridiculous price you offered Davidson for those pickers and tractors, we would have made over ten thousand dollars clear for this quarter . . . with all expenses met."

He moved to the breakfront in the dining area, yanking open the bottom drawer of a cabinet. "I'll find some other customer for those damned machines. Where's the bourbon?"

"I poured it down the sink."

"You *what?*"

"I poured it down the sink." She paused, looking at him. "For God's sake, Roy, stop lying to yourself! You know there's not another customer for those machines. You can't unload them all, not in time. Davidson is the only big grower within fifty miles. No man with less than three thousand acres is going to buy that much machinery. If we could have sold it a piece at a time, we might have had a chance—but we just can't wait any longer."

"Goddamn fifth of good whiskey. A full fifth."

"Will you listen to me? Just once? Those machines must go back to the distributor. There's enough money to pay Ben two weeks in lieu of notice, and to cover the return charges. I gave him notice today."

"You fired our mechanic?" He came toward her, stunned disbelief on his face. "You ruined our business?"

"We haven't got a business, Roy. That's the whole point—the only thing losing Davidson means." She went ahead quickly. "The parts inventory will bring a little. I called Justin Byers at the bank. We are just solvent enough not to have to declare bankruptcy—almost nothing more."

The slap rocked her almost across the arm of her chair. He stood looking down at her, hand back as if to strike her again.

"You stupid bitch! You closed out everything? Gave up *my* business?" He stressed the possessive pronoun. "Without even consulting *me*?"

She came out of the chair, her body trembling with rage. She looked at him for a long moment. When she spoke, her voice was completely flat and cold.

"Don't ever raise your hand to me again, Roy."

"I think I just might kill you!"

"You did that, a long time ago. This is my third resurrection, isn't it? Every time we've had a chance to make something for ourselves—to buy our way into a business of our own and have something that doesn't belong to your father—you run from it and hide among your bottles. This was the best chance we ever had, but the motels could have worked—the outlet stores for the mills could have worked."

She looked contemptuously at him. "*They* could have worked, Roy, *but you wouldn't*. You were too busy playing south-ern gentleman to people who wouldn't spit on you when your money ran out." She moved away from him, going toward the bathroom.

"Where the hell do you think you're going?"

"I'm going in there to be sick! As if everything else was not enough, I think I'm pregnant."

"Oh? Who's the happy father?" His voice was like a whip, flaying her.

In passing him, she came close to him. She turned, and her nails found his face, ripping flesh from his hairline to his chin. "You contemptible—"

His closed fist slammed into her stomach, driving her back and through the narrow door to the bathroom. The mat wrinkled under her feet and she stumbled, turning to catch herself and falling across the high narrow rim of the old-fashioned bathtub. . . .

"The last thing I remember, Doctor Howard, was Roy standing in the bathroom door, screaming horrible things at me." Karen's face was gray with remembered pain. "I came to in the hospital, several hours later."

"Had Roy gotten help for you?"

"The terrible screaming woke Lee up. He got the doctor for both of us. Roy had gone into a seizure. We were both unconscious."

It took a long moment for Karen's struggle to reward her with some regained composure. "I lost the baby," she said in a strangely calm voice. "When I could travel, I brought the children back to Danton. Roy was kept in the hospital. I hadn't seen him after that until he showed up last weekend."

Our time was nearly gone, but I had to press a bit further. "Had he physically abused you before?"

"He'd struck me with his hand—slapped me—twice before that." Her voice was soft and wondering with a tragic and revealing insight. "Each time it was when we failed at something. Each time he denied that he had fathered one of the children. He accused me of having an affair—insisted that some other man had fathered them. The first time it was Sandra, and when the mill outlet business failed he added Beth to the list."

"Did that always lead to it? Failing in business?"

126

"Mostly, I think. But when Roy was drinking he was—" She broke off, her face burning a deep red.

"Impotent is the word I think you're looking for."

Her blush subsided a bit. "Yes. It's not a very nice word, is it?"

"Nor a very nice situation, I'm sure. When did it begin?"

"About the time Beth was born, I think." She found the blush rising again. "It . . . didn't happen all the time, then."

"It came to be all of the time?"

"Nearly so." Her voice had fallen to a whisper. "Perhaps every two or three months he . . ." Her voice strengthened and she continued. "I suppose I withdrew from him. That would hurt his pride, I know."

"Hurt pride led to accusations?"

The flush ran to a deep scarlet, but her voice remained clear. "I'm a normal woman, doctor—with all the needs of a healthy, normal woman." Her voice drained down in volume as the impact of a particular event from the past flooded her mind. . . .

"Roy, I've got to talk to you."

"I don't want talk. I want us in bed, getting sweaty."

"Not till we get something settled." Karen unfolded his arms from around her waist, moving away from the man who stood behind her, nibbling at the back of her neck.

He shrugged, turning toward the sink and pouring himself another drink. "Any more ice?"

"Not unless you learn to put the trays back in the refrigerator. Fix your drink and sit here at the table with me." She waited until he complied, sitting like an unruly child who has been chastised.

"All right, tell me the story," he muttered, his voice resigned and edged with irritation.

"This story concerns sixty lost dollars."

"What sixty dollars?"

"The wages I had to pay the loafers you rounded up to do work that you and our janitor, Willie Fisher, could have done," Karen told him. "You two could have unloaded that shipment yourselves in about two or three hours. You didn't need to put six men on, at ten dollars apiece. I had to take the money out of the

127

food budget—the cash drawer in the store wouldn't cover it."

"I helped you stock the shelves, didn't I? I don't intend to work and sweat like a nigra on the freight dock. Not when there are people for hire."

"If they'd work when you hired them, you'd only have needed one—two at the most. But you find all the bums in the saloons. We can't make a go of this outlet store unless you begin to pay some attention to costs."

"The sale will make it up. It's a twice-a-year windfall."

"Ten thousand second-quality towels. The profit is eight cents apiece. That's eight hundred dollars. You just threw away sixty of that. Twice-a-year windfall? The usual month in this store runs at about four hundred dollars clear. Just how far does that stretch with three children?"

"I don't intend to work like a field hand just so you can show dear old father a net profit. He knows you're smart."

"It's not *his* profit, Roy. It's our living! Yours, mine, the children's. We can't make it with just this one store. We need a second store, then a third. Do you realize we could build these mill outlet stores into a chain? There are a dozen cities big enough to support Dant outlet stores—Savannah, Mobile, Huntsville, Birmingham. We could have them all over the South. Little stores, with one or two employees, netting about five hundred dollars a month. A dozen of them would be making us at least sixty thousand dollars a year."

"Hey, you're a greedy little bitch. That sounds great. Now, why don't you have a drink with me?"

"I'm serious, Roy. I'm trying to show you where we could go in the next five years."

"And in the next five minutes we could be in bed, and involved in all sorts of interesting activities."

"There has to be something ahead, Roy. Some reason to scrape by like we're doing. A way to do it ourselves, instead of having your mother give us things, or your father raise hell and then set us up in a business."

He slammed the empty glass down onto the table. "All right!" he said loudly. "You're right, of course. You couldn't be anything else. My father turned you into a damned adding machine."

He saw her shocked look. It forced him to reconsider. He

rose from the straight chair and came around the table to stand behind her, bending to resume the nuzzling of her neck. He felt her stiffen under his lips.

"I'm not fighting with you—not tonight. We'll get the damned stores and make a fortune big enough to buy out R. B. Dant."

"We can do it, Roy. We can really make it on our own. I can—"

It hit him wrongly. "You!" he exploded. "Always what *you* can do." His fingers closed on her shoulders like clamps. She gasped with the sudden pain.

"I was only trying to say that I could help you to do it." She rose from the chair, trying to reap some salvage from the suddenly deteriorated situation. She moved into his arms. "I want you to do it, honey. I want the world to know you're something very special." She kissed him, deep and searchingly. "And I don't want us fighting about these things. It's just . . ." Karen swallowed a large piece of her pride. ". . . I get impatient for my man to want that world to know how much of a man he really is. . . ."

"He didn't show anyone, doctor. That night, he couldn't even show me. That was the first time he failed, I think. I don't know why. I guess it was because he had been drinking all day."

"Sounded like he was the one campaigning for sex that night."

"We never . . . concealed our appetites from each other, doctor. Until that night—" She broke off, slightly embarrassed.

"He'd been quick, frequent, and demanding." I finished the sentence for her.

"How did you know?"

"Call it a hunch." I smiled an indication that I was aware of her attractiveness. To tell her that frequency, demand, and precocious climax were frequent characteristics of basically dependent men would not have served any purpose in her treatment, at least at that point.

"I . . . can respond, doctor . . ." She was again embarrassed.

"A good, healthy female appetite for sex." I barely paused, feeling I had to offer her some support. "I'd imagine this is very difficult for you to tell, and I don't mean to make it more difficult."

"I'll make it easy for you, Doctor Howard. I know that I

could ruin everything for my children if I were foolish in that way. So I've never been foolish, no matter how . . . er . . . *hungry* I became. I'm just not willing to give that kind of weapon to the Dant family. That's part of the reason why I came back to Danton, instead of taking the children to Denver."

"Why Denver?"

"I lived there before. I still have some family—a cousin and an uncle and my grandfather there. My parents were killed in an automobile accident nine years ago. I could get a job there, very easily. R. B. Dant doesn't own Colorado—just Seminole County."

She stared at me for another penetrating assessment of my trustworthiness. "But what R. B. Dant owns," she said slowly, "he controls. If I had gone to Colorado, he'd have struck back through the children."

"Struck back?"

"He'd have cut them off without a cent."

"You're a capable business woman, Karen. You've proved that several times."

"At my best day, we're talking about perhaps seven hundred dollars a month. The R. B. Dant estate and holdings would mean several millions of dollars. How could I ask my children to settle for a working mother, baby-sitters, and the feeling of being cheated?"

"Is that why they're in a sharecropper shack?"

"Not only that. How did we get into this?"

"I thought the topic was sex."

"No. The topic was foolishly providing R. B. Dant with another weapon. Sex would be just one more lever he would use, if I were so idiotic as to give him the chance. I'm not going to do it. He has too many levers already."

"Levers?"

"Like my chances of finding a job. Very few of the employers around here would hire me if they felt they were antagonizing R. B. Dant."

She stared again, trying to decide if I could be trusted further. "I told you that R. B. Dant has complete control here," she said. "Around here, few people would take the chance to hire me for a nickel a day if they felt they were bucking him. But I came back here, hoping he would relent enough because of his grandchildren to give me some help for a little while. Even when he put me on the spot and told me I could live in that old shack, I went along with it because I figured he was just testing me.

"By the time I realized he meant to rub my nose in the dirt and keep me there until I agreed to play the game his way, it was too late for me to pull out and go anywhere else because of Lee's action in blowing up that pond."

Karen Dant was never again purposefully evasive. From the fourth session on she trusted me. Thereafter, she moved directly into problem situations in each of her sessions. Only when she was unsure of her feelings or her facts did she hesitate or slow down her presentation.

She seemed to be making an effort to be as fair in her statements as she could be. This was demonstrated by her habit of revealing her feelings only after she had factually reported the incidents. Perhaps this was the quality that had put her into a position of trust with R. B. Dant when she was only nineteen and had made her his right hand shortly thereafter.

I came to learn more of him in the following sessions. Karen, more efficiently than any patient I had ever known, set things into an automatic chronology. This simplified my work, but it also had the unexpected value of making the described scenes so vivid that I was more of a witness to the event than a listener for whom she was reconstructing a situation.

I first became aware of this vividness and my own visualization of what was taking place with her account of her first meeting with R. B. Dant after leaving her husband and returning to Danton.

"I was very tired from the drive, having just been released from the hospital in Jackson," she said. "I didn't feel up to discussing Roy or anything else with R. B. that afternoon. What I wanted was a bath and a night of sleep. I deliberately stopped at Manion, fifteen miles from Danton, instead of coming on into town. We checked into a motel there, late in the afternoon. Lee and the girls went to the swimming pool as quickly as they could shower and get into their suits.

"I filled a tub, putting myself into it for a long soak. I have no idea of how long I had been lolling there, trying to relax. I heard the door of the room open, but I thought it was one of the children and paid little attention. I—I should have." Her jaw took the firm set I was coming to know quite well. She pressed herself through the telling of any incident that had been personally embarrassing or distasteful. It was almost like an act of personal subjugation.

"I should have taken my robe into the bathroom—or *something. . . .*"

"Smells right good in here, Karrie."

Karen turned quickly, straightening in the tub until her breasts broke from beneath the foaming suds. Suddenly shamed and scarlet, she hunched down awkwardly, covering herself with her arms. Her flaming face was fixed on the lean, tall man slouching against the frame of the bathroom door.

"What are you doing?"

"Don't fluster yourself none, Karrie. If I never seen tits before, I wouldn't know what they was. Since I have, they don't come as no shock."

"Please. Go out and wait a moment for me. I'll talk to you then."

"Fer Chrissakes, woman. You're my daughter-in-law. Ain't like I was some young buck tryin' to get inta your pants. I just want to hear what you got to say."

"I don't want to talk in here—not like this. I'm—I'm *naked!*"

"Most people are when they bathe, 'ceptin' one ole gal I heard of who was so damn religious she bathed in her drawers so she wouldn't excite herself none. Don't that beat all?"

"Please, R. B. Get my robe for me. Do me the courtesy to let me at least get myself covered. Please!"

For response, he stepped into the bathroom, knocked his pipe dottle out into the toilet, dropped the seat lid, and sat down, facing her.

"Karrie, I reckon we better do some talkin'." He stuffed the empty pipe into his shirt pocket, and with the same hand scratched at his lean jaw. "I figure you and Roy got into some kind of ruckus, somethin' that makes you need some coolin'-off time."

With the first shock of his appearance past, Karen's attention and thoughts snapped to the strategies she had considered during her time in the hospital, following the miscarriage.

"He caused me to lose a child. Your second grandson, R. B. I can't forgive him that." She was recovering her ability to function, despite her embarrassment.

The old man reduced the scratching to running his thumbnail under his jawline. "Don't know if I can forgive him that, either."

She moved toward the topic, sensing an advantage in the directness of her approach. "He lost our child, lost the best chance we'd ever had to make some kind of life on our own. He promised Claude Davidson eight pickers and four tractors at almost ten thousand below what they should have brought in." She covered this card with another trump. "Then he didn't even make the effort to get them in time to deliver on schedule."

"Drinkin', wasn't he?"

She nodded.

"He's one weak son of a bitch, all right. Can't say no to himself, no more'n a kid."

"I closed out the business while it was still solvent. I didn't have to declare us in bankruptcy. All the bills got paid, even my hospital bill."

"You did right on that. He's still in the hospital. That man Byers at the bank was a good choice for you."

The statement was the first indication Karen had that R. B. Dant was fully aware of what had happened in Jackson. "If you knew all of this, why didn't you say so? You know it was the only thing left I could do."

"Reckon it was."

"You know—not reckon. We *both* know. This was the same as five years ago with motels—three years ago with the outlet stores. It's always the same—six months of trying, then quit . . . quit and go out to play like the child you know he is. Like he was tired of his new toy."

"He is a child, Karrie. I agree with you on that. That's why he needs you so much—to take care of him."

"Not any more, R. B. Not ever again."

The movement in the old man's lean, weathered face was almost imperceptible, but there seemed to be a sudden hooding of the gray eyes. "Roy ain't never gonna make it without you."

"Right now I care very little whether he does or not. All I know is that it is all over."

The narrowed, hooded eyes regarded her for a long moment. Suddenly, she felt her nakedness again. She clutched her chest more tightly with her arms. "Please get my robe for me and let me get out of this bathtub."

"Go ahead. I ain't stoppin' you."

"R. B., I'm ashamed."

"Don't know why you should be. You got a damned good body for a woman who's gonna be forty before too long. You're lean in the flanks and soft and full in the hips and chest. Ain't no reason to be ashamed when God gave you somethin' special to be proud of, woman."

"You're going to do it, aren't you? You're going to sit right there until you force me to get out of this tub in front of you."

"I ain't gonna fetch and carry for you, if that's what you mean. No more than you're gonna fetch and carry for Roy anymore." He stared at her for a moment. "Just what do you figure you're gonna do?"

"I'm going to work. I want to support my children. Is that so hard to understand?" His staring made her nervous. "Please go into the other room."

"You just ain't takin' nobody's feelin's into account but your own, are you?" He fumbled out the old pipe again, taking a great deal of time to load it from the pouch he drew from his hip pocket. "Ain't nobody counts but Karrie." He tamped the pipe and struck a match, sucking noisily on the wetness of stem and bowl juices that had accumulated to signal that the pipe needed cleaning. "Just who do you figure to work for?"

Karen's heart sank. She perceived his cold inflection. He had known she would. She had to act, and she realized it. It had to be a frontal assault, a clear declaration of her determination. She set her jaw and forced herself to rise in the tub until she could reach the bath towels lodged in the ring clamp beyond the shower curtain.

"I'm going to divorce Roy, R. B. My mind is made up."

She looked directly at him, and there was no quavering in her voice or in her body.

"You got soap on your ass and bubbles in your made-up mind. I told you that you are his only chance. It just ain't gonna be that way."

She turned toward him, presenting a frontal view, completely exposing breasts, thighs, Venus mound, and the soft blackness of pubis. Somehow she forced herself to resist the temptation to hide behind the towel. She knew she had to match his hardness. Quite ignoring his stare, she efficiently but unhurriedly dried herself with the terry cloth, in no way shielding herself with it. Then she stepped over the rim of the bathtub and went past him into the bedroom, taking her robe from the open but packed suitcase and putting it on.

He had risen and come to the doorway of the bath, again slouching against the frame of the door and sucking at the pipe.

"You got guts, Karrie. I'll give you that. You 'most got enough to be a Dant."

"I don't want to be a Dant. For once in sixteen years, I just want to be myself."

"And yet you want my help."

"Yes, I do. I need a job—somewhere. I need a job to feed and house my children—your grandchildren, R. B."

"I suppose you'd want to move in with ma and me. Have us feed you."

"Until I can find a job and a place of my own. There—there's not much money after clearing things out in Jackson."

"I want Roy's *wife* in my house. That's the way I want it." He sucked hard on the pipe. The wet slap of juices being pulled into his mouth could be heard across the room. "Goddamnit. I got a slug of Indian honey. Tastes like hell." He turned and spat into the draining bathtub. "You comin' home with me on those conditions?"

The hard composure slipped for a moment. Karen shuddered in spite of herself. "No." She looked at him and played the card she had hoped not to have to use. "But if you don't help your grandchildren, it's going to shame you in Seminole County."

"You have got guts enough to be a Dant, by God! Tryin' to blackjack me."

"You're the one who's forcing it. I'm only asking for temporary food and shelter—nothing else."

"Mebbe exceptin' what you think you might have a chance to get from Roy. He'd have to get it from his stupid mother, outa her household allowance. I could sure as hell stop that if I found Roy beggin' to her. Roy ain't got a pot to piss in, and you can't depend on him *or her* in any damned divorce court."

"They are his children. They're your own kin."

"Yeah, but it ain't him you're fightin', Karrie. It's me."

"I don't want to fight with anybody." Her face showed all the fatigue she was feeling. "I just want *out*. I don't want to fight you, R. B. We've always understood each other pretty well. I like you. I don't approve of you, but I like you."

"Then you know better than to buck me, Karrie." He took the pipe from his mouth. "You rightly won't like me so much when you find out you don't understand me at all."

"Is it asking so much? Food and shelter for Roy Dant's children?"

He stood for a long moment, his thin face screwed into a most unusual expression. He never took his eyes from the woman who was facing him across the motel's two double beds. Then his eyes hooded themselves again.

"Food and shelter? All right. I'll see that you have food and shelter. I'll even throw in medical attention. There's a house two miles out beyond the old gin, where that nigra Waybrook used to farm. I'll have a week's groceries there tomorrow. You and the kids can camp out there for a while, so that you can do some serious thinkin'."

"That—shack?"

"You asked for shelter. It's good enough for that. You'd better get there 'fore dark, though—ain't no lights that far out. . . ."

The scene, which she had let me experience as vividly as if I had been there, faded from view and into silence. The mood and moment vanished, and brought us back to the small office of the clinic. Karen Dant was again my patient, rather than the player in a drama her words had formed in my mind.

The silence stretched interminably. Finally, I had to ask the questions that demanded answers.

136

"You went to that shack?"

"Yes."

"It was the only way you could provide for the children?"

I could see a sudden deadening of her eyes. When she finally answered, her voice did not seem firm. "Yes."

The change in her intonation gave me a cue. "There was more to that argument with R. B. Dant, wasn't there, Karen?"

The voice became a strangled whisper. "No. Nothing, really."

"You might find a way to tell me about it."

"I'd . . . rather not. Must I?"

"He had some more potent threat to use. Otherwise, you'd have gone to some agency for help before accepting those terms."

"You . . . you're right, of course." She straightened in her chair. "We threatened each other. He simply had the more intolerable threat." Her voice firmed. "I told him that if he would not help me properly, I'd go on relief and get money for destitute children."

"Why didn't you? You could have."

The pause was one of the longest I'd ever experienced with Karen. She turned her dark eyes to me, and they softened with pain. "Do you know what a 'bright child' is, Doctor Howard?"

"Are you saying you are part Negro?"

"No, not Negro. But with what R. B. Dant could make of my lineage, it would be better if I were. He could ruin my children socially, anywhere in the South."

She held me closely with her eyes, needing to validate me once more as an object of trust. "I told you that I came here from Denver. My mother was Arapaho—full-blooded. That means I'm a half-breed."

"So?"

"Have you seen how the Indian and part-Indian children fare in this state? They're shunned more than Negroes."

"R. B. Dant knows of this? How?"

"R. B. Dant knows anything he can buy or learn about any person he wants to control." The tears clouding her eyes rolled down her cheeks. "That's one of the main reasons I haven't gone ahead with the divorce. I can't let him ruin my children. He's got to accept their rights as his grandchildren. He's got to believe I can't change Roy—I'm not God."

"How did he find out?"

"Probably from my birth certificate, when he had me bonded. Mother's maiden name was Riverwind, though she always went by just Rivers. I suppose he checked on the name. He tries to verify everything."

Again there was the prolonged silence, while Karen reweighed her resistance. "Maybe I should have just given in—it sure would have been much easier." The tremor was in her hands again, as pronounced as in the first interview. "Anything would be easier than to be caught like this. There's just nothing I can do."

"Can't, or won't? Because of the money?"

"Haven't you been listening? My children's reputation is at stake, as well as their inheritance. If I go ahead right now to divorce Roy, the children are ruined with every weapon the old man can use. R. B. could even get an annulment on the grounds that I misrepresented my racial background at the time of the marriage. This state has miscegenation laws. You know what the kind of mud that would throw could do to my children?"

"This *country* has laws about indentured servitude, too."

"In Seminole County?" Her laugh was short, a bitter little machine gun firing a short burst. "We've brought ourselves to a Mexican standoff, doctor. Maybe I should say a Kiowa bargain, as my mother's family might call it. R. B. Dant will give me all the time it takes for me to make up my mind to do things his way, so long as I don't ask for charity from the county and hold him up to ridicule. That's where it stands."

"For how long?"

"For as long as you can help me to stay sane."

Karen could not be shaken from this conviction. During the weeks that followed, she existed in this uneasy bargain, fighting the lonely battle week after week. The emotional drain was drastic, but additional pressures were also brought to bear. Karen found all doors continuing to be closed when she sought work. Even the gasoline she used to drive to the clinic was obtained by selling, item by item, the few things she had in her immediate possession.

Lee had been granted probation, but on conditions of strict restitution. He worked for his grandfather, with all wages applied against the debt. The cost of four sticks of dynamite and the broken padlock appeared on the itemized listing, as well as the estimated cost of rebuilding the fishing pond. He continued his meetings with Fred Carson, and the ventilation and support he drew from the social worker seemed to be enough to keep him functioning—at least he did not violate his probation. His biggest regret was that he could do nothing to help his mother financially, and this help-lessness was the wellspring of constant cold anger.

Fred Carson gave me a picture of the steam boiler in which the fourteen-year-old was trapped. The social worker's description brought to life the inferences I had made through psychological testing. The massive anger I had seen needed no description, but the genesis of that anger—the life events leading up to its eruption —could only be speculations until the boy ventilated his feelings in his own words.

The need Lee Dant had for a strong man with whom to identify was now being filled by his social worker therapist, but we both had only hunches as to where the boy had put that identification before. Certainly it did not seem likely that his father had filled the role, especially as Fred described the break-through episode. . . .

"Mother isn't here. She went into town to try and find a job."

"And you're cutting firewood. Hard work, isn't it, Lee?"

"I don't mind. We'll be needing a lot of it in a few more weeks, when the rains come." The saw bit into another scrap of two-by-four, riding with easy strokes.

"You work well, son. I'm glad you help your mother so much." Roy Dant seated himself on the stump block a few yards away from the sawbuck, looking at the boy and planning an approach.

The boy said nothing. He continued to cut the broken scraps of lumber into stovewood length.

" 'Course, you and your mother wouldn't have to live like this if she wasn't so damned stubborn. You wouldn't be getting your hands all full of splinters, and your sisters wouldn't be wash-ing their own clothes."

Roy gestured across the barnyard toward the back of the

weathered house, where his two daughters were hanging wet clothing on a sagging line. Beth, the younger sister, patiently moved a wooden crate to climb upon to reach the line. "You children sure have to pay for your mother's foolishness, don't you?"

The boy stiffened. The smooth stroke of the saw suddenly became a harsh thrust. The handsaw blade bound and sang a harsher screeching sound in the hard dry wood.

"We're doing all right, *father*." Lee stressed the title as a warning. He felt uncomfortable, vaguely disloyal.

"I want us all back together again," Roy Dant said, missing the caution signal entirely. "Together, where I can take care of all of us."

"That's for mother to decide." The boy's voice was cold.

"It's for me to decide. I'm the head of this family!" Even as he blustered them forth, both the boy and the man knew the words were empty.

"Then why aren't *you* buying the food?" Lee's cold voice gave way to heat—sudden, eruptive, and scalding. "Why don't *you* get us a decent place to live? Why does everything have to come from grandpa?"

Roy Dant's features turned white, then flamed red. He lunged up from the stump. "I won't have you talk to me that way! I'm your father! I'll beat your smart ass bloody!"

The remaining length of the splintered two-by-four lay in the sawbuck—three feet of tapered timber. Roy's advance on his son was suddenly halted by the sight of the club snapping into the boy's hands.

"Get out of here. I'm not a *woman*. I fight back!"

They stood immobile, glaring at each other. Roy Dant outweighed his own son by forty pounds, but the stance of the lean, hard-muscled youth with the heavy club froze his action.

"Get away from us," the boy repeated. "Let us alone." The words were balls of alien ice, pelting at the man. "It's all your fault!"

"It is not. I'm not responsible for your having to live like this. Your mother did it when she ran away and came begging to your grandfather."

Tears welled up in the boy's eyes. "Get out of here, dad.

Don't make me hit you." He tightened his grip on the heavy club. "Just go on back to grandpa's and get drunk or whatever you want. Just you let us alone, and *tell him to let us alone.*"

"I'll remember this, boy. Don't think I won't."

"I *want* you to. I want you to remember. I fight back!"

Roy Dant looked at his son, uncomprehending. Then he turned and moved quickly back to his car, starting it and spinning the wheels in the soft dirt of the barnyard. The drifting cloud of dust settled on the wet laundry hanging on the line.

Lee Dant dropped the club, then threw his body onto the ground beside it. Tears of rage and shame flooded his eyes, and his firmed, lean shoulders racked with sobs. Between the heaving spasms, his thoughts formed themselves into words. *"I fight back. Somebody's got to fight back. . . ."*

"That's the way it was, Jim. That's what happened just before he dynamited the dam." Fred Carson's face was lighted by the trust he'd won, but saddened by the cost of the reported action. "He stole the dynamite that night, and blew the dike out of the pond."

"How do you read it?"

"He had to hit somebody, someway. He couldn't have hit his father. It would have been like picking on a cripple. He had to take a swing at somebody. R. B. Dant was the only one Lee felt was strong enough to fight."

"He's a lot of boy."

"Check. I hope I do a better job of filling the bill for my own boy." Carson smiled his boyish smile. "How's it going with his mother?"

"Pretty good, I think. But I'm worried about how broke they are. She's hocking things to buy gas to come here."

"She ought to get out of Seminole County, somehow." He looked at me to see if I agreed. "She's up against it here."

"Let's get Derek and Marty in on it in the morning to see if we can come up with any ideas."

A subsequent staff conference led to reducing the frequency of Karen's and Lee's visits to the clinic. We reluctantly went to every other week to try to save her the cost of the fifty-mile trip to obtain therapy.

I braced her, on the next session after we had spaced the visits, with the question of her leaving the area.

"Haven't you had enough yet? Why haven't you picked up and gone back to Denver?"

"I wish to Heaven I had, when I had the chance. I really can't now—no matter what?" Her voice turned it into a question, it seemed.

"No matter what R. B. Dant wants?"

She looked wistfully at me. I might have expected tears from another patient, but not Karen. I continued with a question.

"Do you still think the price of leaving is too high?"

"It would mean abandoning my children. I couldn't take them with me. Lee's probation restricts him to Seminole County, and Roy managed to get a restraining order stopping me from relocating the girls without his written permission." Her jaw set. "Every move has been anticipated and blocked."

She paused for a moment, then shifted the subject slightly. "It doesn't help to have Roy 'checking' on me every week, and telling me what an idiot I am to live as I'm living when things could be so different. Strange, isn't it? Sometimes I get so lonely for an adult to talk to that I'm even glad to see *him*."

"Or to come here and talk with me?"

She nodded, her hands still trembling.

"Are you fearful of losing that, too?" I looked at her, trying to decipher the basis of the fear. "Are you afraid we might be put under pressure from the Dants?"

"I'm sorry. I don't mean that." Her denial was quick and strong. Perhaps it betrayed more uncertainty because of the fact that it did come so quickly.

"All right, Karen. It's a legitimate question and you have a right to an answer. If our board of directors could be reached—and I don't think they could—they would lose the entire staff instantly. No therapist would submit. We're just not that hungry. Every state in the union is desperate for professionals, and no professional worth his salt is afraid to say no. The only real answer to blackmail is to refuse to honor it."

"You don't know R. B. Dant."

"I know which cat gets chased."

"What?"

"Which cat gets chased. It's the one that runs."

"Am I running?"

"No. I don't think you are. You're trying to stay hunched down and frozen, hoping to outlast someone with nearly limitless resources. Every day your holding becomes a little bit weaker. Lee's forced work builds him toward explosion, the girls are undoubtedly irritated, irritating, and demanding, and your belly is full of worms."

She flared at me. "I don't have a *belly!* I hate that word! I have an abdomen or a stomach. I do not have a belly!"

This was the first time Karen had been truly angry with me. Her reaction was out of proportion. I had to follow it up. "See how much on edge you are? Those resources are strained, too. Now, why should that word hit you so hard?"

The suddenness of my responses took her aback, and she became confused and apologetic. "I'm sorry. I didn't mean to flare at you that way."

"Don't be sorry. It's time you quit holding the lid on your feelings. Now, what about the word belly?"

"It's coarse—crude."

"That's not all."

"No." Her anger found its proper target, flowing out in a flood of pain that projected the scene vividly. Again the words made me a witness, not one hearing a report. . . .

"Ain't no reason for you to be so unfriendly." The voice was deep and raspy, yet it contained a cold, hard underwhine, like a saw biting into a pine knot. "I ain't meanin' no harm, Miz Mc-Cullough."

"All right. Let us leave it at that."

"I was just offerin' to see you safe home—you and yer purty little girl—seein's how Tom's gone on that Cheyenne job."

"I thank you for your concern, but we are quite able to take care of ourselves, Mr. Wade."

"Downright unfriendly, you are."

"I thanked you for your concern, and told you that we did not require your protection. I don't feel that there is anything more to say."

"By God, you sure do talk ladylike for a squaw!"

143

"You've been drinking. You're not yourself, so I'll let that remark pass and not tell Mr. McCullough of it. Now let us pass, Wade!"

The whine of his voice came through, insinuating and hard. He planted himself in the narrow lane of concrete walk a foot above the muddy bed of the street, his red face flaming. "I don't take no orders from you, Indian. You walk down there in the mud. I goddamn well don't give the sidewalk to anybody's red bitch!"

Karen lunged toward the man, her hands rising. "You can't say those things to my momma!"

The mother's hand caught her, whirling the small girl around. "No, Karen!" Her voice was sharp, but it did not rise in pitch. "Go back to your saloon and your bottle, Wade. You've upset my daughter, and you've said entirely too much."

The ten-year-old girl stood rigid, facing the man who blocked their passage. Her mother's hand was still tightly clenching her upper arm. "You're a . . . *you're a bad man,* Mr. Wade. You—" She broke off, not knowing words to use in a situation she had never before faced.

"Shut up, kid! One of these days you'll have some half-breed bastard in your belly—just like your maw!"

Karen's face went white. From the corner of her eye, she saw her mother's hand flash to her hair, pulling out the eight-inch hatpin that held up her waist-length black hair. In half a step, the mother reached Wade. Her hand flashed upward in a driving arc.

Wade's scream was an animal thing. The force of the thrust drove him backward, and he stumbled from the raised sidewalk. In falling, he twisted, sprawling face down in the muddy street.

Her mother followed like a cat. Her heavy Cuban-heeled shoe stomped into Wade's head, just behind his left ear. The force of the kick accomplished two things: Wade was rendered unconscious, and the kick rolled him so that he now lay face up in the mud, the hatpin sticking out of his shoulder.

Mildred Riverwinds McCullough bent to him, pulling the hatpin from his flesh. She looked at him for a moment and then wiped the blood from the weapon on the front of his shirt. Only then did she look back at the terrified girl on the sidewalk.

"Is he dead, momma? Did you *kill* him?"

"No. He'll live, unless he's still here in Brodie when your father gets home."

Mildred calmly replaced the hatpin, coiling her braided hair into a neat bun atop her head. Then she stepped back onto the sidewalk, taking Karen's shoulders and pulling her to her side.

"Why did he do that, momma? Why did he say such awful things?"

"Are you ashamed of me, Karen? Do you mind that I'm a squaw?"

"You're not a squaw, momma. You're my momma."

"I'm Arapaho, Karen. I'm a full-blooded Indian woman. To some men, that means I'm like a dog or a horse. That's why they are so . . ." she groped for a word the child would understand, ". . . *mean.*"

"Am I—"

"An Indian? You are partly so. That is why it is so important that you take great care to be neat and clean—and to speak correctly, as I have taught you to do. Otherwise, you're just another dirty Indian—a half-breed."

"What did he mean, momma? A half-breed bastard in my belly? What is that?"

A flicker of pain went across Mildred McCullough's smooth face. "Come along home, my very special child. It is too soon, but there are many things that this will force me to tell you. You have a right to know. Now you *must* know."

"But you fought him, momma. You fought with him and hurt him."

The flicker of pain died, and the face went sad and calm. "There are times, Karen, when there is nothing left to do but fight."

"He could have hurt you. I was so frightened."

"Yes. He could have hurt me. That is true. But had I done nothing, he would have hurt me far more. That is the lesson you can learn of such unpleasant things as this. One must always do the thing that serves one's pride, Karen. To do anything else, or to fail to do, *that is cowardice.* . . ."

Following this revelation, Karen sat for a long time in a strange kind of reverie. I sat watching her feel her way through the paths of memory, learning something of herself. The expressions of successive insights formed and dissolved in her face, fleeting markers of the emergence of her own identity, scars of the bitter lessons and warm flushes of the more tender ones she had learned.

At last, she spoke. "I've hated crudeness and vile words since that time, just as momma did."

"Yes. You've learned to be neat, and oh, *so proper.*"

"You're mocking me."

"No, I'm not. I'm only trying to show you the other lesson your mother was trying to teach you. The one you need to use in your own life."

"That there are times when one must fight?"

"Unless you prefer to stand on the sidewalk and beg for what is your right."

"I'm not begging."

"Are you ready to walk in the mud, then?"

"No!" The flare was there. "I'd see them in hell first!" She quickly extinguished the flare. "But I can't do it. How could I give away my children's future. They'd have nothing!"

"How could your mother let you see her ready to kill a man if she had to do so? *How could she risk your not understanding?*" I held her tightly with my eyes. "Did you think she was bad, or cruel, or vicious?"

"Certainly not. She did the only thing there was to do."

"So why do you feel your children can't understand what you must do?"

"They're so . . . young."

"Yes. In fact, the youngest is only two years older than you were when you learned the facts of life from your mother—that anything which does not serve your pride is cowardice." I did not let up. "Can you really believe your children have so little awareness or understanding—so little strength that they cannot learn a lesson from *this kind* of unpleasantness?"

"But what can I do? I'm blocked at every turn."

"Make your choice. Either walk in the mud, or find *your* hatpin."

I had not expected to see Karen until her next appointment,

two weeks following the vivid session. I do not know why I had not anticipated the massive counterpunch that she would draw when she made her first decisive move to divorce Roy Dant.

It was nearly midnight when the phone rang at my home. I put aside the book I had been reading and turned down the stereo enough to be able to hear.

"Doctor Howard? This is Lee Dant."

"Yes, Lee. What's happened?"

"My mother's in the hospital, doctor. She needs you."

"Was there an accident?"

"No. I'm sure she wasn't in an accident. She just lies there and won't say a word. You've got to help her!"

"Seminole Hospital?"

"Yes."

"I'll be there as soon as I can. Who's her doctor?"

"Doctor Lloyd is the one we called. He's still with her."

"I'll call him, and then come right over."

I pressed the cradle button on the telephone, let it up, and dialed the hospital. When the switchboard operator answered, I identified myself and asked for Dr. Lloyd. It took a few moments before he was on the line.

"Jim Howard, Dave. What's happened to Karen Dant?"

"I don't know. She seems like she's in deep shock—dazed and mute."

"Have you sedated her?"

"Not yet. I'd like to know what the hell's going on before I give any kind of medication."

"Let me come and see her. I've been working with her for almost five months. Give me a chart order for consultation. If this gets consolidated, we'll have a hell of a problem. I want to come over right now."

"Consolidated?"

"We'll talk about it when I get there. Okay?"

"Sure. I didn't know she was your patient. I was going to try and get a psychiatric consultation on her tomorrow. Come on over, I'll wait for you."

"I can't tell you why, Dave, but write it as an order that I am to see her. Please, it's important."

"All right, if you're going to be legalistic about it."

"I'll explain when I get there—about ten minutes."

I cradled the receiver. I knew R. B. Dant was on the board of the hospital, but I also knew that he could not change a physician's treatment order and bar me from seeing Karen. I put on my shoes, made a hasty explanation to my wife, then got in my car for the brief drive to the hospital.

On the way, I tried to think of what unusual pressure might have made Karen react with this kind of collapse. I remembered the first staff meeting in which the Dant situation was discussed. Then I had conjectured suicide or physical collapse. I tried to sort out the many impressions that had led me to that early hunch. One thing was certain; Karen had withdrawn from the fight. She no longer felt capable of staying in the unequal contest.

She lay on the hospital bed, unmoving. Even through the thin sheet, I could see the rigidity of her body. Her eyes were fixed on some point in the ceiling. She did not react when Dr. Lloyd and I came into the room.

I moved to the bed, standing beside her, taking her hand. It was set, as if it had been molded of hard plastic. I squeezed it. There was no answering contraction in her muscles. I pressed the ball of my thumb deep into the palm of her hand. Even this produced no contracture.

"Karen? It's Doctor Howard."

There was no response. Her eyes remained fixed on the ceiling. I tried again and received no response. Then I motioned Dr. Lloyd to the hallway, stepping ahead of him.

"Is every muscle locked up like that hand?"

"Yes. Her whole musculature is in spasm. I've never seen anything like it." Dr. Lloyd's voice was concerned. "Even catatonic states don't get that complete, do they?"

"No. Hysteric ones do, though. You found no physical injury?"

"No. I thought of all the obvious things. There's no indication of an overdose of anything, either."

"Reflexes?"

"All the tonic ones are just that massive. I can't elicit any soft reflexes. They just *aren't there.*"

He looked at me. "What can we do about it?"

"I've got one idea. I don't know if it will work. If she still trusts me, it will. If she doesn't, then you probably will get a catatonic state, instead of a hysteric one."

"What puts someone into a state like this one, Jim?"

"Ever see a boxer go rigid after taking one in the solar plexus—right in the breadbasket?"

"Was she hit?"

"Not physically. She's reacting physically to whatever punch she took emotionally. It's just as if she had been caught right in the belly."

My words came out without plan, but the sound of them taught me what had happened. "Right in the *belly!* That's what got to her." I was talking to myself and didn't give Dave Lloyd time to question it. "Come on in, doctor. I'm about to be either the goddamnedest fool or the luckiest son of a bitch alive."

"What are you going to do?"

"I'm going to play it by ear—whatever my guts tell me to say or do or try."

"Can I help?"

"Yeah. Get something that would sedate her quickly, just in case my guts tell me wrong."

"Amytal sodium? That's quick."

"Drugs are your department, doctor. I just hope to hell we aren't going to need them."

In a few minutes we were ready. I took a deep breath, grinned at Dave Lloyd with a confidence I was far from feeling, and went back into Karen's room. This time, I went directly to the bed and sat on the edge of it. I didn't take Karen's hand. I put my two hands under the back of her neck. The heavy muscles there were like steel springs, set firmly under my hands. She made no move, nor did she try to speak.

My hands gently kneaded at the muscles of her neck, but she did not relax or lessen the massive rigidity of her body. Her fixed stare did not move or track, but held to its ceiling spot. I let my hands slip beneath her shoulders and lifted her to a sitting position, drawing her head against my shoulder.

Softly, as one would speak to a child, I began to talk to her, my hands stroking at her rigid back muscles. For a very long time

I held her like that. How long it was, I do not know. I was not doing a hypnotic induction; I was attempting to achieve some progressive relaxation. The minutes passed.

Then the tension broke. Karen collapsed against my shoulder. I held her, and wasn't even aware that she was crying until I felt the wetness soaking through my shirt. The tears were a silent draining, with no sobs.

Her muscles had suddenly given up all their strength. I had to tighten my arms around her small body to keep her in a sitting position. I continued to talk, trying to gentle her as one might soothe a frightened animal. The silent drainage passed after a time, and quiet sobs began. Only when the sobs were being choked back was there an indication that Karen was making a fight for conscious control of herself.

"It's so *ugly.*" These were the first words that could be strained from the quiet sobbing.

"That you've been told you were going to be called a tramp and an adulteress in a countersuit? That they were going to try to make you an unfit mother and take the children away from you?"

I spoke my hunch aloud. "They're threatening you with the loss of your children."

I got almost immediate verification for my hunch. She went wide-eyed, starting back from me, looking at my face. "How did you know? Who told you?"

"Nobody. What else could make you freeze like this?"

"It's too ugly. I can't put the children through that!" Her voice was rising. "I'm giving up. Don't you see that I have to give it up—do anything they want?"

I eased my arms from holding her, putting my hands on top of her shoulders, fingers pressing through the thin hospital gown and biting into her flesh. I held her roughly for a moment, looking at her. Then I let her down onto the hospital bed and took her hands in mine.

"Tell me about it, Karen."

"I went to an attorney. That was Thursday afternoon. He agreed to handle my divorce. Then, this morning, R. B. Dant came to the farm to tell me to withdraw it. He told me what would happen to me. He asked how I could prove that no men were visiting the farm—giving me money—paying for—for—"

"For sex. Of course. A woman without work, no income, who lives alone, a long way from town. He could build a convincing case, I'm sure."

"That's why I'm going to withdraw the divorce."

"The hell you are. When are you going to *fight?*"

"Can't you understand? I've got nothing to fight with!"

"Just for once, dammit, think like a female instead of a lady. You've got to protect yourself, and your kids. You've got all the weapons you need! You've got an assault and manslaughter charge to make against Roy Dant—he struck you and you miscarried. He's a known seizure victim, yet he still holds a driver's license, endangering others. These are medical *facts*—on record in hospitals. The alcoholism, the business failures—even the things you know about R. B. Dant's business. Half a dozen men in the South would pay a great deal to learn about that."

"I couldn't do that. I couldn't tell any of that!"

"You won't have to tell. Any more than the Dants will tell about you. One thing R. B. Dant wants to protect is his image—the way he looks to other people. He's perfectly willing to be an unofficial son of a bitch, but a *certified son of a bitch?* He'd never let anyone have the chance to put that stamp on him."

"How can I do that? Where would I get that much strength?"

"Out of your Scotch stubbornness, your Irish pride, and your calm Arapaho *belly.* You've got the strength to do whatever has to be done, woman. Just like your mother before you."

"And not be the cat that is chased?"

I grinned at her. "At least you didn't take my head off for referring to your abdomen."

She smiled wanly. "It doesn't sound very nice, not even now."

I grinned at her. "I'm agreeable to your getting one good night's sleep in that bed, but if you think you're going to hide there to keep from being the kind of person you know you've got to be, you'd better think some more. You wouldn't be able to live with you."

The showdown with R. B. Dant was not long postponed. Karen was able to report on it the following week when I saw her. She had a more relaxed air than I could ever remember.

151

"I faced R. B. It was over in less than fifteen minutes, doctor."

"What happened? How did you handle it?"

"I called his office and set an appointment. Then I just told him."

"You make it sound like a minor thing."

"It wasn't minor. But for the first time I think I estimated him correctly. I asked him why he felt that I would continue to let him bluff me out of the game."

Her description went on, and her face lighted almost like a projection screen, allowing me to visualize the encounter. . . .

"Just what in Christ's name makes you think I'm bluffin', Karrie?"

"You wouldn't risk the consequences."

"You tryin' to blackjack me again?"

"Not unless you force it."

"Force what? You got nothin' to gain—ever'thing to lose. You know that."

"You have it backward. I have myself to gain. You're the one with a great deal to lose."

He took a moment to fumble with his old pipe, trying to assess the difference in the woman he had cowed so thoroughly a few days before. His pale eyes stayed on her, but the set of her face put him on the defensive. "I ain't got a thing to lose."

"You're very sure of that, R. B.?" Her voice was full, even, and cool. "How long did I work for you?"

"You know that. That don't make no difference now. You don't work for me now."

"I did work for you long enough to remember how you got several contracts without being the low bidder."

His eyes hooded in the familiar style, concealing his inner mind's workings with genuine poker player's skill. "That's pretty dangerous talk, Karrie."

"Then Roy, keeping a driver's license when he's known to be subject to seizures. But that's minor, I guess." She stared directly at Dant, forcing him to remove the hood from his eyes. "But there is a very interesting law about causing the death of an unborn child—that's not so minor."

152

"You can't make nothin' like that stick in court."

"Hospital records, police report, ambulance report—all public records, if they were put together." She let her face go under the shade of her own suddenly hooded eyes. "But I don't think they'd have to be put all together. What do you think, R. B.?"

"Just what is it you're asking?"

"For you to get the hell out of my way. I'm going to divorce Roy Dant, no matter how dirty you try to make it."

"Now, Karrie. You talk like I was mean."

"You're what you are. All I'm saying is that I'm getting out, no matter what it costs."

R. B. Dant sucked at his cold pipe, making a wet kind of sound. Then he removed it from his face and sat facing her. He stared for a long moment, then threw in his hand. "You have guts enough to be a Dant—willin' to get into a pissin' contest with a skunk if you have to."

"On your terms, R. B. You have the choice of weapons."

He nodded, slowly. "No choice to be made."

"And the children?"

"I wasn't never gonna do nothin' to harm them, Karrie."

"We understand each other, then?"

The expression that crossed the old man's lean, stubble-bearded face was one rarely seen by anyone who knew him.

"Goddamn, Karrie. You're one hell of a woman."

I saw Karen several times in the weeks following, while her quiet and uncontested divorce was going through the courts. These were sustaining contacts. Our therapeutic work had been done when she made a fundamental discovery of herself—that she was not for sale. She made her decision and carried it through.

The actual divorce was something of an anticlimax. It came one week after Lee was released from his probation. Gracious in use of the power she held, Karen took minimal support for the children, and even mended what fences she could for their future relationship with their grandparents.

She came to see me one more time. It was the day before she and the children left Danton to move to Colorado. It was her time to "graduate" and we both knew it. She promoted me from doctor to friend that day. Perhaps a better term would be from doctor to "cherished stranger."

I couldn't help but notice her grooming. She was as crisp and impeccable as she had always been, but there was something far less mechanistic about it. She had relaxed, even to the point of permitting one wisp of her dark hair to elude her comb and her setting spray.

Somehow, that fitted her very well.

*

Karen needed, and discovered, an entitlement to act in her own behalf. When she found herself in an unfair situation, she sought for strength within herself. She made a declaration of personal independence. From early in her life, she had had an internal assurance of her own competence, and a knowledge of her rights. To meet her problems, she needed only to translate these well-established personality characteristics into the decisions that could resolve her dilemma. True, her confidence had been eroded. But when it was rebuilt, it took up its own quite adequate function. She had a history of having made use of her own known strengths.

Yet there are others who have never learned what their own internal strengths are, or how to use them. No background of felt personal assurance aids them or allows them self-reliance. Each early thrust for identity and independence is quickly turned into a humiliating demonstration of their weakness. They dare not show any strength, at the risk of being held arrogant and sinful. This "sin" means summary punishment, often very severe.

Some primitive tribes have massive suppression as a cultural imperative in the rearing of the young. It is significant that these primitives find ways of relieving the suppression through periods of ritual license and freedom—recesses from suppression by means of orgies or festivals of nonaccountability. These allow the unexpressible to be expressed, and the emotional steam to be drained with minimum damage.

In our American culture, however, there are subgroups within the total society that uniformly suppress without the good sense of balance adopted by the primitives. They do not

155

provide the "safety valve." Often these subgroups are organized around a stringent sectarian religion, using the authority of scripture to buttress suppressive practices and the resultant cultural neurosis to support and insulate the faith they follow. In essence, they make God as angry as they themselves.

Given such rigidity, ascension to a feeling of self is incomplete at best. Usually it is marked with the guilt of rebellion to a degree that leads the young to practice self-exorcism of the demons of personality—aggressiveness, creativity, pride, curiosity, individuality, sexuality, intellectual mastery. This subjugation of self becomes a constant preoccupation. Without some leavening expression of feeling, the vessel bursts under pressures it cannot contain.

The usual result is that the young seize the power to act. Girls force parental consent to marriage by deliberately incurring pregnancies. Boys often physically assault their fathers as a final act before running away into a world for which they are not prepared. In time, they find a part of themselves, and come to trust their findings sufficiently to exist. But the ingrained experience leads them all too often to recapitulate the rigors for their own wives and children. These are like the "walking wounded."

But not all casualties can be self-evacuated. Some "basket cases" exist, even in holy wars. In such battlegrounds, the best evidence of the innate strength of all human beings is that there are not more like Joseph. . . .

PART FOUR

* JOSEPH *

Weigh a Pound of Fog

THE BOY LAY FACE DOWN ON THE HILLSIDE, HIS FORTY-EIGHT pounds pressing into the deep growth of kudzu vine that had been planted to slow the erosion of the red clay. He was panting, spent, and crying. He tried to lie very quietly, but the pounding of his heart echoed in his temples. He was certain that the noise of his heartbeat would cause him to be found. *All of Seminole County can hear my heart*, he thought.

He tried to stop his breath, too. In a vague way he was grateful that God had made kudzu a broad-leafed plant into which any small and frightened thing could burrow. The long strands of the vine could be lifted to permit his small passage. Once, he remembered, he had gotten all the way to the highway, more than half a mile from his house. On that day, he had lain in the kudzu for seven hours. He would never have been discovered if he could have forced himself to run across the highway. But he had been too fearful of being seen. In the end, it was his belly that had betrayed him. He doubted that the Lord had gone forty days in the wilderness without food.

He thought of that time again, and the double whipping he had received when he mentioned the thought to momma. She had brought him a plate of peas and a big square of cold corn bread after the first whipping—the one for running away.

"I should not feed such a boy. But you have had your punishment for being disobedient and running from your father."

"Yes, momma."

"Can you sit up? I will oil your cuts and keep them clean."

157

"I . . . I will try, momma." The seven-year-old tried to lift himself with his hands, callused tools that would have fitted a farm boy twice his age. He used his hands and arms to reduce the pull at the skin across his back and buttocks, but still he winced. "Could you do it if I stand up? It is mostly on my legs and—" He broke off, shamed to refer to his buttocks by a word for which he had been previously punished.

The tired, saddened woman put the plate of black-eyed peas and the corn bread on the low tool bench, then helped her son to raise himself from the floor of the granary. He stood naked before her. His clothing was carefully hung on the peg where he had placed it when he stripped on his father's command. The stripes of the whip were deep and cruel. Where the tiny "tickler" of the lash had curled on the side of his thigh, blood suppurated.

She took the bottle of camphorated oil from her apron pocket, pouring some into her palm and rubbing her hands together before touching his back softly. "You were very wicked, Joseph."

"Yes, momma."

"As wicked as when you went naked in the horse trough with that evil little girl."

"We did not mean to sin, momma. It was very hot. We wanted to cool ourselves."

"Displaying your naked bodies? Experiencing the temptation of lust? Do you not remember what our preacher said about nakedness?"

"I did not know then, momma. I was five. I am seven now, and I know what sinfulness is. Then, I don't think I did."

"We must train you, Joseph. 'Train up a child when he is young, and when he grows old, he will not depart from goodness.' "

She rubbed harder against the cuts. The child winced, bringing a stab of guilt to the mother who had caused him pain. "Eat your food."

The boy mumbled a prayer of grace, then fell to the plate of food, stuffing spoonfuls of peas into his mouth. "It is very good," he said between mouthfuls. "I was very hungry."

"Our Lord was hungry in the wilderness, yet he was without sin. For forty days he was tempted, with Satan mocking him to turn stones into bread that he might eat. You were gone only for the time from breakfast until now—stealing hours of sinful pleasures when there were chores for you to do. Yet you complain of hunger?"

"I bet the Lord complained, too. I don't think he could go no forty days."

The woman's face flamed. "How dare you to say this? This is sin! Doubting our Lord and the Holy Book!"

She pushed him roughly from under the hands that had been tending to his welts. He reeled across the uneven floor of the granary. The sudden movement of his bruised legs caused him to shriek with a sudden upsurge of pain.

She was at the door of the outbuilding, calling toward the barn. Joseph trembled. He had made a serious mistake without intending to do so. His father would come soon, and the punishment would be worse. Quickly he gobbled at the plate of food, lest he be accused of the sin of wastefulness as well.

Now he thought of that time as he lay under the kudzu. He recalled all the other times when he had tried to run away. With a bitter wisdom, he knew that he could not remain on the earth in the shelter of the vines. His sobs stopped.

If I make them come for me, he thought, *I shall be punished more.*

Reluctantly the eight-year-old lifted himself from the shelter of the friendly vines and moved toward the distant barn. He forced his steps in order that he would not lag and lose his resolve, likewise willing himself to square his small shoulders as he moved along. The distance seemed to stretch interminably. He pressed himself to walk still faster.

He reached the hay rope hanging from the overhead boom. His father was nowhere to be seen. Then he could hear it, the heavy panting breath of the man, and the clash of the hayfork against the concrete of the barn floor.

Papa is still working. Could it be he did not know I ran away?

The thought became action. He clambered up the rope as quickly as he could bring one hand above the other, hauling himself back into the loft of soft hay. He reached the pulley track and swung himself into the barn, crossing the loose hay to the open drop where he had been pitching down the hay, when the sinful thought came to him.

"Joseph! Put down more hay!"

Heart in his throat, the boy answered. "Yes, papa."

He stood at the edge of the chute, forcing himself to take the short-handled pitchfork into his sweat-greased hands. He drove it into the loose green alfalfa, dragging and lifting a mass of hay twice his size to the drop.

The man below looked up. "You are a lazy one. I go to the house for my cup of coffee, and come back to find the hay only half down. Were you sleeping in the loft?"

"No, papa."

The fork flew in the boy's hands. Loose hay came through the drop in a steady stream.

"That is better. You can pitch hay when you want to."

The voice carried pride, but Joseph did not read it so. To the boy it was almost as cruel as the lash of the whip. He stared at the short-handled, three-tined fork in his hand, remembering the broad, sweat-soaked back of his father below him. Again he remembered the horrid, sinful thought. The near perfect illusion of the moment when he had stood at the edge of the drop, fork in his hand, and heard Satan's voice telling him how easy it would be to hurl it like a spear.

He forced the thought aside, burying it under a virtual torrent of hay spilling over the edge of the drop. He worked frantically, trying hard to atone—to make the sinful thought go away.

"Enough, Joseph! That's enough for a *month!*" Peter Vandenkirk's shout was pleased, his bass laughter filling the huge barn. "Come on down, my son."

The boy flung the pitchfork away from the hole, driving it spear-style into the hay. Then he shuffled across the ladder, descending to the concrete floor of the barn.

His father reached for him, surprised that the boy seemed to shrink from him for a moment. He tousled the youngster's head and shoved him into the deep pile of loose hay, laughing.

Joseph should have felt joy, not shame. But the memory of the murderous thought was too intense. He gained his feet and staggered across the mound of hay, falling to his knees and putting his arms around the thick waist of his father. "Forgive me, papa," the boy said. "I'm sorry that I did not work well enough."

160

It was a long time before I heard of these early events from Joseph. Neither of his parents had marked his flights and his punishments as any significant deviation or problem in his early life. My first knowledge or awareness of Joseph was a request from the medical director, Derek Welton, that I administer psychological testing.

It came as a result of one of those situations that sometimes occur in public clinics—an emergency appointment following some kind of bizarre behavior. The whole focus of the clinic then is to determine what is happening as quickly as possible.

The arrival precipitated the emergency. We had had no advance notice that a boy, his parents, and a minister were all arriving. The ongoing work of the clinic had to be bent to fit the situation. Dr. Welton was seeing the parents; Martin Fells, P.S.W. (Psychiatric Social Worker), was seeing the minister; and I was charged with seeing Joseph, even though it could be only a brief visit.

I calculated the probable time for him to take a self-administered personality inventory as the first unit of testing. This was a matter of necessity, not of choice. My schedule was loaded for the early hours, and I estimated that I could proceed with two other patients while Joseph answered the more than five hundred questions included in the Minnesota Multiphasic Personality Inventory. After the two patients, I could join Joseph and administer projective testing.

He said very little, seemingly attentive and quite polite, as we first met. I took him into the staff library, where he could work without interruption, explained the test to him, and excused myself. I met with my first patient, and in the ten minutes between patients I stepped back into the library to offer encouragement and check on his speed of progress.

Joseph was gone. The IBM answer sheet lay on the table, test booklet beside it, open to the second page. Joseph had left a message, partly printed, partly longhand, for me.

The text of the message was scattered over the paper:

TAKING THIS WAS
"Is" pretty rough, but I can't manage it

and I feel very 'good' talking with you people
thank you $=$
"OVER"
lets face it
Christ said I wouldn't have to do it $+ =$ Joseph
I promise you that I will /
never do a thing like what I did
again.
but doctor smith said that you
were just going talk
but I wonder I say this
because I mean it and I'm sure
the Lord understands me
because I've taken him as my Lord and
Savior and I no that
I will never do a thing like
this again, but would I have to
take this test its pretty HARDOME

I hurried back to the office and the reception area. Joseph was nowhere to be seen.

"Did either of you see Joseph Vandenkirk leave?" I aimed the question at the two secretaries.

"He's gone? His parents are still in with Dr. Welton, and the minister is still with Mr. Fells." Mrs. Lenahan was upset, but in command as always, moving quickly toward the possible conclusions.

"He may be waiting in their car," Mrs. Grey added. "Or maybe he went to the bathroom."

I toured the center quickly, but no rest rooms or unoccupied space led me to Joseph. I went to the small parking lot, checking in all of the cars there. He was still missing, so I walked back into the building.

"No luck," I told the secretaries. "I'd better tell Dr. Welton." I picked up the phone and dialed the medical director's extension.

"Yes?"

"Derek, the boy has skipped out. I think he was hallucinating, from the note he left for me. You'd better tell his parents. He's not in the building or in the parking lot. I looked in every car."

"How long has he been gone?"

"Maybe a half hour. I went on with my first patient, leaving him to take the personality inventory, as I told you I would. He just walked out."

There was a pause. I could overhear Dr. Welton explaining what had happened to Joseph's parents. Then he came back on the line. "We'll come out right away. Mr. Vandenkirk thinks he knows where the boy would go. It's not the first time."

"He hasn't gone home," I said. "They live thirty miles out— on beyond Manion."

"We'll come out."

"I'll meet you in the hall."

I strode from the office, just as Dr. Welton's door opened. I had my first look at Peter and Katje Vandenkirk. He was a stocky man of medium height, with sand-colored hair and a face burned to a deep mahogany by the Dixie sun and long hours spent in the fields. His clean white shirt seemed barely to contain his wide shoulders and bulging arms.

Katje Vandenkirk, his wife, was nearly as tall as her husband, but the resemblance ended there. She was slender and work worn. I noted that she carried herself very well, seeming almost to glide rather than walk. Her sun-streaked hair was drawn into a tight knot at the back of her neck, accenting the slender throat and the sharp cutting of her tearstained face.

"I'm sorry, sir," I said to the father. "When I went back to see how Joseph was getting along, he was gone."

He nodded. "It is not the first time, Dr. . . .?" His voice carried a rising inflection.

"Howard," I supplied. "Nevertheless, I should have arranged for one of the office girls to stay with him. I apologize."

"Danton is not a big place, doctor," the slender woman said. "We can find Joseph." Her voice was smooth and reassuringly calm.

"He will be in the park, *jah?*" The man was not asking his wife for anything but a confirmation. "By the cannon in the park he will be—as the time before."

"I'd like to go with you, if I may. I feel that I may have frightened Joseph."

"He is . . . not well, doctor. For a long time, he is not well."

"I'm recommending hospitalization, Jim." The medical direc-

163

tor's voice was even. "When Joseph is functioning better, then we can follow him on an outpatient basis here."

"Tell Pastor Diekhoff we will come back soon?" Peter Vandenkirk asked Dr. Welton.

"Of course."

I took a moment to ask Mrs. Grey to reschedule my second patient, if she could not wait. Then I rejoined the Vandenkirks. We went to their car. Automatically, Mrs. Vandenkirk took the rear seat, leaving the right front door open for me.

"My car is not good, doctor. I'm sorry."

"It is fine, Mr. Vandenkirk. A car is a tool for most of us who work for our living." I looked at him curiously, wondering why the man felt the need to apologize to me. "What makes you so sure that Joseph has gone to the park?"

"There is a cannon there. Joseph has spoken of it many times. Each time we come to Danton, he wishes to see it."

Katje Vandenkirk had spoken her second sentence since her nod of introduction. She added her third. "My grandfather was a cannon shooter in the War Between the States. Joseph has felt since he was a little boy that this was the cannon his great-grandfather had loaded and fired. It is a harmless idea, is it not?" Her voice was faintly worried that I would disagree.

"Boy silliness," Peter Vandenkirk said. "Always what is real is not good enough. Always there must be fairy tales of wars and of killing—old wars and killing. His brother in Vietnam is not to be heard in Joseph's talk—only great charges of men in blue and couriers on horses' backs. More better he would think about the Lord's battles with Satan."

"How much older is your son in Vietnam?"

"Six years," the mother supplied. "Henrik was sergeant in only one year. He might even have been officer, if he wanted. He is very smart—our boy."

"Take care not to show unworthy pride, woman."

"If we find Joseph in the park," I said, "may I talk with him for a moment before we have to leave?"

"Dr. Welton called up long-distance to fix it so Joseph would go to the hospital. It is over a hundred miles. I have animals to feed and milk tonight. Time is very little, doctor." The sentence marked the first break in Peter Vandenkirk's apologetic tone. "Work does not wait. The animals will be in pain if not milked—that would be sinful. 'If a man careth not for his oxen, that man is not a good man in the sight of God.' "

"I understand. I just thought I might have frightened Joseph, so I want to make sure he is not more upset by what has happened."

"Your ox to care for, doctor?"

"A human being who needs help, Mr. Vandenkirk."

His response was a mumble. I felt I knew a part of what the father was feeling—what was stirring inside that great barrel of a chest. But if we were to be of any value to his son, perhaps to others in his family, I had to make sure by bringing it out into the open and clarifying it.

"I know you have feelings about asking for help for mental troubles. Perhaps we should talk about that."

"I talked with Dr. Welton. He says my boy must go to the hospital for crazy people. But he is a good boy. He works like a man, and *he fears God.*"

"It is a hard thing to face—hospitalization of a child."

Katje Vandenkirk broke into the conversation. "Never in our family was there disgrace. Joseph has not sinned so. Why should it be that he is punished with your mental illness?"

"Punishment? Call it fear, call it shame, call it guilty feelings —urges, impulses that Joseph feels and cannot control in any other way. Maybe it is all of those things and more. This illness may be all that Joseph can do under the circumstances he feels inside of himself and in his life."

"All he can do? To go crazy?"

"To get *sick!* To be sick so that he has a place to hide from what he feels and fears."

"We have been good parents to Joseph. Always we have tried to protect him from fear—to keep him straight and clean in the sight of God and man."

"Of course you have. All who love their children do what they can to help them."

"So how have we failed him, doctor?" Katje demanded.

"I don't know that you have. I've never really talked to

Joseph. I don't know what his feelings are—what is happening inside him. That's the reason I want to talk with him—even if only for five minutes."

"He should pray and work hard. It will be God who will lift this burden from his spirit."

"God makes your seeds to grow, Mr. Vandenkirk. But it is your labor to plow, disc, harrow, and plant them. *You* cooperate by doing what you can. Why are you so sure that no man can help Joseph?"

"It is a curse, your illness. My son has sinned. He is being punished."

"Three years ago there was a drought. All the farmers lost crops. Had all of you sinned? Were the God-fearing hurt less than the sinful? Were Cajun farms, Catholic farms, Dutch farms, Irish farms in Seminole County *all* subject to punishment by God? How about the Negro farmers? Didn't they lose along with all the others?"

"Of course."

"Of course they did. Why do you feel that those of us who try to help others are so far from doing God's work? Is it because we work across desks, rather than across the dragbars of tractors?"

"By the sweat of your brow shall ye have bread."

"Brows sweat on the inside, too, Mr. Vandenkirk. Our tools are in our heads and our tongues—but we *work* with them."

He slowed the car to a crawl, taking his eyes from the road to snap a glance at me. "You say much, doctor. But are you a Christian? Do you believe?" He looked back at the road and slowed the car to a stop at the curb.

"If the God in which you believe allows me to help your son, would it matter what I believed?"

"So much talk I cannot follow all at once. My son is a child of God. I ask if you are one also."

"We are all children of God, Mr. Vandenkirk—more alike than we can ever be different. Our faiths may differ, but whatever view we have of God does not matter. What matters is what God's view of us may be."

He looked at me for a long moment, veins bulging in his sunburned forehead. "I believe what you say, doctor. Let us find my son."

166

He started the car again, driving the remaining blocks to the Danton city park. The silence was not broken again until he brought the car to a halt at the edge of the park. Then he glanced at me.

"We love our son, doctor. He is always to know this. Our ways are . . . our ways. They do not change like the seasons. But our son must bear his trials and learn to be what he is to be. May the Lord bless your effort."

"Thank you."

"He will be under the cannon—there." He gestured across the park. "I am sure of this. We will wait here for you to bring him to us, that we may take him to the hospital."

I nodded, then left the car. I walked through the pine and magnolia trees toward the cannon, wondering why I had felt constrained to sell Joseph's parents on the idea of seeking to understand Joseph's problem in human rather than divine terms. Perhaps I was angry because they could see so little gray in a black-and-white world. Yet, even as I thought this, I remembered the ride's end—with an admission of love and concern, and the entrustment of their son to a stranger.

The boy was under the cannon, as his father had predicted. He was on his knees, shoulders against the crossbar of the carriage. His head was slumped forward, his arms outstretched to touch the spokes of the wide-set wheels. He seemed to take no notice of my approach. When I was near enough, I noticed that his eyes were closed and his lips moving, as if in prayer.

I paused. When his lips stopped, I spoke. "Joseph?"

There was no reaction. I spoke again, more firmly. His head turned toward the sound and his eyes opened.

"This was my great-grandfather's cannon, Dr. Howard. He killed many Yankees with it."

"Possibly he did, Joseph." I squatted down beside the wheel, looking at him through the spokes. "How do you think of this cannon?"

"It's for killing. Killing is wrong. *Thou shalt not kill*—that's a commandment."

At seventeen, Joseph had nearly all his growth. He was not stocky, like his father, but rather had the slender gracefulness of his mother. He was perhaps half a head taller than either of them.

Despite his slender stature, his shoulders were broad; yoked as they were to the caisson bar, I could see the muscles that had developed through his years of laboring with hayforks, grain shovels, gelding pliers, and feed bags.

"Thou shalt not kill. Blessed are the peacemakers, for they shall be called the children of God."

"Your parents are here, waiting for us."

"I know."

"Before we go to join them, could we talk a little?"

"No more tests. Christ told me I didn't have to take none of them tests."

"No more tests, Joseph. But I would like to talk with you—just talk—for a few minutes."

"All right, doctor."

"Could we sit on that bench?"

"When I finish a real good prayer. It will only take a minute." He closed his eyes, his lips moving again. After a moment or two, he brought his arms down from the wheels, walking on his knees until he was clear of the caisson and barrel, then rising to his feet. He was nearly as tall as I. We moved to the bench and sat down.

"Why didn't nobody believe me, doctor? That I'd never do it again?"

"Do what, Joseph?"

"What I done! I can't talk about it." His lips were dry, and he licked at them with a flicking tongue as fast as a snake's, then rolled them together several times. "God forgave me. I took the Lord Jesus for my personal savior, and He forgave me."

"That's a good feeling—to feel you have been forgiven for something you have done wrong."

He nodded, silent. I asked the question. "How did you know that God had forgiven you what you did?"

"God came to me. He told me."

"When did God come to you first? How long have you seen Him?"

"Last year, when I was in the hospital with pneumonia."

"Did you hear His voice?"

"Sure. It's beautiful."

"Tell me about it."

168

"He sat right there on the edge of my bed, and He touched me. He told me I wasn't goin' to hell, that I was forgiven."

"What did He look like?" I tried to slow the pace of my questions. We sat in the shade of the morning, under the budding magnolia tree. It was peaceful—Joseph had chosen his hiding place well.

"He looked like somethin' real clean. His clothes was white as that fresh magnolia blossom, only brighter. He had blood on his forehead and in His hair and on His hands. But He was as shiny as sun on the water." He looked at me, moistening his lips again. "It was so beautiful."

"Have you ever seen Him again?"

"Sure. I seen Him lots of times. Never up that close, though." He closed his eyes for a moment. "Anytime I want to see Him, I just have to pray hard, then look up in the sky. He's always there."

"Does He always talk to you?"

"Most of the time. Sometimes He just looks at me with a kinda smile. I know things is all right then."

I lighted a cigarette, stalling for a little more time to make sure of what I was going to say. The subject had to be faced, but I felt Joseph and I were tuned in on each other, and I didn't want to break that. I thought about it, then realized there was no other way to approach the problem.

"Do you know why your folks and Reverend Diekhoff brought you to the mental health center?"

"I guess it was because of Sunday night. The church kids don't believe I seen God, and they wouldn't listen when I told them God was a good thing to be with. We were all talkin'. I got up and told about what God looked like, and what He said to me. Pastor Diekhoff, he tried to get me to stop."

Joseph was into a narrative, and I was able to visualize the scene as he talked. He started before the evening church meeting. . . .

Heat lay over the southern town like a damp towel applied before a shave, and even the feeble breeze was wilted. The country-side seemed even hotter, with the red dust lying open as a harlot, hoping for ravishment by rain. Yet the rain did not come on

Sunday, as the Hollander farmers always hoped—that God would nourish their fields without interfering with the six days in which they would work. It was a day for calm, like all Sundays in the Dutch area of Seminole County, yet calmness was braised into a brittle thing by that August afternoon.

Evening chores completed early, Joseph Vandenkirk was preparing himself, as he had done every Sunday afternoon he could remember. He scrubbed at his knuckles to be sure he would go into the Lord's house with clean hands. The point of his clasp knife raked again and again under his nails, with generous soapings and soakings between the scraping actions. He looked at his hands, hard callused and darkened by the daily pounding of the southern sun. The calluses stood like yellow patches at the bases and on the joints of his fingers.

"Christ's hands must have been like mine," he thought in a voice he did not hear. "He was a carpenter—a worker with tools. How good of God the Father to let His Son know honest work." He stared at his hands, fascinated. *"Are these the hands of God?"*

He remembered one of the forbidden stories in the magazine his father had been so upset about. Joseph had read, slowly and with difficulty, most of the magazine before it was cast away. In the one story, the hands of a dead man still sought to clutch at the hero—even when he had slashed them off with a sword.

"Do hands live?" he mumbled.

He stared at his hands, placing one atop the other, back to palm. "Christ's hands were callused and showed the signs of work. My hands show the hard calluses of work. *My hands are the hands of Christ.*"

He thought for a long time. "No. My hands show no wounds. There are no marks of the nails." He took his clasp knife up again, pricking at the center of his palm. "There is where Christ has the bloody holes in His hands."

"Joseph! Soon we go to church. You must hurry."

"Yes, momma."

He closed the clasp knife and shoved it quickly into his back pocket. He rinsed his hands one more time, then applied the stiff brush vigorously to his cropped blond hair, trying to make it all bend in one direction, rather than show as tufts of stubble piled helter-skelter on his head.

Quickly he donned his shirt and tie, tying the stiff fabric clumsily and in too large a knot. His jacket followed, and he felt momentarily ashamed at the smallness of it, and the way his huge hands dangled from his wrists which protruded from the sleeve. He turned to look quickly into the mirror, rubbed one shoe tip on the back of one trouser leg, then the other shoe on the opposite leg. He moved toward the stairs.

On the way to Manion, where the church was located, Joseph was silent for a long time. So silent that both of his parents noticed.

"You are troubled, Joseph?"

"No, papa. I was thinking about the hands of Jesus."

"The *hands?*"

"Yes, momma. He was a carpenter. He would have had blisters and calluses, wouldn't He?"

Peter Vandenkirk smiled and shrugged his shoulders. "A man who works toughens his hands." He lifted one of his own large hands from the steering wheel and regarded it. "It is a sign of honest labor."

"Then Christ would have had calluses—like yours, or *mine.*"

"God would know of such things, my son. But such would be the truth with any workingman." The older man nodded with something approaching approval. "It is good that you think of Christ, since He died because of you."

Silence fell again while the old car rumbled toward Manion at a slow pace. Peter Vandenkirk did not speak further, Katje knew better than to intrude, and Joseph returned to his thoughts. It was not until they turned into the graveled parking lot of the small church that more words passed between father and son.

"After the congregation has met in prayer," Peter said, "when you are with the other boys and girls and good Pastor Diekhoff, you might speak this thought you have of Christ. It might help those who scorn to work hard."

"Yes, papa."

They went into the well-worn wooden church, nodding gravely to their neighbors and taking their places on the hard oak pews. Joseph was glad they had come early, so that they could have the hard bench near the organ. He could feel the bass vibrations of the instrument, shaking the walls and the floor. He thought of the vibrations as if they reflected the voice of God—full, deep, vibrating shivers. *It is the favored spot of God.*

The evening service was far shorter than the two-hour Sunday morning service, for it was to be followed by the church meetings held separately for the family heads, the women, and the young people. The women's meeting would be short, so that they might prepare food in the dining hall in the basement for all the congregation. The men stayed in the nave of the church. Children, from eight to twenty, met in the frame annex building for continuing instruction by the pastor.

Before they split into their respective groups, Joseph put his hands, palms out, against the heads of the screws of the hymnal rack, pressing them to feel the heavy tremors of the organ as the congregation sang the final hymns. The round screwheads jumped and fluttered against his palms. *Those are the places of the nails.*

When the congregation broke into its component meetings, sixteen children began to move toward the annex building. They trooped silently from the church, reluctant to make an unnecessary noise until they were out of the house of God. But on the stairs outside the building Willem Van Voort jostled against Joseph, making the taller boy stumble and half run down the last eight steps to the concrete walk below. He caught himself with the pipe handrail to keep from falling, but bumped into Betty Kleinschmidt's full, round breasts.

He flushed violently. "I'm sorry," he mumbled.

"You couldn't help it, Joseph. Willem pushed you. We saw it all." She tossed her head, and her breasts jiggled deliciously. "He's such a smart aleck." Her voice was strident.

Willem could not help but hear. He was just coming to the foot of the stairs. "It was an accident. I didn't look where I was going."

Nedra Kleinschmidt came to her sister's defense. "You did it deliberately, Willem Van Voort. You just like to be mean."

"No one should be mean," Joseph said. "Not ever."

"You should apologize to Joseph and beg his pardon." Betty pronounced sentence as if she were a judge.

"He ought to apologize to you. It was your big tits he made sure he ran into."

172

Joseph's hand rose by itself, without his being aware of its action. It doubled into a fist and smashed at Willem's face. The pudgy boy jerked his head, taking the blow on his shoulder. The force of Joseph's punch drove him across the walkway to the side of the annex building. The frame siding rang hollowly with the slam of his body.

"I'll get you for that, Vandenkirk!" Willem pushed himself away from the wall, coming for Joseph.

"STOP!" Reverend Diekhoff's voice cut through the summer heat like a lash. "You are in the house of God! Lift not your hand against your brother!"

The burly young minister came striding from the rear entry of the church onto the walkway. He stood between the two boys. "I do not know what this is about, and I do not care. You will not show anger here!"

"Willem pushed Joseph down the stairs," Nedra Kleinschmidt said in ten-year-old absolutism. "Then he said a bad thing, too." She glanced at Willem with genuine malice. "That's when Joseph hit him."

"I do not wish to hear of it. Come inside, all of you."

Dampened, with all prospect of excitement suddenly gone, the reluctant children put themselves into a semblance of order and entered the Sunday school building. They took their places around the circle of straight chairs. Van Voort and Joseph were exactly opposite each other.

Pastor Diekhoff's opening prayer was a long one, centered on seeking the help of God for those so weak as to give in to Satan's temptations to violence and the sin of Cain. His heavy voice droned for a long time, and then the prayer was finished.

Joseph was in turmoil. He could still feel the warm cushioning softness of Betty Kleinschmidt's breasts against his chest. He forced that thought away from him, trying to devote his attention to the pastor's words. Of the entire prayer, he caught only the last lines:

"Keep us free from sins of anger and lust, O Lord. Give us strength to seek forgiveness from those against whom we sin with angry thoughts and deeds. We are but weak and sinful creatures who would be pleasing in Your sight. We fear Your vengeance for our sinful ways. Help us to put anger from our hearts, lest we be damned to eternal punishment, and never behold Thy radiant face. Amen."

Joseph realized what he had to do. He had to free his mind of the urge to smash Willem Van Voort's face into pulp.

"You are on your feet, Joseph. Do you wish to speak?"

"Yes, pastor. I want to ask that Willem forgive me my sinful anger."

"Willem?"

"He——" The boy stammered, looked at his preacher's stern face. "——is forgiven. If he will but forgive me for *accidentally* shoving him."

"It is well. We shall hear no more of this." The stocky week-day farmer–Sunday preacher looked at the two boys for a moment. Van Voort sat down, but Joseph remained standing.

"There is more, Joseph?"

"I have had a thought about our Lord. My father said I should speak of it to the children here."

"Yes?"

"Our Lord was a carpenter. He would have worked hard at His job, wouldn't He?"

"Indeed, He would."

"Working with our hands, blisters and calluses happen to all of us. Would not our Lord's hands have been hardened with work and the handling of His tools?"

Van Voort's laughter was choked back. Joseph went on. "It would be that to work hard was right for our Lord, and it must be right for us to work hard, too."

"Thank you, Joseph."

Van Voort's snicker was clearly audible. He had turned his face away, but his derogation was obvious. Joseph stared across the circle at the overweight boy.

"I think that is very good, Joseph," Betty Kleinschmidt said, coming quickly to her feet.

Joseph saw the unbound breasts bounce and he shuddered. It was an effort to force his eyes away.

"Joseph thinks of our Lord. He's probably closer to him than a good many other people." Betty's glance toward Willem gave ultimate emphasis to her remark.

Nedra rose to her feet, abetting her older sister. "She's right! What Joseph said is very good."

"God is a good thing to be with," Joseph said quickly. "He keeps us from sinning. I know, because *I seen God!* He came to me one night, plain as the pastor. I seen and talked to Him."

"That's a lie!" Van Voort's voice was sharp, rising above the sudden hubbub of noises coming from the young people.

"It is not a lie! I seen God! When I was in the pneumonia ward at the hospital . . . there was a man in the hall whose wife had had a baby. He didn't want that baby. He hollered at the doctor, told him to take that baby away and give it to somebody or to kill it. I wanted to make him stop talkin' like that. He was cussin' and sayin' he didn't want no baby. He didn't want no wife or anything. He was takin' the Lord's name in vain. I wanted to get out of my bed an' make him stop. I wanted to make him shut up with his sinnin' talk like that."

"That's enough, Joseph. We've got to get on with our meeting," the pastor remonstrated.

"Right after I tell 'em how good it is to know God personal. Knowin' He's my Lord and Savior makes all the difference. He came right to me, sat on the edge of my bed. He was all in white, real shiny. He talked to me, just like I'm talkin' to you all now. Our own Jesus came and told me I shouldn't go and stop that man."

"Yeah?" Willem's voice dripped acid. "What did you do?"

"I told God I was sorry for thinkin' that way, and asked Him to forgive me."

"That's enough, Joseph." The pastor's voice was sharp.

"He looked right at me. Then He put His bleeding hand on my forehead and pushed me back down onto my bed. He said, *'You must pray and I will forgive you, and I will pray and ask you to forgive me.'* "

The preacher's big hands took Joseph's shoulders. "All right, Joseph. Now sit down, and we'll go on with the meeting."

"But they got to know it's good to be with God. We all should be with God! It's a good thing."

"You're crazy!" cried Willem.

The meeting was a bedlam. All of the children were trying to talk at once.

"I seen Him, preacher! I really seen Him!"

Diekhoff's face was agonized. He looked at the boy's uncomprehending eyes. "Stop, Joseph. *Please stop!*"

"God is good. I seen Him, and I know. . . ."

Joseph and I sat on the park bench. He was looking at me. "I do see Him, Dr. Howard. Whenever I want. Even when I don't see Him, He talks to me."

I stubbed out my cigarette, watching the boy's flushed face. His voice was flat and insistent.

"I want you to tell all of this to your doctor, Joseph—how you felt and what you did. Tell him about hearing the voice of God."

"Ain't you gonna be my doctor?"

"When you come back from the hospital."

"Hospital?"

"Yes, Joseph. Until you get your feelings under control so they won't be causing you so much trouble, you'll be in the hospital at Francisville. There'll be a chance to rest and think all this through while you're there."

"I better ask God about that."

"I'm sure He'll agree. Your father and mother are waiting now to take you there. When you're feeling better, you'll come back here. If you want me to be your doctor, I will be."

He was tense, his body driving into the bench. He seemed to be at the point of running away. "I ain't crazy. God really did come to me. He told me things were all right, that I didn't have to take no tests."

"I know you believe that, Joseph. I hope we can always be honest with each other."

"It is right to be honest, doctor. Do you think I'm crazy?"

"I think you're *sick,* Joseph, and that you should go to the hospital. When you come back home, then we can talk of all these things." I looked at him for a long time. His face was a study in despair. "You wanted me to be honest with you. I'll try to be that always, if you'll try to be honest with me."

"My parents want me to go there?"

I nodded.

He rose from the bench. "We should go, then, and not keep papa waiting."

I gained my feet, and we stood there facing each other for an awkward moment. Joseph extended his hand.

"You could be wrong, doctor. I'm not very smart, but I know what I seen and heard."

I took his hand and shook it. "We'll talk about that when you get back, Joseph."

Several months after Joseph went to Francisville, we at Seminole Mental Health Center were notified he was going to be released. Since we were to be the agency for follow-up care, an extensive record of his hospitalization was transmitted to us several weeks before his discharge. Dr. Welton discussed all the vital data with me, and we planned the future management of Joseph's treatment.

"I imagine he'll have some trouble getting at his angry feelings, Jim. He's become so thoroughly saturated by that flattened life-style he just can't let himself talk back to anyone."

"I agree. He's probably madder than hell at me. I was the last one from here he saw before going to the hospital. He probably feels I'm responsible for whatever happened there."

"According to the reports, his hospital stay wasn't too bad. They put him on Thorazine, and he stabilized in about ten days. His letters to his parents showed that. He was out of contact for only a couple of days, and then they always passed hospital censorship."

"What were the letters like at first?"

"Full of the things God was telling him. Sort of like that note he left for you."

"Did they give him shock treatments?"

"No."

"Good." I was relieved to learn that he had not been given electroconvulsive treatment, feeling as I do that it is very much a last-resort policy. "I'm sure as hell glad about that. I've got a hunch he would just solidify his religious preoccupations with it—that it was some sort of death and rebirth thing."

"That may be a pretty good hunch. Dr. Reader's notes

indicate that Joseph asked for it. He's supposed to have said that 'it would make the past like another life, and purify me.' "

"We've still got the problem of helping him drain out his feelings, though."

"What do you find in the psychological test results from the hospital?"

I took the sheaf of papers, reviewing them for the fifth time in the four days we had had them. "According to the staff psychologist's conclusions, Joseph is at the bottom of the normal range of intelligence, with specific trouble in reading and understanding what he reads. He's better with his hands than most boys his age. The projective tests suggest he's sensitive and confused by his feelings, with a lot of smothered hostility and sort of a 'burned child' way of withdrawing from his feelings. I guess he's never had an outlet for them."

"The hospital chaplain disagreed with his being discharged."

"How come, Derek?"

"He feels the boy just learned to say that he wasn't upset or thinking about religion. That he kind of 'took flight back into normalcy'—that there's a lot under the surface that wasn't tapped."

"Mostly those angry feelings you were talking about, I guess."

"I've got a hunch I'll be the target, Jim—not you. I was the one who told his parents he should be hospitalized. You were the guy who went to the park and talked to him about cannons and Christ." Derek Welton smiled his slow, boyish smile. "That elects me to the black hat, Jim. You wind up with the white Stetson again." His grin broadened. "Funny how often you seem to arrange to be the good guy."

"Like that Max Shulman character, I *nice* for a living."

"Okay," he said, continuing the game. "But next time I get the white horse and you have to take a dirty horse."

In clinic settings, where more than one staff member is often involved in the treatment of a patient, frequently the patient will use one staff member as a target for hostile feelings, and not aim them at his own primary therapist. As these patients come to trust therapy and the acceptance given their feelings, then the hotter feelings can be expressed to the practitioner with whom the patient is working most closely.

It was a very long time in coming with Joseph. The ingrained suppression of his feelings was so deeply conditioned in him that he found no way to make a direct attack on Dr. Welton, even as remote from his treatment as the medical director seemed to be. Joseph first showed faint antagonism toward Dr. Reader, the psychiatrist who had treated him at Francisville State Hospital. When he discovered I was not going to scold or punish him for this mild criticism, he moved gently toward showing his anger with Dr. Welton. The session in which he revealed that first faint displeased reaction was very strange.

He opened the session by being highly critical of "the hoodlums" who lived around Manion, the nearest village to the Vandenkirk farm.

"They was in our back lane the other night. I could hear 'em yellin' and laughin'."

"Who are they, Joseph?"

"Them kids from Manion and the other side of town—Walters, Murphy, Davis—that bunch of hoodlums. The ones that's always in so much trouble at school."

"What were they doing in your lane?"

"Sinnin', I guess. There was girls laughin'. Next mornin' I found a whole bunch of beer cans." His voice was flat and inexpressive, as it had been for all the weeks we had been working together.

"Sinning?"

"Kissin' and pettin'—like that."

"Having intercourse?" I took the longer stride.

"What's that?" His voice lightened slightly with curiosity.

Now I was committed. I had to follow through. "Screwing the girls. Having sex relations with them."

"Adultery?"

"It can't be adultery unless one or the other is married. The Bible term is fornication."

"So that's what that word is." His voice was so low that he seemed to be speaking to himself. He looked at me and made the pronouncement that was old when Solomon's temple wasn't even an architectural drawing. "Lustin' after each other."

"Not just lusting, Joseph. Doing something about it." I

179

watched him intently, trying to remember the limits of his vocabulary and his understanding. "Like a stallion on a mare, or a bull on a heifer. It's a fact of nature."

"It ain't natural to lust."

"Yes, it is. What man has done is to set up rules according to what he feels God has told him about right and wrong. But the feelings are still there."

"Nobody ever told me nothin' like that before."

"Not even the doctors at Francisville?"

"I didn't listen much to what they said. It sounded like it was somethin' bad, most of the time. Dr. Reader was always goin' on about my tellin' him what I felt about girls." He closed off the topic abruptly. "I don't think he did me no good with all the talk."

"Maybe you weren't ready to talk about those things."

"I figure a psychology doctor can do you more good than a psychiatrist. I never got nothin' from talkin' with Dr. Reader. From you—you tell me things."

"You want to learn about things? Anytime I know anything, I'll tell you. I'll tell you if I don't know, too. But first I've got to know what it is you want to learn before I know what to talk about."

"How come them psychiatrists always want you to tell about girls and things like that?"

"Because those are feelings people have and must learn to live with. Sometimes they feel things real strong, and don't know what to do about it. That makes them get upset. If we know the things that upset people, sometimes we can help them to straighten out their lives."

"That could be, I reckon." He looked at me for a moment, then leaned forward across the desk. "I got kind of scared when Dr. Reader kept tryin' to get me to talk about that kind of stuff. I don't like them feelin's, and didn't want him pickin' at me."

"Picking at you about your feelings about sex?"

"Sometimes I used to have dreams about sinful things. That scares me, too."

"You still have those dreams?"

He flushed. It was the first physiologic sign I had seen in him other than his tense muscles. "Sometimes. I pray that I won't.

One time there was stuff on the sheet. Momma accused me of doin' it to myself deliberately."

"Did you tell her about having a dream?"

The flush became a blast of blood under his skin. "No! 'Course not! It was an evil thing. Satan and his handmaids sneaked in and made me dream. I seen 'em in the dream, all naked and touchin' each other. It was Satin's doin'."

"Your own body produced that reaction, Joseph. Very naturally."

"It's a sin! 'Better to save thy seed for the belly of a whore than to cast it forth upon the ground.' People shouldn't never play with theirselves."

"Better read your Bible again, Joseph. That isn't what that part means."

"That's what the Bible says." His voice grew offended.

"Wait a minute. What was the situation? Hadn't Onan's brother died without having a child? The widow was not barren or unable to have one. According to the law of that time, Onan was supposed to give her a child—to breed her. But he withdrew —pulled out of her—and let his seed spill onto the ground. He didn't want to give his brother's wife a child. That's what God was punishing him for—not for masturbating."

"Masturbating?"

"Jacking off."

"You know the Bible, doctor?"

"Some. But be sure you know the difference between these things. When Onan displeased God, it was because he failed to do what God had commanded—not because he had glands that produced seed that went to waste."

"It's nasty stuff, anyhow." Joseph swallowed convulsively.

"You just swallowed, Joseph."

"My mouth was full of spit. I had to do that or else spit in the wastebasket."

"Right. It was a perfectly normal action, wasn't it?"
"Sure."

I put one of Professor Gordon Allport's examples to work. "What if you had spit into a cup? Would you drink it?"

"No. It would be dirty."

"If the cup was clean?" I pinned his eyes. "It was a natural product of your own body. You can easily swallow it when it's in your mouth, but you aren't able to imagine drinking it?"

He paused. "I guess that's kind of silly, ain't it?"

"So is the idea that your other glands aren't supposed to put out any fluids at any time. You're a healthy physical man, Joseph. All of your parts work."

He was quiet for a long moment. "Sometimes I done it . . . I , . . masturbated."

"I'd be surprised if you hadn't. What about it?"

"I fight not to. I try to control myself. But then I'd get to thinkin' and get all excited. I couldn't stop myself. I pray to God to forgive me."

"You water stock on your farm?"

"Sure."

"Ever forget to turn off the pump and let the trough run over?"

"Yeah."

"What kind of sin would you call having the trough spill over?"

"Sin?" His face was genuinely puzzled. "That ain't no sin. Ain't nothin' around the trough that a little water can hurt."

"Ain't nothin' around your body that a little overflow is going to hurt, either."

The silence stretched long. We stared at each other closely. The session was nearly over. For the first time, Joseph had begun some movement against his fears and his feelings. I waited a long time before I spoke again.

"We'll have to quit for today, Joseph. But you said you thought a psychologist could do you more good than a psychiatrist. Do you really think that, or were you just mad at Dr. Reader?"

"It's wrong to be mad at people. Bad."

"Who said that?"

"Christ, the preacher, my folks—everybody."

"Don't include Christ. He got mad enough to wreck the tables of the money changers in the temple. He argued with the scribes and Pharisees. He even got mad at people He loved."

"He did not!"

"What about the night in the garden? He knew He was going to be taken away and killed. He wanted His two beloved disciples

182

to stay awake and keep Him company. They went to sleep on Him. Didn't He show some anger when He said, 'Cans't thou not watch with me but for one hour?' He was angry that they were letting Him down when He needed them." I looked at Joseph closely, watching for a reaction. "I think He had a right to be angry, then."

"But He says if a man hits you on one cheek, you've got to turn the other."

"Right. He said that's what you've got to *do*. Not what you've got to feel. All He says is that if you take the obligation of a Christian, you *do* the Christian thing. He doesn't say anything about whether or not you might *feel* angry when you get hit."

The reaction came. It was slow, spreading across his face. His eyes lighted and the fine muscles of his cheeks and forehead relaxed for one of the few times I had ever seen. For the first time since I had known him, I saw a genuine smile break across Joseph's somber face.

"I was havin' anger toward Dr. Reader."

I nodded, and our session was over.

Following that session with Joseph, I felt there might be a way to go—a wedge to open the shell of fear in which he had been encased. In sessions following, I tried to force the wedge a bit more deeply, hoping to spread the casing to allow the healthy part of his personality to obtain some fresh air, if not a chance to emerge. For a few of our hours, it seemed if we were making some progress. Joseph managed to describe some of his feelings about the earlier running-away episodes.

"I really don't know why I done it. I could never go very far away and I sure couldn't stay away."

"Maybe that was because you didn't really want to go away."

"I don't know. I was tryin' to do God's will—tryin' to be good and not sin. But I didn't know God's will or what it was then."

"What do you mean?"

"I wasn't old enough. God didn't see fit to come to me till I was almost lost in sin."

"Lost in sin? You've never told me about it."

"I won't never let myself sin again."

"You mean masturbation?"

"Worse than that. I can't talk about it."

"You'll have to decide that, Joseph. But was it so much of a sin as all that? Did you kill someone?"

"No!" His voice was still flattened, but there was a surge of power in the denial. "I broke . . . a commandment."

"Thou shalt not commit adultery?"

"No. I—" He broke off.

"Raised up a false image?"

He sucked in an enormous breath. It grated in his chest with a rasping sound. He held the breath so long that I began to grow concerned.

When his voice came again, it was even more harsh and mechanical, with no inflection at all. His constant pitch was as insistent as striking a single note, over and over. It built the scene for me far more vividly than if his intonation had fitted the confession he was making to me.

"I broke three of God's commandments—all in the same day. . . ."

"Another piece of pie, Joseph?"

"No, ma'am, Mrs. Diekhoff. I already had two. It's very good."

The preacher's plump wife grinned. "Never did see a fifteen-year-old who couldn't eat a whole pie at one sitting. Not in this part of the country, anyhow."

She smiled at the boy, her young face lighted and unlined. Joseph felt very warm under her glance. His eyes met hers momentarily, then quickly shifted back to the plate. He took his fork and flattened it against the dish, gathering thickened apple juices and cinnamon between the tines.

"How about some more milk, then?"

"No, thank you. I just come over to see if the pastor needed help with his hay cuttin'. Papa said I should."

"Mr. Diekhoff went into Danton to get somethin' for his mower. I don't know what." Her voice was light and bubbly, unlike his mother's soft, gray tones. "Seems that man of mine spends more time tryin' to fix up his machinery than any other farmer in Seminole County."

184

"Maybe he's doin' the Lord's work, somewhere."

"Could be. But just the same, he's got a farm to run like every other man. He's gotta be a farmer on weekdays, and he'd ought to remember that, too."

"He's a powerful fine preacher, Mrs. Diekhoff. Makes you feel the Lord's bein' real close."

Her smile flashed again. She passed behind his chair on her way to the sink and ruffled her hand across his coarse, short-cropped hair. "Thank you, Joseph. He'll be real pleased to hear about that."

The touch was only a gesture in passing, but Joseph flushed deeply, feeling the red color rising in his face. He coughed to cover his embarrassment. As he choked in his next breath, the heavy tang of cinnamon-laden juices in his mouth went into his throat. The cough became a series of coughs, genuine attempts to rid his throat of the foreign substance.

Martha Diekhoff turned back from her sink, moving toward the boy. "Are you all right?"

Joseph hacked continuously, the cinnamon strangling his voice. "Down my Sunday throat," he managed to gasp between spasms of the cough.

The plump woman came toward him, taking him by the shoulders, pulling him against her apron front. Her flat hand slapped lightly but quickly between his shoulder blades, sharp little blows. With each strike, Joseph's face was buried more deeply into the softness of her belly. The fresh-washed, powdery scent of her snapped into his nostrils. Struggling to free himself, his hands rose, pushing at her well-muscled thighs.

"I'm all right," he sputtered, still gagging. He had to make her move away from him, had to escape the heat of her body through the summer-weight cotton dress. He struggled to his feet, going quickly toward the sink. On his arrival, he opened the tap, catching water in his hand, trying to work swallows down his throat between the ripping coughs rising from it.

The minister's wife went quickly to the cupboard, bringing a glass. She handed it to Joseph. He caught it full of water and drank, sputteringly. With her free hand she drew a handkerchief from her apron pocket, giving it to the boy.

Joseph, his coughs subsiding, forced his body against the

edge of the sink, shamed by the sudden and unexpected erection that bulged in his tight jeans.

She remained close, watching him to make sure his paroxysms had truly been relieved. He could not bring himself to look at her, nor to move away from the sink. He drank another glass of water, hastily, trying to calm himself. Another glass was made to last much longer—but not long enough.

It was the clatter of the old pickup truck in the yard lot that broke the tension. Martha Diekhoff glanced through the window, then went to the door to look out toward her husband. The movement gave Joseph the blessed moment of freedom to get away from the sink. He jammed her handkerchief into his hip pocket, then regained the chair, shoving his legs and hips beneath the old table so that his shame might not show. Only then did her presence in the door draw his eyes. The morning sun etched Martha Diekhoff's firm legs through the light summer dress, the short apron interrupting the display eight inches above her knees.

The heavy-shouldered pastor strode into the house, his blue eyes twinkling. "An hour I'm gone to town, and I find a man in my place when I return."

Joseph's blush flamed, guiltily. "Good morning, pastor."

"Good morning to you, Joseph. It's good to see you."

"Papa sent me to see if you need some help with hayin'."

"That man's a good neighbor—and a good man." The preacher thought for a moment. "I'll probably start cutting on Thursday, so as to have it done some time Friday. Then, if the Lord sees fit to give us three more good dry weeks, it'll be ready for the barn." He grinned at the boy. "Sure wouldn't look right to have a devil's fire on the minister's place, would it?"

"*Devil's fire?* What's that, pastor?"

"An old expression my father used. If you put green hay into the barn while it's damp, there's a chance of spontaneous combustion setting the barn on fire. It gives off a lot of heat. I wouldn't want my barn burned down. Since sparrows don't carry matches, and no farmer worth his salt would risk smoking in the haymow, the old folks used to call it the work of the devil." His grin widened. "My father used to have a lot of foolish ideas about what made things happen. He was a stubborn, superstitious old

Dutchman." The grin faded a little. "He was a good farmer, and a God-fearing man, with some old-fashioned ideas. But," his voice was again resolute, his apologies made, "he was stubborn— just like I am."

Or like my papa? Joseph thought. His erection had disappeared, buried in the guilt of the uneasy thought. He blurted out his speech in sudden jabbing sound. "I'll tell my papa that you want me Thursday, with the tractor and the cutter bar. Will it be all right if I come as late as six thirty? I've got my early chores to do first."

"If you come any earlier, I'm liable to think you're stuck on Mrs. Diekhoff." The blue-eyed man smiled, looking appreciatively at his young wife. Then he turned back to Joseph. "That would be fine, Joseph. I thank your father for being so generous with your time."

Henry Diekhoff could not help but notice the boy's embarrassed and uncomfortable face. He presumed it was the unequal nature of the loan of work that made the boy seem so on edge. After a moment the minister added, "Since your father got his cutting done week before last, I'd like you to tell him I'll bring my rake and help him winrow it ready for the bailer whenever he says it's ready."

Joseph read this as a dismissal. He stood, awkwardly extended his hand to the minister, thanked Mrs. Diekhoff for the pie and milk, then bolted out the open screen door of the kitchen. Thirty feet from the house, he paused weakly, leaning against the post of the house gate. He could still hear the voices of the minister and his wife.

"That's a good boy," the preacher was saying. "He's sure kind of *different,* but he's a good boy."

"What do you mean, different? Weren't you kind of gawky and unsure of yourself when you were around fifteen? Or were you born eighty-five years old?" Her voice was pleased, bantering, musical.

Joseph could hear the sound of the preacher's hand, slapping Martha Diekhoff's rump. "I'll show you who's eighty-five."

Together they laughed. Her voice was like reeds and finger cymbals, and his like the bass pipes of some mighty organ.

Joseph, his face scarlet, fled across the Diekhoff's barn lot, hurdling the fence into the pastureland that lay between the two farms. He ran halfway across the long pasture before he threw himself down on the bank of the little creek, sobbing from humiliation.

I ain't different. I ain't no different from anybody else— no more unsure of myself. Why'd they have to say that? Why'd she have to rub up against me that way? Why'd she stand in the light that way?

Joseph caught himself suddenly. "That's sin," he said aloud. "I wanted her to touch me. I wanted her to hold me against her."

He thought about it, mental images leaping into the disturbed pool of his composure like startled frogs. It took him some time to translate it and assign himself the specific sin. "I broke the commandment. *I coveted my neighbor's wife.*"

He rolled onto his back, looking at the sky, waiting for God's hammer blow to smash him into perdition. But the morning sky stayed blue, with faint wisps of cloud over the low hills of back-country pine scrub. "I'm sorry, God. Truly I'm sorry. I don't mean to be a sinner."

He vaulted to his feet, falling forward onto his knees. He clasped his hands before him and began to pray for forgiveness. He prayed a very long time, knuckles white with the tension of his own laced fingers. No feeling or relief came. Joseph changed his prayer. "Don't turn Your face from me, God. Don't leave me in the darkness of my sinnin' ways."

No solace came into his feelings, and his fright was not eased—no great sign of guilt appeared on his forehead, but neither did the feeling of forgiveness come to him.

Joseph rose uneasily. He reached into his pocket for his handkerchief to wipe the sudden perspiration from his upper lip. But the cloth his hand brought from his pocket was not his own wadded bit of rag, but the smaller one with the embroidered bluebird in the corner. He stared at it, then raised it to wipe his lips. The faint wisp of sachet touched his nostrils again, searing them like a branding iron. He recognized the same sweet smell he had known when his face was buried in Martha Diekhoff's body. His heart leaped for a moment, feeling strangely light. Then the awfulness of his sin smote him down.

188

"I'm coveting again. I have not driven the sinful thought from my heart. No wonder I cannot be forgiven." He looked at the vibrant bluebird stitched onto the plain cotton handkerchief. "And I stole her handkerchief. I'm a thief. I *stole—I broke another commandment!*" His voice was almost a shout.

Prayer wouldn't help, he knew. He threw the handkerchief from him, hurling it with all his strength, but the cloth responded by opening and catching the air like a sail. The breeze brought it back toward his feet, spreading it before him to show him the needlework bluebird in one of its cotton corners, and the initials M.D. in another.

Joseph broke into a run again, forcing himself to flee the place. Yet he had not traveled fifty yards when he stopped. Slowly he walked back to the edge of the creek. His stolen treasure lay before him, its edge lapped by the breeze. He picked it up, gingerly, folded it carefully. He put it into the other rear pocket of his jeans, forcing it deep into the tightly compressed pouch.

"Maybe if I give it back, the Lord'll forgive me. I didn't mean to be no thief." He said the words aloud.

It was his thoughts that mocked him. *Didn't you? You didn't want to be an adulterer? You didn't covet your neighbor's wife? You don't lust after the preacher's wife? Your sin is the same as when you went naked into the horse trough. That stolen handkerchief is dirtied with your lustful sweat.*

"I can wash it. I can make it clean again."

Too bad you can't do as much for your own soul.

He moved, almost staggering, toward his father's farm. He found himself dragging, fighting the mental battle with himself.

"Joseph! Where have you been so long?" Peter Vandenkirk's voice was harsh and loud.

"I—"

"You knew you were to come back as soon as you had talked to the preacher."

"Yes, papa."

"An hour I've waited, with much to be done. You call that a way to do your father's bidding?"

"No, papa."

"I don't wonder you blush with shame. Peter Vandenkirk's son—and this is the way you honor your father?"

The awesome detachment of Joseph's voice, flattened and mechanical, drew my attention back to the boy sitting in my office. I looked at him closely, noticing his uncompromised and moving position in the chair. It was as if he were denying any personal involvement with the report that had led to my vivid visual re-creation of the scene.

"Did you tell your father anything about this, Joseph? Any of the feelings?"

"No!" This was the first hint of emphasis in the entire narrative.

"You didn't think that he could have understood that Mrs. Diekhoff was attractive, and that you responded to her?"

"That was the Devil's work—makin' me feel that way."

"Devil's work?"

He seemed to think about that for a moment, then looked back at me, meeting my eyes directly for the first time in the session.

"No. I guess I thought it was then. It was later that I realized it had to be the Lord tryin' me. I failed Him."

"What do you mean?"

"I didn't do nothin' about my sin. I didn't talk it over with the preacher, or nothin'."

"How could you? It was his wife who prompted those feelings. You couldn't tell a man something like that."

"It shouldn't make no difference. He's my preacher. He ain't like ordinary people." His voice was not quite so flat, but still it had no variation or life showing in it.

"Did you go to work his fields—help him haying?"

"Sure. Papa told me to do it, you know. I worked hard, too."

"I'm sure you did."

"We cut all the hay on Thursday." He looked down at his hands. "I stayed to see that it was all down by the end of the day."

"So you wouldn't have to go back on Friday and risk seeing Mrs. Diekhoff again?"

His eyes flashed from his hands to my face. He made no reply, so I went on. "I had a teacher one time. I thought she was about the finest woman that God ever put on earth. I used to

190

dream about her all through the day, to the point where I wouldn't hear a word she said in class."

"You thought lustful thoughts? *You* sinned?"

"Remember the talk we had about masturbation a couple of weeks ago?"

"Yeah." He nodded.

"When you thought about Mrs. Diekhoff," I said carefully, "did you think about having sex with her, or just about holding her and protecting her—taking care of her?"

"I don't know."

"Think about her now. Do you really think about making love to her? Or do you think about being close to her—being important to her?" I slowed, but only for a fractional moment. "Don't you really just want to be nice to her? To have her like you? I'd be willing to bet that your daydreams never went beyond having her kiss you or touch your hair. Maybe you imagined her putting her arms around you."

The flush that rose in his cheeks signaled that I was on the right track. "I never thought of doin' anything bad to her."

"I'm sure you didn't. Tell me, Joseph, did you ever look up the word *covet* in the dictionary?"

"No. It means to want or desire."

"If you looked in the dictionary, you'd find that it means to desire to take unlawfully."

"I had desire for her—desire to be close to her."

"But not to take her unlawfully or to steal her from Mr. Diekhoff. That's the whole point of this, Joseph."

"There ain't no point. God told me he forgave me my sins, so that's all there is to that. He appeared to me and told me my sins were forgiven and washed away."

"Can we talk about that next time? Next week?"

Joseph nodded, and the session was over. For a long time after he had left the office, I sat thinking of what he had told me. Two years of softening his memories of being fifteen had not given him perspective on his attraction to the preacher's wife. How could it, when I could look back over thirty years and remember my own frightening awkwardness of that time? Then, values such as those Joseph's culture so rigidly held were much closer to being the norm. If thirty years had not dimmed my memory, how could

Joseph, at seventeen, have accepted the suddenly erect penis and the hunger for Martha Diekhoff that had blasted into his awareness?

I was thankful that Joseph's appointment was set just before my lunch period. It gave me a bit of time to realign my thinking and my feelings before having to face a different situation with a different patient.

I had been heartened by the progress Joseph had made in ventilating the memories that were so crowded with pain. It seemed to me that this kind of progress might well continue as Joseph found himself. However, as is all too often the case, I was wrong. Resistance developed in the next session. Joseph was almost mute. We sat for the larger part of the next hour with no words flowing between us. I asked him, in several different ways, but he denied me permission to enter into his thoughts and feelings. It was nearly the end of the session before he spoke at all, at least of anything pertaining to himself or to his feelings.

It came when I finally asked the question that I might well have asked at the beginning, had I not been so lulled by the progress we had been making, and the rapport we seemed to have built in the sessions that had preceded this one.

"Are you angry with me, Joseph?"

He shot me a quizzical look from his half-averted face, but still he responded with silence.

"Did something in our last session make you angry with me?"

He shook his head, then answered as if forced to speak. "It happened after that. I had to talk it over with God."

"What's that?"

"The lust your words put into my heart."

"Lust for Mrs. Diekhoff?"

"No. I went to thinkin' about takin' somebody unlawful. Even you said that would be covetin'."

"Even I said that?"

"Maybe it was especially you. I never thought of takin' nobody unlawful, or by force. Now I have. But God, He said it was all right . . . all right that I thought that, not that I done it. I seen this picture in a magazine at the drugstore—she was naked!"

"And you wanted to touch the woman in the picture."

"Yeah. But God, He reminded me that you'd told me about that kinda stuff." He looked at me more directly. "That's why I don't think I'll come here to talk to you anymore." He held me now with a fixed stare. "I got God to talk these things over with."

He had aimed it right back at me. I murmured my own silent prayer that my guts were right—that Joseph was ready to be confronted with the fact of his own illness.

"That's part of the way in which you are sick, Joseph. When I got too close to helping you look at all your feelings—good ones and bad ones—you turn away to *talk with God.*"

He stared at me as if I had struck him. I had made a complete commitment to unvarnished confrontation. From this point on, no retreat would be possible. I could not recover or backtrack with Joseph. Now, I had to push on.

"But that voice of God you hear is within your own mind. It comes directly out of *your own feelings.* I don't want you to quit coming, because I honestly believe that you cannot continue to hold yourself together without letting go of some of these feelings. You've got to get them out into the open. You must examine them for what they really are—not for what you are afraid they are."

"You're sayin' there ain't no God!"

"I'm saying nothing of the kind! What I am saying is that God is not your enemy."

"Of course not! He's my Lord and Savior. I took him for my Lord and Savior and he'll keep me from sin."

"You can keep yourself from sin. By the free choice that God gave you. You don't need miracles or visions of God to be a good man—you *are* a good man. You *are* a child of God. What I am saying is that you'll go on believing every urge or feeling you have is wrong and in need of special forgiveness as long as you forget that God loves this world and His creatures. When you do that, and feel sinful, then you have to make a special case for yourself."

"I don't forget nothin' like God's love."

"Then what was that *great sin* you committed before you had to make yourself believe you had a personal kind of contact with God?"

"I don't know what you're talkin' about."

"You've said, more than once, that you had done something too bad to talk about. Now, what was it?"

"God forgave me that. I don't have to tell you."

"You didn't have to tell your father, either, did you?" It was more than a shot in the dark. The curious total submission to his father, the absence of the usual teen-age rebellious strivings for liberation and independence from parents, was a hallmark of Joseph.

On this occasion his voice was not flat. "I set fire to the barn! I burned it down."

"When?"

"Last year—three or four months before I came here the first time."

"Before you first thought you had talked with God?"

"Yes. God didn't come to me till I was in the hospital with pneumonia—that was three or four months after I burned the barn." Joseph lapsed into silence.

I waited for what seemed a very long time. Joseph was staring at me. I returned his gaze. When he spoke again, his voice had dropped to a near whisper, yet his words came without hesitation and quite audibly.

"He sent me out to clean the stalls. I turned the animals out into the pasture, then started to work. There was urine and manure layin' in the straw, an' on the concrete. I took a fork and went to diggin' at it. Where it wasn't wet and stinkin' it was dry and dustin'. I got to sneezin' and coughin'. I couldn't stand that smell for nothin'. If it made me sneeze, I knew it would make him sick."

"Your father would get sick?"

"Yeah. I scraped the fork on the concrete floor. It hit a spark."

"That caught the barn on fire?"

"No."

"Then what happened?"

"I just got the thought from that spark. If this damned barn wasn't here, nobody wouldn't have to sneeze or get sick from the smell of the sour straw and the dust. There was a place in the floor where it had caved in. The piss stayed in it and the bed straw'd be wet and finally I couldn't take it, so I burned the barn down."

"Did you ever tell your father about it?"

"That's when I lied. I broke my fourth commandment. He asked me if I knew anything about it, and I—*I bore false witness*. I told him I didn't know nothin' about it. But it wasn't no sparrow carryin' a match. It was me as lit the barn down."

Narrative rolled from the boy, in the odd combination of teen-age argot and stilted biblical prose I had come to expect from Joseph. The oddness of the language somehow made his remembered confrontation with his "sinful act" more vivid. The flat strangeness of speech forced the past to be again the living present. . . .

"The animals! Joseph! Save the animals!" Peter Vandenkirk's voice created huge waves of sound, trying by sheer force of sound to drown and quench the flames of the burning barn.

For a moment the boy stood, frozen in panic and awe. He saw a spiral of flame rise from the open upper hay door, then curl along the steel track of the boom. The pulley rope was inside the cylinder of flame, like a rod within a glass jar.

"Help me, boy!" The shout rose louder. Peter Vandenkirk was throwing his shoulder at the door of the barn, trying to force it open. "We've got to save the animals!"

Joseph was assailed by an impulse to run away, yet he found himself running toward the flaming structure. He heaved his weight against the edge of the door. Together he and his father forced the heavy door along its track, sliding it out of the way.

"The animals are out, papa. They're safe!" Joseph's voice was a shriek. "I turned them out when I started to clean the barn. They are safe!"

"*Gut!* First tools, then bags of feed. Save everything we can!" Peter Vandenkirk vanished inside the barn, returning in seconds with a heavy tool chest hugged to his chest. He dashed past the boy, running to the center of the barn lot. Then he dropped the chest and wheeled to return.

"Get in there, boy! Save things!"

Joseph faced the door, appalled by the sheets of flame that draped the mangers. A crackling roar filled the interior of the barn. Then he was beyond hesitation. He dashed to the workbench and seized tools from the board above it—wrenches, sledges, hammers, and auger bits were jerked from their cradles.

He staggered toward the door with them, spilling some of the smaller ones from his load. For a moment he paused as if to recover them, then fled from the searing heat of the blazing hay. He half dropped, half threw his load to the ground and came back for another.

His father was on his third trip, a huge grain bag over his shoulder. "Hurry, Joseph. Hurry!"

The boy plowed into the barn, head down, then out again, furrowing the dust and flying sparks of hay with the two grain bags he was dragging at his sides. He ran furiously in and out of the barn, not carrying but dragging sacks of alfalfa pellets, laying mesh, calf feed, sorghum meal. His father aped his technique, dragging rather than carrying, huge hands clenching the sacks by their eared corners. Between them they carved deep channels in the dust.

"The gasoline, papa! The gasoline!"

"Get water. Keep it cool. I'll get the tractor."

Joseph threw the pump switch by the cattle trough, and the jet pump whirred, water spilling into the tank. Milk and feed buckets splashed into the pool. Joseph, a bucket in each hand, raced toward the cumbersome wooden cradle topped by the three-hundred-gallon fuel tank that stood at the end of the barn. He sluiced the water in a high arc, letting it crash down on the tank, then hurried back for more.

Katje Vandenkirk was in the barn lot now, running with a bucket of water. She passed Joseph on his return for more water.

"I called the firemen!" she yelled in passing, not pausing until she had heaved her water over the tank.

The tractor roared, its cleated wheels spinning in the soft dust of the barn lot. Peter twisted the machine in a tight circle. "The chain, Joseph! Hook the chain!"

Joseph sluiced his tenth pail of water over the tank, then grappled for the heavy chain of the tank cradle. Making one end secure, he hurdled the chain to run to the far side of the wooden structure and seize the other end, making it fast to the dragbar with the pivot bolt, completing the loop around the base of the tall cradle.

Peter Vandenkirk moved the tractor to take up the slack, then slowly began to drag the heavy, timbered tower away from the barn with a steady pull from the heavy machine. He would have liked to race away, but feared to upset the top-heavy tower and tank, thus adding gasoline to the fire. It seemed to take forever. Joseph sluiced another pail of water over the tank, running alongside the slowly moving structure.

Suddenly, the wall of the barn was ripped open by the heat, and sparks and sheds of burning hay escaped into the air. The pine slab walls were rupturing before the torchlike flames from the haymow. Katje Vandenkirk's bucket made sizzling sounds as she flung water onto a flaming ember that came to rest briefly on the tank. The ponderous drag slid farther away from the barn with maddening slowness.

When the tank had been dragged a safe distance, Joseph turned his attention to the small shed lying downwind from the blazing barn. It was a lung-searing torture to speed toward that building. Air filled with ash and embers wrapped him. He entered the shed and pulled out the wheeled rig of acetylene welding equipment, running with the cumbersome cart until he had outdistanced the tractor and the gasoline tank.

Then he was back at the cattle trough. His mother dashed water over him where his clothing was smoking. He seized his buckets and ran to sluice the smaller shed.

Farmers from nearby farms began to arrive then, and the pails of water multiplied. Wet grain bags were used to beat at the flying sparks that blew against the other buildings in the barn lot. Katje Vandenkirk doused the men who came to the trough with buckets, and Pastor Diekhoff simply leaped into the trough and out, soaking himself completely as he joined the bucket brigade.

The battle continued for twenty frenzied minutes before the great surge came. The roof fell through the barn, showering flames and sparks in all directions with a great whoosh of sudden wind. Five minutes more of concerted action, and the danger was past. No other buildings would be lost. Plastic pipe was connected and laid to build a muddy lake like a moat around the bonfire of the great barn. Steam erupted with a great hissing noise where the moat and flame met. From the other well, the garden hose was stretched, and the pressure tank that provided the Vandenkirks' house with water pressure pumped a puny stream at the edges of the fire.

The fire truck from Manion's volunteer brigade arrived then. The heavy pumper truck with its thick hose laid a great steamy fog over the fire heap that had been a barn, sucking the water trough dry as soon as it had exhausted its small on-board supply. The foam tank was emptied as well, and fire ceased to be a threat.

Joseph collapsed, panting, on the pile of feed bags, smoke-seared lungs aching, eyes running tears.

His father's hand smashed onto his shoulder like a huge clamp, jerking him to his feet.

"You were smoking in the barn, jah?" The voice was cold and angry. "You *burned* the barn!"

Great fear clutched at Joseph's belly. "No, papa. No!" He looked at his father's angry face. "I do not smoke, papa! I didn't do it!"

"Who would burn a barn should be in prison! If I find such a man, I will put him in the penitentiary!"

"I did not burn the barn, papa. I didn't." Joseph's mind scrambled like a small animal, frantic for exemption, for escape from his father's furious rage. "Don't put me in prison, papa! I didn't do it. It—it was—" His mind found words and his tongue flashed them past his lips. "—it was devil's fire!" He screamed the last. "Nobody did it. Nobody did it! It was devil's fire!"

"What is devil's fire? You blame your sin on Satan?" Peter Vandenkirk's hand raised to strike.

The arcing hand was caught by Pastor Diekhoff. "Wait, Peter!"

"This is my business, pastor. He is *my* son!"

"He could be telling the truth. There is devil's fire!"

"No!"

"Spontaneous combustion! Green hay will do that some-times!"

"That's what the pastor told me, papa." Joseph's voice was trembling, words tumbling from his mouth like scurrying animals bent on escape. "If hay isn't dry enough, it can catch on fire!"

The upraised hand came down, slowly, as the minister released it. Peter Vandenkirk loosed the great vise of his other hand from the boy's shoulder. "The hay dried two weeks only—it *should* have been longer." He looked at his son's pleading face.

Then he nodded. "Go clean out the garage. Make space enough to hold the bags of feed."

Joseph, his legs feeling like cooked spaghetti, his belly seemingly acrawl with worms, face and throat like scalded meat, escaped to his assigned task. He was grateful for the respite. He would have been shamed if he had been where he could hear his father's pride-filled remark to the men who had come to fight the fire and stayed to watch the interrogation.

"Did ever a boy work so? I could not have saved so much without him—and the gasoline tank would have exploded. He brought out almost all of the feed. He is a boy who works as a man *should* work. . . ."

I waited a very long time, looking at Joseph across my desk. He seemed lost in memory, but his words had ceased to flow. Finally, I interceded.

"Did you ever tell your father what had happened?"

"I . . . couldn't. I . . . can't." He raised his eyes to meet mine, showing me tears standing in them. "It wasn't only the commandment I broke that day. I bore false witness, but then I never made no"—he stumbled on the word—"restitution."

"Restitution?" I was surprised by a word that seemed well beyond Joseph's usual vocabulary or understanding.

"I failed God there, too. In the Bible He says, 'If fire break out, and catch in the thorns, so that the stacks of corn or the standing corn, or the field be consumed, he that kindled the fire shall surely make restitution.' I ain't payin' and I ain't paid nothin'. They ain't no way for me to pay for that corn that was in the feed bin and burned up."

It was typical of Joseph to think of literal corn—American grain crop corn—and the hopper feed bin as a stack. But for the great shame and remorse burning in his face, I might have smiled. Instead I simply looked at him, as he continued to stare at me.

Finally he spoke. "I should have told him, I guess."

"You were very frightened. I imagine you really would have needed help with that one, wouldn't you?"

"God, He helped me. He come to me. He told me I was forgiven."

"When was that? When you were in the hospital?"

"Yeah. A couple months after the fire. I hadn't been sleepin' good and I just got weak. I got a fever and was real sick. They put me in the hospital. That's when God come, like I told you before."

"When you thought you heard a man ask the doctor to give his child away? That a father could turn away from his own son? That a man would want his child dead or out of his life?"

"Yeah, that happened there, too."

"Because you thought if your dad found out what you'd done, he'd send you to the pen? *He'd get rid of you?*"

"That's when God came to me. He came right to my bed an' told me I didn't have to worry about doin' nothin' to stop that man from givin' his child away or tellin' the doctor to kill it."

"What was the thing you felt he said—exactly?"

"I'll never forget that. The man said, 'I don't give a damn about my baby. I wish it would die. We got another kid, and I don't care if this one does die. I'd like to sell that little baby. I'd like to get about nine hundred dollars for it. Then I wouldn't have to pay no bills, and I wouldn't care if it died or not after that.' " Joseph plunged ahead, his voice racing. "I thought, *there's a guy tryin' first to kill his baby, then tryin' to sell it*. They'd took him out of the pen to come and see his baby 'fore it died. His wife, she was about a nervous wreck. He'd hit that baby. I heard him say, 'If it dies, well, then I killed it.' Nobody should hit a little baby."

"Even for going into the horse trough to cool off?"

He did not seem to notice or hear what I had said. He went on describing the imagined situation.

"The baby did die—the doctors couldn't fix it up. When they told the man the baby was dead, he told them to just put it in a cardboard box somewhere and get rid of it. After a while, he sort of recognized what he was sayin'. Then he went nuts—he was screamin' that he had killed the baby, and that he was goin' back to the pen. He broke down and cried a lot. He said he'd never do it again if he could only get a fair trial."

"You almost had to have a miracle then, didn't you, Joseph?"

The boy looked at me strangely, the light dying in his eyes.

"You were here in the Danton hospital last year, Joseph.

There was no case of child beating anywhere around here at the time you were in the hospital. There was no injured baby here at that time."

"God came to me then. He really did."

"I believe you feel that. You needed something to help you when you were so frightened—when you felt so guilty and so sinful."

"He came to the doorway and said, 'I want to help you. Forget all your sins. We all sinned in our lives, and I'll forgive you.' But then He come toward my bed, all shinin' with light. He says, 'You must pray, and *you'll have to forgive me at the same time that I'll be prayin' and forgivin' you.'* He shook my hand, then put His torn-up hand on my forehead and sat down on the edge of my bed. *I know there is a God.*"

"Why did God ask you to forgive Him? What was His trespass against you?" I snapped my question at Joseph, forcing his attention.

"Tryin' my soul with all of them sinful thoughts."

"Is that what God said?"

"He made me think: Did momma and papa ever do me wrong? Ever treat me like a jailbird? Ever claim they didn't want me or wished that I would die? Did they work to help me? To give me things for my future? Help me be what I wanted to be?"

His attention was on me, eyes riveted to my face. "An' what did I do to repay them? I burnt down the barn because I was . . ."

"Furious with them."

He looked fixedly at me while a questioning expression spread across his tanned young face. Joseph was not able to integrate the shift of confrontation I was making. Another patient, more alert to the implications of his own thoughts, might well supply his own confrontations. Joseph, set in his rigid defenses, would require a frontal assault. I took a deep breath.

"What do you mean?" he asked.

"Let me put a few things in order for you, first. You had felt, all of your life, that you were walking a tightrope between being a sinner and doing God's will?"

"Everybody's got to keep from sin. 'Narrow is the path.' I always felt like that."

"And when you thought you had sinned by coveting the

preacher's wife, you couldn't see it as just the kind of crush any boy might have on a pretty woman who was nice to him? A woman who never asked anything of him but whether or not he'd like another piece of pie? A woman who could laugh and joke with her husband about his age or his seriousness?"

"What I felt for Mrs. Diekhoff was a real strong feelin'."

"Of course it was. Why else would you have had to punish yourself for being so *sinful* as to find your body responding to a warm and friendly woman? What did you think when you bumped into Betty Kleinschmidt? That time Willem Van Voort pushed you down the stairs?"

"I didn't think nothin'. I was nervous and upset about that."

"And when you saw that naked woman's picture?"

"I . . . don't know."

"In fact, Joseph, *just one sin wasn't enough.* You put her handkerchief into your pocket automatically. Her husband had just come home and you were embarrassed, and in a spot where you could be more shamed. But when you found it in your pocket later, you had to see the fact that you had it as being a deliberate and planned theft.

"Then, when you got on home, your father scolded you. You were so completely upset that you were ready to feel guilty about anything at all—including the dishonoring of your parents."

"Maybe. Maybe I did." His voice was filled with wonder.

"It's a terrible thing to feel alone with that much sin and guilt. To feel that you are that much of a sinner."

His face was lighting to match his suddenly enlivened eyes. I drove home the confrontation, not waiting for him to develop it.

"In a situation where you feel that much alone, you *need* a powerful friend. You've got to have somebody more powerful than preachers or fathers or mothers or doctors or policemen or *anyone.*"

"That's the way it was when He come to me. I was steeped in sin. He come to me. I said to Him, 'Dad . . . er . . . *God!* I need your help. I got to be forgiven my sins.'"

This was the confirmation I was looking for. I called the slip of the tongue to Joseph's attention. "You said *dad,* Joseph. You didn't say God! It was your father's forgiveness you wanted, wasn't it? You wanted his forgiveness for burning the barn! For every angry thought you'd ever had about *him!* You needed your father to say it was all right! That he wouldn't send you away to the penitentiary! That your father wouldn't refuse to be your father any longer, in spite of your having done an angry thing.

"When you ran away as a child, you always came back to take your whipping. It was your father you needed. You needed the times when he could show you love and tenderness. Those times were there, Joseph. It wasn't all whippings and chores, was it? Didn't your father claim you could work as well as any man from the time you were a little boy? When you got sick, didn't he put everything aside to help you? Didn't he show pride in you? Pay you wages? Send you to help neighbors so that the whole community would think well of Joseph Vandenkirk?

"Was God telling you things you wanted to hear from your father? That you were forgiven? That he wanted your forgiveness for the times he didn't understand you? Or the times he asked something that was too much for you?

"Didn't you have to confess to *God* what you were afraid to confess to your father? That you could be angry with him? That he sometimes hurt you without even knowing of your hurts? That you needed to know that your folks are as proud of you as they are of your brother Henrik in Vietnam? That you hungered for a knowledge of the love and feeling they have for you?"

Joseph was half out of his chair, his face alight. The muscles of that face were confused with the conflicting commands his feelings were giving them. Joseph did not know whether he wanted to laugh, cry, or curse. He dropped his head forward onto the desk and sobbed.

We were there for a very long time. The boy with his head down, crouched in his chair. His shoulders were heaving with quiet sobs that wracked his body, while I leaned forward, my hand on his shoulder, fingers pressing firmly against his work-banded muscles.

Finally Joseph lifted his head. He stared at me for a long moment.

"I . . . I got to tell this to my pa . . . to my *dad*. But I don't know how to put it so's to be sure he'll understand it all." He smiled wistfully, through a face still seeping drops of tears. "Maybe I don't understand it all so good, myself."

"I never heard you call him dad before, Joseph. It was always papa."

"*Papa* is what a child calls his father. If I'm ever gonna be a man, I can't go on like a child. I just gotta tell him, try to explain what happened."

"Would you like me to explain it to him?"

"I . . . I want to tell him. I'm just afraid I can't do it right."

"Is your *dad* in Danton today?"

"Yeah. He's supposed to pick me up at noon."

I pointed to the desk clock. It indicated Joseph and I had continued to ten minutes to one, not the standard hour.

"Then he's probably out in the waiting room, Joseph. Why don't you ask your dad to come on in? We'll both tell him."

*

The loneliness Joseph felt demanded that he invest his feelings in something outside of himself. He was fearful of transmitting his feelings to others, yet the lonely condition we all share forced him into his unreal association with an all-powerful, all-knowing God. His hallucinated Savior calmed him, supporting him in the fashion in which he needed to be sustained. Only with the release Joseph gained in hallucinating forgiveness could he make his fumbling contact with fallible, far-from-omnipotent humans.

We all share loneliness as a constant condition. Trapped as we are within our skins, barred from direct contact with all that exists beyond that dermic barricade, given only our perception and its sensations as our merchants of reality, we experience the continuing tension of our isolation. We seek to relieve this tension by finding routes to exchange our feelings. To do this, we build language, art, music, philosophy, sex, work, love, religion—all our forms of communication. Taken as a whole, we call this our "culture."

When these pressures grow without adequate relief, we somehow redouble our efforts for contact. We begin to hold communions of less direct and namable kinds. We are not fulfilled by these more primitive acts. Daydreamed vengeance does not restore our internal peace. Imagined arms do not warm and gratify us.

Yet no one of us is exempt from primitive impulses. We use our illusions when reality does not fulfill us. At times we do not even admit that we have needs remaining unful-

filled in reality, and deny that we are expressing them in fantasy and illusion.

It was precisely this that happened in the journey with Julia. . . .

PART FIVE

* JULIA *

"...and sweet the wines of May..."

THE TALL, WELL-SHOULDERED MAN REACHED FOR HER HAND, lounging back into the weight-worn taxi seat in the same motion. The girl responded to his touch, putting her right hand atop the stacked fingers, pressing at his large knuckles.

"It's been a very special day, Joel." Her voice was softened even below its usual level. He glanced at her, pleased to watch the liquefaction of her dark brown eyes.

"It has, hasn't it?" He smiled at her. "I'm glad the concert was what you had hoped it would be."

"Grieg . . . says something to me." Her body relaxed, merging gracefully with the man's shoulder and the seat back. "But the chance of having a whole day with you seems definitely to call for Grieg."

He returned her pleased expression, glad that she could openly appreciate a stolen Sunday. "I had to promise Gary two days off next week in exchange. He wants to hunt when the bird season opens." He slipped into a burlesque southern accent. "Yoah comp-ney do fetch a maighty high figuah, Miz Girard."

She joined the game. "Awl that cost foah lil' ol' me?" She tittered like an antebellum belle. "Mistuh Geye-rahd, how you do run on." Her fingers squeezed the back of his hand again. The accent was put aside. "I like it."

"Did you take your Dramamine?" His voice had cleared, also.

"Yes. I wouldn't risk getting airsick and spoiling our first day together in weeks. I took one this morning, too—before we came over."

"It's a lot calmer during the morning flights. When the earth begins to radiate heat, later in the day, it can get a little bumpy."

The man leaned forward, directing the cabdriver through the gate and onto the line toward the parked aircraft. "It's that 182 in the second line."

"That what?"

Joel blushed, forgetting that not everyone would be as familiar with aircraft as a small-city light plane dealer. "That green and white high-wing aircraft in the second row. It's a Cessna 182."

"Oh." The driver's confusion cleared. "That's a pretty one."

"Thanks."

They left the taxi, Joel paying the driver and adding a bit to the tip for the compliment to his plane. Then they stood, two young people beside an airplane, looking back at the city and reluctant to move. The late afternoon sun was cooling, hanging above the horizon as if suspended in the crystal sky by the thin ribbons of high clouds.

"I like being married to you," Julia said softly.

Joel turned, sweeping her off her feet and whirling her around, feet well off the ground.

"Idiot! Stop that!"

"I just want to see if that motion sickness stuff fills the bill," he said, flashing a boyish grin. He stopped whirling her about and pulled her even tighter to him. "I like being married to you, too. That's why I want to check out that Dramamine, since I have other kinds of motion in mind for later."

She had her feet on the ground again, but put her hands up and behind his neck, pulling his tawny head down slightly to kiss him. "It seems likely we have the same motions in mind." Her face was alight. "What less could I do for a gallant young aviator type who flies away with me for a day of lobster salad, Anjou wine, and beautiful music?"

She dropped back into the southern belle game. "Youah do shuhely know how to puhsuade a guhl, Jo-el Geye-rahd, Ah sweah."

208

"Then youh get yo puhty lil' tail intuh my flyin' muh-chine, foah youh lose awl thet puhsuasion. Ah'm gone tayke you to yo home 'n' make babies with youh—with youah kine puhmission, ma'am."

A stab of feeling ripped Julia. She threw it off, seeking to make herself stay with the Dixie-fried conversational game.

"Suh! Youh vio-laytin' mah modesty."

"Ah plans to vio-layte youah body, too. Get in thet ay-re-o-plane."

Joel did not recognize the turn the game had taken. Neither did Julia. She only knew that the bright glare of afternoon sun-light ripped at her eyes, and that her muscles tensed and entrails tightened into banded knots as the Cessna wallowed mildly in the thermals of the late October day. It spoiled the glow she had been experiencing, and she resented it.

By the time the aircraft had covered half the distance to Leighton, she was uncomfortable. Two-thirds of the way along she was miserable. Her head throbbed. With difficulty she fought back the retching until they landed.

For several minutes after the gentlest of approaches and touchdowns, she sat in the airplane. Joel had taxied to the face of the hangar marked "Girard Flying Service." He left the plane and came around to her side, ducking the strut and opening her door.

She turned her pained face toward him. "I'm sorry, darling. Truly I am."

Julia Girard did not recognize a relationship between this kind of memory and the problems that had brought her to Seminole Mental Health Center. We had worked together for some weeks before the unique blockage was clear enough to either of us to be discussed.

She had, of course, given me the present problems and a few clues to her battles with herself in our first meeting. She had offered them in a taut, hostile manner, expressing her feelings about being referred for treatment in the kind of shorthand the therapist must learn before he can have the temerity to transcribe.

I thought back to my first meeting with Julia Girard, some

months earlier. There was little difficulty in recalling the impact of that encounter.

Her slimness, the way she carried herself, the expertly altered uniform she wore made Julia appear to be tall. She moved as if she had no weight, but was energy restrained by the white nylon of her laboratory technician's uniform. Her dark hair was carefully rolled to shoulder length. Her face revealed a faint touch of makeup, well applied. These things, conspiring with frightened eyes and set features, gave Julia a calculated advantage.

Her eyes were mobile, flashing up as I entered the room. The skin was faintly colored, glowing as fine marble does—from beneath its white surface sheen. From the V of her uniform, her throat rose to a face that would have delighted a sculptor. Her bone structure was firm, yet delicate and finely chiseled. The eyes were generously spaced, and at the tip of a straight, blending line of nose, the nostrils flared slightly.

I did not note all this in my first view of Julia Girard. I doubt if anyone could be aware of anything but her total impact. She was a stunning woman.

I found my voice after a moment. "Mrs. Girard? Won't you come in?"

She nodded, moving from her chair as if she were on smooth springs. She said nothing.

"I'm Dr. Howard. My office is at the end of the hall."

My words sounded inane, suddenly. I wondered how many of the patients I had met in three years at Seminole Mental Health Center had also regarded them as flat and artificial.

She did not speak until we were in my office. I gestured her to a chair, then took my own seat. I looked at her expectantly, waiting for her to begin. It took several moments. She drew her lower lip between her teeth and bit it, soundly.

"I was awake all night, just knowing I was to come here today. Now I can't think of anything to say."

"You were nervous about having been referred to us?"

"I don't know what to say—what kind of things would be important for you to know." For the first time she raised her eyes to meet mine. "It just seems so ridiculous to me."

"Ridiculous?"

"Seeing a psychologist to talk about a physical problem."

It was not an unusual beginning, I thought. Many patients have a great deal of difficulty in considering the impact of their emotions on their physical operation. ' The referral letter we have from Dr. Madison states he can find no physical explanation for these recurrent headaches you have."

"He just hasn't found one—that's all. There has to be a reason for migrainous arthralgia. It isn't just a matter of being tense and nervous."

"Perhaps. Yet being anxious and tense may well contribute to the pain you experience with these headaches."

"I know where that tension comes from, doctor. It's my job." She looked at me for a moment. "I . . . I have trouble getting along with people. The people I have to work with are especially . . . er . . . difficult."

"You're a nurse?" I inquired, gesturing at her uniform.

"Technician—hematology. I do blood work."

I marked the faint condescension in the tone as she defined the term for me. "At Leighton Hospital?"

"Yes."

"You seem a little young for that line of work."

"I finished my laboratory training when I was seventeen."

Mentally I marked the speed. Julia Girard was an achiever. To have undertaken the eighteen months of training the state required to get a technician's license, she would have had to finish high school before she was sixteen, then gone directly to her training. That kind of achievement would imply excellent intelligence.

"Where did you take your training?"

"Atlanta. I also worked there for a year before coming to Leighton two years ago."

"Which hospital?"

For a moment she seemed flustered. "Not in a hospital. I worked for Dr. Fred Beatty and Dr. Paul King. They maintained their own pathology laboratory—at least for chemistry and radiology."

I nodded. "And how long have you been at Leighton? I mean as a staff technician."

"For eight months, full time. Before that I worked on call for almost two years—seventeen months, really."

I marked that, also. Julia would be precise in report, perhaps from her training, but equally likely from her own internal sense of order.

"And you say that you have a problem getting along with your co-workers. What kind of trouble?"

I could see the tension flood back into her body. Julia Girard responded quickly, and I saw the nonverbal resistance to answering the question. She took her arms from the sides of the chair and lightly folded them across her chest, as if to close off the whole area of conflict with her fellow workers. Yet, consciously, she forced herself to reply to my query. Again she pulled her lower lip between her teeth and administered a bite. When she did speak, her voice was sharp.

"They . . . gossip. Not only that, but it is stupid gossip. The inanity per square inch in that place is unbelievable. I try to just be there and do my work. They keep wanting conversation—by which they mean talking about someone else. I don't like that, and I won't do it."

"So you withdraw from them, and they resent it?" Mentally I noted something different from what my question implied. My own reaction to the impact of Julia made me certain that she would be very much resented on sight. A substantial percentage of women would dislike her because she was stunning. Another percentage would resent the authoritative crispness that would not seem "fitten" in one so young.

Others would find displeasure in her firm, well-modulated voice that showed no trace of the South. Her vocabulary, also— leading her to precision like "inanity" and "migrainous arthralgia" rather than "stupid" or "migraine headache"—would have set her apart and increased the percentage of those irritated by the difficulties of competing with her.

Preliminary deductions crowded in on me. There was friction in her work situation, and it left her both frightened and angry. It was also quite probable that Julia, in her youth, was making it quite clear that she considered herself superior in mien, mentality, and manner.

212

"They do resent it. They're quite narrow, really. The whole style of life of someone like Mrs. Harrigan is so prosaic and dull that I feel like vomiting when she wants to 'chat.' God! How I hate that word chat."

"You sound quite angry with her. What's behind it?"

"I *know* my job. I do my job. Why must she keep prating about having a relaxed attitude with the patients? Relaxed, hell! Let the doctors have the bedside manner. To me, they're just so many veins and such and such a lipoprotein profile. I do my job with them and get out. I don't feel I'm required to make conversation with them."

I remembered having visited Leighton Hospital early in my beginning days with the center, before my schedule was too crowded for exploration and consultation. Leighton, as a city, was slightly larger than Danton, and its hospital reflected this. Yet it was still a small hospital, with a small-town manner in its approach to the friends and neighbors of the community who might be its temporary residents. To be an isolated, noninteracting technician in the small town was not a thing Julia would find feasible.

"It *is* a small town," I reminded her.

"So my mother-in-law is always telling me." She aped a voice, with gentle irony. *"It's a small town, dear. People will be friendly if you give them the chance."* She snorted. "Who needs such a chance?" She was showing some real irritation when she fell back into her own voice.

"How long have you been married, Julia?"

"Three years. We married in Atlanta. I left Dr. Beatty a few weeks later—when Joel was able to get what he wanted in Leighton."

"You don't mind if I call you Julia? It's a little forced to say Mrs. Girard with every question." She nodded and I went on. "Is your husband connected with the Girard Department Store?"

"That's his father. Joel has a small interest, but he runs his own business." There was pride in her voice. "He operates Leighton Airport."

She looked at me, as if deciding to make use of the initial interview. "Joel is . . . proud. He wants us to make it on our own. He won't be beholden to his father or anyone else."

"Good for him." I decided on a prod, to study Julia's reaction level. "Of course, if he's Phil Girard's son, his position is definitely secure in Leighton."

It produced the flare I had expected. "If Harrigan and those other biddies at the hospital regard me as a snob, it's because they think the same damned thing. But it's not true!" She clenched her teeth and gave me a look designed to cut. "I told you my man was proud. So am I." It was definitely a warning.

"Good. But what is this about being a snob?"

"Anyone who keeps to himself is a snob in their eyes, I guess." She snorted again. "If they think I'm such a snob, they should go to some of the Girard 'family parties.' Those people are so patronizing it makes me ill."

"Ill? That's a place your headaches come from?"

"No. I mean that's another place where I think I want to throw up." She glanced at me again, the anger fading and a qualitative appraisal in her dark eyes. "I always get the same question, so neatly put that I feel choked. They ask me if I'm pregnant in a million different ways. You'd think my having a baby was some kind of a group project of the whole Girard clan."

Her voice was no less modulated and inflected, but there was a kind of fury underneath the soft tones. It was less genial than when she had mocked her mother-in-law's advisement. She looked at me intently, her eyes flashing sparks. "I'm not pregnant, God knows. About three or four times a year I have to hear that same damned question. They want a dynasty, and I'm supposed to provide the heir to the throne."

The sparks in her eyes seemed to be drowned in the rising film of tears that now veiled their surface. Her voice dropped to a deep-throated moan of pain. "I want a child, Dr. Howard. I want to have a baby!"

"Does Joel feel that way, too?"

She nodded, not trusting herself to speak. It took a moment, then she resumed as if talking to herself. "We've had tests on top of tests—here, Atlanta, Baltimore, and New Orleans. I've kept charts on my vaginal temperature till I know my cycle by heart."

She pinned me with her still filmy eyes. "Not one of those tests reveals any reason why I shouldn't have been pregnant three times in the three years. But it just doesn't happen."

214

I thought about it for a moment. "That's the real reason for this referral, isn't it? Dr. Madison feels your tension level and those headaches are keeping you from conceiving."

"Didn't he say so?" She was questioning with desperation in her voice.

"Not in those words. He did mention tension headaches, the premenstrual syndrome, *middleschmerz.*"

"Middleschmerz? What has my staining in mid-cycle to do with this? It doesn't happen often, and it surely isn't any problem. We just expect it. After all, most women have *two* ovaries, doctor. It's not uncommon."

"That's not the appropriate explanation, Julia. The tension level may be."

She sighed. "I don't believe it. But that's why I'm here." She looked at me as if waiting for me to convince her that there was such a condition as psychological infertility. Then tears welled up in her eyes again. "It's embarrassing. I've always resented talking about . . . intimate things."

"I realize it is difficult. Tell it as you will, and when you wish."

"I *wish* to find out. If there is a way you can help, a little embarrassment is a small price." She stabilized both her voice and her tears. "Paula Adams is pregnant again. She's having the second one in that same three years."

"She is?"

"One of the few people with whom I enjoy talking. She's my next-door neighbor. We take some classes together at the junior college—on nights when she can find someone to baby-sit, that is."

"You're taking some college work?"

"Joel works till about ten three nights a week. I need to do something to occupy my time." She seemed to be moving away from the topic of pregnancy, but I thought it best to bring her back to it.

"She's pregnant?"

"Yes. I don't really know why she'd want to be. If you knew her husband and saw the two little beasts she has already, you'd wonder why she'd want a third."

"Sounds as if you feel both ways about having a child."

"I don't really. I'm ambivalent about a lot of things, but

not about that." She looked away, as if to soften a confession of which I might not approve. "To be truthful, I wasn't going to take Dr. Madison's advice about coming here. Paula was the one who talked me into coming. She saw Mr. Carson here last year. It helped her considerably."

"I hope we'll be able to help you, too, Julia. It may take some time for us to find out if we can."

"Why can't I have a baby?" There was pain in her voice, sudden and plaintive, though her tone was soft.

"I don't know. Emotional barriers to conception aren't as rare as most people might think. But each one is a different situation—there's no automatic solution."

I looked at her closely. "We'll do our best to help. It's not an easy process. It will take time. But I am sure therapy will help you with other things along the way."

She seemed to answer my observation with a start, as if she was pulling herself back into the defensive. "What things?"

"Your feelings about Leighton, the people there—in-laws, supervisors, the people you work with—maybe a number of other rough spots."

I had taken a first gamble. It paid off in sparks. "Don't expect to turn me into some sweet little southern belle. I'm what I am!"

"Of course. But you should also know what that is."

Her rising attack was never launched. I saw her relax a bit in her chair and went ahead with structuring the outline of therapy.

"I don't expect to make you into anything other than what you are. You may make some changes in yourself when you come to understand some of the reasons for the kinds of difficulties you have encountered."

"How would that help?"

"It's always better to have some freedom of choice in your responses than not to have it."

"I do as I damned well please, anyhow."

"Then why are you so defense-prone that you have to argue the point? If it really pleases you, why do you need to bristle?"

She paused, weighing the remark. It took a considerable time. Finally, Julia nodded. "How do we begin?"

"We've already begun. For today, we set a schedule of appointments, discuss fee and all of the necessary details. In the

216

next few sessions, we'll be attempting to build some sort of bridge your feelings can cross—to try and get those feelings translated into words we both can understand."

We set a time and a fee appropriate to the income of a young married couple. I rose, signaling the time was up. She came from her chair easily, offering her hand. For the first time I had the advantage of a fully lighted smile. Her face relaxed, gentling to indicate that we had a beginning of really effective contact. I found myself smiling at her, too.

"I'm pretty bitchy sometimes."

"I think I already had a sample. It is manifested mostly in your tone—not your words."

"I'm glad you didn't use a lot of technical analytic jargon."

"I speak English, mostly. If a technical term says it better, then it's worth using, once we both agree on its meaning." I released her firm hand and moved to open the door again.

"I'll see you Tuesday."

"Unless I lose my nerve again."

Julia was in my office on Tuesday, and nearly every Tuesday thereafter ended with her appointment. This late hour was given to accommodate her work schedule, but I discovered it also made an extremely pleasant last appointment on my schedule.

She was exceptional in many ways other than her stunning appearance. She had wit, charm, and enough hostility to supply a devil's legion. I admired the way she contained it, keeping it at bay and letting people feel only the points, rather than the full thrusts of that hostility.

Julia was also well armored, but the armor was designed to keep others at a distance. Sometimes I attributed this to the unconscious snobbery of the young. More often I saw it as the signal of deeper pain. Generally, she fell back into verbal fencing when she was not ready to move against her feelings, and I found her as skilled at this as any patient I had ever known. It took a conscious effort for me not to be trapped in delightful but empty intellectual games. These would have limited value in treating her.

Julia had definite impact. It touched those who met her in many spheres. Not the least was her subtle and unintended challenge to every man. She was a lovely woman, spectacular in appearance, with a sharpness of mind and quickness of wit. Such a woman, out of place in a small town and seeking the completion of self through bearing a child, could rouse any man. The combination of her assets and her lacks would provide some appeal to the man, whether he sought confirmation of his virility, his intelligence, his capacity to be a social creature, or the gratification of his wish to master the rare and difficult.

I was astounded by her reading range. Further astonishment came in seeing the fashion in which she processed information and related concepts across the lines of fields of knowledge. When she questioned, it was an exacting probe. When she induced relationships, they were structured, with the follow-up deductions rarely overlooking any of the facts.

In time, I began to see how her intellect functioned. In the Adlerian sense, it provided compensation routing to superior feelings about herself. Furthermore, she had in her intelligence an effective adversary to combat her unfulfilled loneliness, so that she was not forced to compromise herself to the level of back-fence conversation.

Yet there was also the functional element of allowing her to test and retest me as a therapist. Her testing was adroit. It might well have continued indefinitely, but for the fact that her life forced a breakthrough to the emotional rather than the mental interchange.

Being in a room with Julia was a thing so immediate that I had difficulty in focusing on other times. Her disciplined intellectual presentation was so formalized that there was a further problem in re-creating and visualizing the events she reported. Since the attempt to know by inserting my imagination into the *gestalt*—the pattern—of the reporting of a significant experience was my favored route in understanding what was happening with a particular patient's feelings, I felt the lack with Julia. I was almost consciously seeking to make it happen. Perhaps that was why it did not occur.

This day was different. Julia was upset, and it showed in all the tense moves of her slim body as she entered the office. She gestured at the bloodstains on the front of her uniform even as she sat down in a continuous flow of motion that had begun in the waiting room.

"I'm a damned mess."

"Accident in the lab?"

For a moment she hesitated. When she spoke again, I knew that my wait had been rewarded. The tone, the inflection, the feeling of the first sentence projected us into the scene. . . .

"Ah'm afraid of needles, Miz Girahd." The voice was flatly harsh, like dry sandy soil under one's bare feet.

"I'll be as gentle as I can, Miss Ambler." Julia looked at the young girl. "But your doctor ordered me to get a blood sample."

"Ah'll faint. I jes' know Ah will."

"Sit here in the chair, please. I'll be ready for you in a moment." Julia kept her voice crisp and professional. "There's nothing to be afraid of. It will all be over in five minutes."

The girl saw the instrument tray and began to cry, sobbing as she lowered her pregnancy-distorted body into the chair. "Nothin' to be afraid of," she gasped between sobs. "Ah got ever'thing to be afraid of. Mah dahydee like to kill me when he found out that . . . Ah was in the fam'ly way." She took a moment to sob some more. "Ah got a baby kickin' in mah belly. It hurts. Nobody likes me 'cause Ah'm pregnant. Mah dahydee, he won' speak to me, 'n' mah momma hates me, too."

"You're pregnant. It happens to a lot of women." Julia's voice was icy as she sought to maintain her calm.

"But Ah'm only seventeen. I don' want no baby! Donnie—he run off to Nashville when he found out Ah was in the fam'ly way." The girl's voice ran on, sobbing. "Ah'm just ruint. Ever'body knows that I done it." Her face was marked with tears, wet streaks furrowing the puffy, sand-colored cheeks. "Just that one time with Donnie, and now I gotta have a baybee. Whay did it happen to me?"

Julia could not trust herself to speak. She turned and busied herself with the lab tray, putting her back toward the chair, so that Gladys Ambler would not be able to see her angry face. She fought to control herself, praying that the girl would shut up, but knowing that she was going to babble.

"Nobody'll evah want me naow. Ah'm ruint—that's what."

The girl's voice became harsher, more demanding of Julia's attention. "Mah own dahydee spit in mah face! Yeass he did. He *spit* in mah face!" The pause was dramatic. "Ah don' want to have no baby."

Julia could stand it no longer. She whirled to face the girl, angry words forming in her throat. "Don't you realize hundreds of women would give anything they have to be bearing a child? You're a selfish little brat, thinking only of *yourself!*"

"It don' matter. It don' matter none at all. Ah don' want no baby. Let one of them hundred woman have it—let her have her belly all swole up an' ugly!"

"You're pregnant, and you're going to have that baby. Yelling your head off won't change that."

The girl looked up at the technician, finding a focus for her hatred outside of herself. "A lot you care. You' married to a rich man's son. You don' have to be facin' no shame lak Ah do. In a fam'ly way with the fathuh run off to keep from marryin' you."

Julia had to look directly at the girl. "Fathers *always* run away!" she snapped. "Every woman is alone when she's with child!"

The uniformed technician advanced on the girl, twisting the tubing around her upper arm, forcing the vein to bulge under the sun-toughened skin. "Now just let me do my job—then you can go and bellyache to somebody else."

"You got no raight to talk to me that way!"

"Hold your arm still."

"Ah tol' you Ah was afraid of needles. Ah'll *faint*."

"Go ahead and faint. If it bothers you so much, just look the other way."

Julia's hands were tense, trembling. She began the puncture, seating the needle in the vein. With the penetration, the girl's muscles tightened. When Julia sought to broach the vein, Gladys Ambler jerked her arm against the tube. The medium-diameter needle snapped. Blood spurted in a tiny jet, spattering the front of Julia's uniform.

"You hurt me!" The voice was accusatory.

"Hold still, Miss Ambler." The voice was a set of cutting edges, dipped in ice. It froze the girl in place.

Using forceps, Julia caught and extracted the stub of the

needle. She reswabbed the area, turned, and took another slip tube and needle, expertly lancing it into the vein. As quickly as she could, she drew the necessary samples.

"Ah'm goin' to repoht you to my doctuh."

"I'm sorry that I hurt you. Needles do break, sometimes."

"Ah'm goin' to tell him how you talked to me."

"It is your privilege." Julia's voice was contemptuous and defied further comment. "Now hold that compress in place until I can put an adhesive bandage over it. Then you can leave to make your complaint."

The operation of placing the small bandage was brief, and the girl escaped, muttering her way out of the room. Julia stood for a long time, shame flooding through her face. She was more angry with herself than with the patient. It took longer for her to gain control of herself than she was allowed, for the door that had banged closed behind the patient was opened again to admit Julia's supervisor, chief technician Mae Harrigan. The plump, round-faced woman closed the door and stood just inside the small room, staring at the dark-haired technician.

"What happened in here, Julia?"

"I lost my temper."

"So I gathered. That little girl was fit to be tied." The older woman walked into the room, standing beside the service chair.

"She's not a little girl," Julia said. "In another five or six weeks she's going to be a mother. She'd damned well better quit her whining for sympathy and be prepared to go through with the job."

"I know she's a pain in the butt. She does it every time she has to come to prenatal." Mae Harrigan's voice was sympathetic, but it moved on into the official tone. "But, dammit, Julia, you've got to use some tact in handling patients. We don't have to like them, but they're individually entitled to the best we can give them in care *and manner.*"

Julia nodded, then felt for a moment that she should attempt an explanation. "She jerked her arm just when I got into the vein. I had hold of the shell, and the needle snapped. That's all there was to it."

"I'm not talking about the broken needle—that's no big thing.

I'm talking about what you said to her. That's the thing that bothers me. You just don't get along with people, Julia. I want things to run smooth in this department."

Mae Harrigan felt ill at ease. She did not like dressing down any subordinate, but she was uncomfortable when confronting Julia's glassy exterior. She didn't feel that she knew this girl, and it bothered her intensely. Her voice became less certain, as if she could not decide whether to be more lax or more harsh. "Her father is likely to raise hell."

"Who? Him? He beat her mercilessly when she came home"— Julia mocked the girl's tone —"*in the fam'ly way.*" She snorted harshly. "When she first came to prenatal, three months ago, she was so battered and bruised that I thought someone would have him arrested."

"That's between them. All we have to do is to make sure our feelings here don't get *us* in any trouble. You've got to make some changes in your attitude about these women in prenatal."

"I told you when you hired me that I didn't want to work prenatal. Can't you schedule Ruby for that, instead of me?"

"You're first lab tech. We've been over that before. You were hired to be used in the full range of service, and you're not being paid to get into arguments with patients, no matter how impossible they may seem."

The flat pronouncement gave Julia no further room for argument. "All right," she said, her tone resigned. "I'll give more TLC, in spite of all the crap."

"That's right—TLC, *tender, loving care.*" Mae Harrigan's voice reflected the fact that she felt a bit more secure. She could afford to be more generous. "It won't be reported—this time. I managed to calm her down." Her voice softened a bit more. "I don't want to lose you, Julia. You are a good worker. And I don't want to have to give you hell. But this is a small town. It isn't Atlanta. Here we have to get along with people. Will you please just try?"

"I'll try."

"Really try. It's got to be more than just a bare try. This is a place where we all have to live and work together and get along with each other. You sometimes don't seem to *want* to fit in."

222

Julia did not reply, and the older woman prodded her again with the observation, "Do you want to fit in?"

"No. I really don't want to *fit in*. I want whatever place I have because of what I can do in the way of work—not because I know who's sleeping with the chief resident or is available to the administrator. I don't want to make small talk, or be phony in the things I say. It's as simple as that."

"That wasn't what I meant. You know that!"

"Yes," Julia said in a tired tone. "I don't mean to harp at you, Mrs. Harrigan. But do we really have to play 'Dear Abby' to these people? Most of the time I'm polite, and I try to be as efficient as I can."

The supervisor's eyes narrowed, and her glance was one of appraisal. "What was it she said to you to upset you so much?"

"It wasn't any specific thing. It was her whole demanding, whining attitude that got to me. I lost my temper and I should not have lost it. I'm sorry."

"All right," Mae Harrigan said. "But I'd find it easier to accept your apology if you didn't have to clench your teeth to give it." She looked at the slender girl for a long moment, then turned and left the room without another word. . . .

Julia looked across my desk at me, her dark eyes snapping with remembered anger. "That's the kind of thing that goes on, Dr. Howard."

"Sounded to me like Mrs. Harrigan was only doing her job."

"Yes. I know that. I guess that's part of what infuriates me all the more—that I took it out on her. It was really that silly little bitch—that walking baby factory. She was such a baby herself that she made me ill. All that talk about her *dahydee*. That's how she pronounced it, like a baby."

"Sure it wasn't her talking about her pregnancy? Or the fact that she is pregnant?"

She nodded, wearily. "Yes. I resent that, too. I resent any woman in pregnancy, because I'm not."

"You're not hiding behind your intellectual barricades today," I said. "You really can let out your feelings sometimes, can't you?"

"If I'm angry enough, I guess." Her voice softened more

than I could remember having heard. "Maybe when something like this happens I can let down my guard." She looked at me again, her eyes melting. "I imagine you get tired of my not coming to the point of this whole thing."

"What is the point, Julia?"

"Her father beat her when she turned up pregnant. He beat her badly."

"And?"

She didn't reply for a moment, and as it stretched, I added to my question. "Did your father ever beat you?"

"No. My father didn't do a damned thing about anything. I—I guess that's it. Somehow it seems worse than a beating."

"What do you mean?"

"At least her father had some kind of feeling that could let her know where she stood. Maybe it was a feeling about what she'd done—maybe something about himself—but, anyhow, he did *do something.*"

"A pretty drastic something."

"He expressed something of what he felt. He . . . wasn't a smiling blob. She at least could understand what he did."

"You seem to be saying something specific."

The pause was long and heavy with remembrances. Whatever flashed across the surface of Julia's mind reflected in her lovely face. That face became a kaleidoscope of constantly changing expression, altering its tone so rapidly that the configurations giving such fleeting glimpses of yesterday could not be identified. The expressions seemed to alter her face structurally, dropping the mask of sophisticated loveliness. Her words, when they came, were things that painted another scene. . . .

Julia saw the gray sedan in the driveway of the old frame house she called home. Her grandmother and aunt were there. It wasn't the time she wanted them there. She wrinkled her nose, partly in distaste and partly to screw up courage to tell herself that she didn't care what they thought. *It's not really their affair,* she thought. *No matter how late I am.*

Nevertheless, she tugged at her skirt until it hung at the

proper midknee length, rather than two inches above. Then she eased her sweater from the waistband of the skirt, letting it blouse rather than cut sharp lines of her sixteen-year-old breasts. She wished that she had remembered to take some cloves in her handbag. She knew the sharp-nosed and somewhat disapproving woman relatives would detect the odor of the two cans of beer she had drunk with such a show of bravado.

It was very late, she realized. The disc jockey after midnight had an infuriating habit of giving the time. She'd heard it after almost every record on Bill's car radio on the way home. *As if his music weren't insipid enough, he has to keep reminding me that I'm out beyond curfew—again.* She wrinkled her nose once more, set her face, then walked the remaining distance into the house. She threw the door open, entering.

"Hi, mom. Hi, dad."

She could feel the disapproval of her grandmother and aunt, their eyes resting on her like those of pawnshop appraisers. She could almost feel their scrutiny assess the condition of her skirt, her breasts, her face.

"Where have you been?" Her father's voice was strange and forced. "Do you realize it's after one in the morning?"

"That's what the man said on the car radio, just as we got back to town."

"*Back* to town? What makes you think you had permission to go out of town? Where did you go?"

Julia could feel her face flushing. She glanced toward her mother, but decided that there was no help to be had from the thin woman when she saw the slender, aristocratic hands kneading at themselves, forcing themselves into a ball in the mother's lap.

She quickly scanned the others. The grandmother and aunt were still checking for visible signs of damage and did not meet her eyes. Her father, broad shouldered, handsome, and red-faced, was fulfilling his role as a chastising agent of the older generation.

"I said," he demanded, "where did you go?"

"We drove to Mobile and went to a drive-in movie. It stank."

There was no change in the expressions of the three women. Aunt and grandmother sat in judgment, and it was obvious that they had cast their brother and son in the role of inquisitor.

"With that Bill Phillips?"

"Yes. I've been dating him for about three months, off and on. You know that." She tried to hold her temper, tried to convince herself that this would be like any of the other questionings, but she knew the presence of his family made that impossible for her father.

"He drinks. Was he drinking tonight?"

"He's not a *drunk,* father." The tone and implication made it clear that she was prepared to criticize her father's drinking, if he were to press the issue too hard.

"Was he drinking?"

"He had two cans of beer." She looked at him, unable to resist cutting back at him, but not yet ready to shame him for his own fondness for drinking. "So did I. What's such a big thing about two cans of three-two beer? He's old enough to buy it."

"Old enough to go to jail for giving it to a sixteen-year-old girl, too." Grandmother Darrell had broken a promise to herself. She hadn't let her son handle it.

Julia's eyes flashed toward the woman, then back to her father. He was even more red-faced now. "Christ, yes. And he could be in worse trouble for taking a sixteen-year-old across a state line."

Julia's barely restrained temper broke. "Not unless he intended to seduce me or sell me! He didn't do either one!"

"That's enough! I won't have you talking that way!"

"So why are you making so much of my being out late tonight? You never did before. Is it that tonight you have an audience? If you'd told me about it I'd have worn a *red* dress."

"Stop that!" Alice Darrell's voice was pained. "You're talking to your father." She stopped herself, suddenly, as if she had overstepped her place.

"Then why is he trying to make me feel like something cheap? He's never told me when to be in before. All the times I've gone to drive-in movies—the times I've gone out with boys not half as nice as Bill Phillips—he's *never said a word.*"

Richard Darrell's voice was cold. "That's enough, young lady. Go to your room. We'll talk more about this tomorrow, when you've had a chance to think it over."

"You won't have an audience tomorrow." Julia snapped it at him, one last confrontation.

She had pushed him too far. She knew it even before his huge hand slapped across her face. For a moment they stood, face to face. Julia fought back tears forming in her eyes, taking bitter gratification from the stricken look in her father's face and unwilling to allow him to know that she was as hurt as he. She whirled on the grandmother and aunt. "I hope you liked the performance," she said coldly.

Without haste, she moved to the stairs, climbing them to her room. It was as she reached the top step that she heard the judgment of the tribunal.

Her grandmother's voice was projected loudly enough to make sure Julia heard the verdict. "You've got to take a very strict line with that child, Richard. You let her get away with anything." . . .

The Julia of seven years later—the one in my office—had tears in her eyes. This time they flowed softly, without being forced back. Her narrative stopped, and it was a long time before the vivid scene faded back to the present. Finally, she spoke.

"That's my father, Dr. Howard. If he had an audience, he tried to act as he thought a father should act. Most of the time he just struggled to be whatever he thought other people wanted him to be—a smiling blob of putty. My mother was the only one with any real inner strength, but she lacked physical stamina. She acted as if she actually believed he was the man she could believe in."

Our hour was up. Indeed, we had run overtime. It was Julia who noticed it first. "I'll have made you late for dinner again. I'm sorry."

"No problem. I schedule you at the end of the day for both of us. It's more convenient for me and it fits your work schedule." I smiled at her, hoping to put her a bit more at ease with the distress she had felt in making me late. "No one is waiting for an appointment, so a little overtime doesn't make much difference."

She returned my smile, taking a tissue from the white professional package on the desk corner and touching at the wetness of her bright cheeks. "I didn't mean to do this," she said trying to regain her brittle intellectualizing.

"I'm glad you did let your feelings out. You're not all iron woman after all, are you? That's good. I'm a therapist, not a blacksmith."

"Perhaps so, but I have the feeling that if you needed to hammer, you'd do it."

I shrugged, and we ended the session. I sat for a long time after Julia had left the office, trying to make the pieces fit. I didn't have much luck. I presumed that I was reacting to the change that had allowed me to view one of the sources of Julia's early pain—her defensiveness. All I could conclude was that she had turned to intellectualizing because of the pain she had experienced in her efforts to learn who she was and what her place should be.

As I had expected, she shied away from the topic of her father for many subsequent sessions. In fact, she devoted little time or space to any of the recountings of her early days. I learned little that was not on the original application and social services report.

She was one of five children—the oldest—of a used-car salesman and his wife. The parental marriage was of uncertain quality, with the father working most of the time in other cities, and on occasional weekends being at home. She did acknowledge he was a good auto salesman and that, while money was not plentiful, the family had never known any serious want.

I was not pleased with the way Julia had returned to evasion. I thought back over the scene in which she had so severely tested her father's authority and could not help but wonder if some of this was now directed toward me—that somehow she was seeking to test my strength.

In the ensuing weeks of intellectual games, I came to the conclusion that this was precisely the situation. I had given a great deal of thought to Julia and her problem. I determined to wait for an opening, then move her directly to the first questions of her referral—psychological infertility and reactive headaches.

Julia was late this particular spring day. She was, as usual, the last patient set in my schedule. I found myself reacting to her tardiness. It was a day when I had kept strictly to my time rations, cutting my breaks between patients wherever possible. By doing this, I had picked up almost half an hour.

Extra time in an "ego mill" is a luxury, and enabled me to get some overdue correspondence handled. When Julia was late, I had the feeling that I might as well have typed another letter or done a testing report if I had known that she would not be on time. It did not occur to me to consider my reaction petty. Certainly I did not remember that she had to drive nearly forty miles from Leighton to Danton in order to keep the appointment.

I went to the old staff room and drew a bitter cup of overage coffee. It had been fresh eight hours before. Mrs. Grey, among her other duties, made coffee a half hour before our morning staff meetings began. I took the cup to the library, sitting with it before me for a moment to allow it to cool sufficiently before I risked placing my lips against the old mug. I glanced at the current journals, noting the titles of articles my colleagues were recommending with pencil checks on the tables of contents. But this particular day none of them sounded interesting enough to hold my attention.

I tried the coffee. My lips burned in proof that I had not waited long enough, though the time seemed to be dragging. I put the coffee mug back onto the table, determined to wait it out. While it cooled, I walked back to the central office. Mrs. Grey was typing, Mrs. Lenahan, returning charts to the filing cabinet.

"Something you need, Dr. Howard?"

"Not really, Grace. Thank you. I'm just waiting for my coffee to cool."

She glanced out the window at the soft day's light. "Beautiful day for getting away early, if your last appointment doesn't show. Maybe you could get in nine holes of golf." She grinned at me, the secret grin of one golf bug to another. "I'm going to try."

"It's an idea," I answered somewhat coldly. "But I have a lot of paper work. I don't have the luxury of getting away at four thirty every day."

I hadn't meant to make it sound sarcastic. Somehow it did. I could feel the flush of guilt rising in me. Grace Lenahan and Marilyn Grey deserved every consideration. In the three years I'd been with Seminole Mental Health Center, they had made my job many times easier by the kind of smooth teamwork they gave automatically. My remark was petty. I knew it would be impossible to run a pressured situation like an outpatient clinic without women like them. I tried, lamely, to cover my rudeness.

"Hell, I have no right to complain. I was looking for work when I took this job. Have a good game."

She smiled, unoffended. "We all must have been looking for it. The patient census was over two hundred this month, and nine new referrals are on deck for next week."

I looked at my watch, checking it against the wall clock, which showed fifteen minutes past four. "Maybe Mrs. Girard is going to no-show me."

I felt Mrs. Lenahan looking at me. Her voice seemed a bit strange. "It would be the first time. She always calls if she has to cancel an appointment. She didn't call today."

I looked back at her, nodded, then walked to my office. I sat down, reaching for a chart to post. I hadn't written a single line when the buzzer on the intercom sounded.

"Mrs. Girard is here."

I rose to walk back to the waiting room. Julia was at the counter, writing a check for her fee. I stood in the door, waiting for her. When she had finished and taken her receipt, she turned toward me. "I'm late. Sorry."

"The hour is set; whatever part of it you don't use, you lose."

She was still in uniform. As she came toward me, I noticed there were bloodstains on the white nylon. Her face seemed to be flushed and strained, as if she were expecting me to scold her.

I nodded, turning back toward the office. She came quickly, passing close in front of me, then preceding me. I caught the faint delight of her perfume and, as if her scent were a leash, strode behind her down the hallway. Her slimness was outlined by the afternoon light streaming through the open door at the end of the hall. The light outlined her slender waist, the boyish narrowness of her hips, the soft flare of her rib cage. When she paused at the door of my office, I could see her suntanned flesh through the white nylon of uniform and slip.

When she was seated, she leaned forward. It was apparent that something was on her mind. I took my own chair and waited.

For a moment, her words were stilted, and she seemed to be casting for a quite different topic than the one on her mind. Her attention went to the bloodstains. She gestured at them impatiently.

"I should have had time to change." Her tone was disgusted. "I hate that job."

"What happened?"

"I had to take prenatal clinic again—after they'd promised not to assign me. I broke another needle in a patient. She spurted blood like an animal."

"It happens, sometimes."

"The patient started screaming at me, just like Ambler's snotty bitch of a daughter." Julia's lower lip was trembling.

"I suppose Harrigan read you off about it." I remembered the several occasions when Julia had described conflicts with her supervisor.

"The conditions were sterile. I make very sure of things like that. Some of the one-time needles are defective."

I waited, giving no indication of reaction. She was uncomfortable with that. I recognized her implicit request for something supportive from me. When she saw it was not coming, she went on.

"I know my job, Dr. Howard."

"Even in prenatal? How long has it been since you broke a needle in anything but a pregnant woman?" I pinned her with it. "It does bother you, otherwise you wouldn't have asked to be relieved of that little section of your job."

For a long moment she was silent. Finally she did speak, and her voice was flattened. "Yes. It bothers me. It bothers me that all those stupid farm wives can shuck out children like ears of corn. They do it easily, idiotically, and so goddamned frequently. I can't get pregnant, no matter what I dislike, like, do, or don't do." She swung her head around, lifting her face to mine. Tears stood in her soft eyes, and the modulation came back into her voice. "Of course, it bothers me. I can't stand having them talk about how it will be to have a child, or what their current children are like. How can they be so blind? Their children are probably little monsters, like Paula Adams's *kinder*."

"The family next door?"

"What's she got to show for it? Three kids, with a husband

who's just too busy to come home. Eight or nine weeks straight, she's alone, and she's stuck with them. Kids like that should entitle her to risk pay as an animal trainer."

"But Joel comes home, doesn't he?" I looked closely at her, hunting for some reaction to the mention of her husband's name.

"Yes." Her voice was soft. "He's always home as soon as he finishes work."

"So how are your situations alike?"

"They aren't. That's the trouble. She can have kids by a man who couldn't care less for them, or for her. I have a man I love, and we're equally desperate to have a child. But nothing, absolutely nothing happens."

"You don't mean you don't have sex relations."

"We want a baby, doctor. Of course, we have sex."

"Do you?"

"Don't start that again. I'm not afraid to get pregnant. I want a baby."

"And when is it that you have your headaches?"

She sighed. "About a week after my period."

"Starting in the late afternoon."

"It's that damned job of mine!"

"That's a cop-out!"

"It is not! We had sex—intercourse—twice during that period last month. This month, too."

"What about the headaches? They did get worse on those nights, didn't they?"

"Yes. They always do. It's difficult to make love then, but we've been doing it."

"And when you do, you're tense, in pain, and unable to relax."

"Usually."

"You mean invariably, don't you?" I pressed at her. "And Joel?"

"He . . . he's kind. He's a wonderful man, doctor. I love my husband."

I charged ahead on the point. "So much that you let him make a sperm deposit in you, even if your head is splitting. Even if you're so sick at your stomach that you want to vomit."

"I—suppose so."

"Doesn't it strike you as odd that this sickness coincides with your time of most probable impregnation? When ovulation has provided your half of the material for a baby?"

Tears were glistening in her eyes. "I told you. I don't avoid Joel then. Since you pointed that out the first time, I've given all I could, in spite of headaches, backache, and nausea. I just don't get pregnant!" The tear in her left eye tore loose, sliding down her cheek. Her voice dropped to a near whisper. "I *can't* have a baby."

"Can't, or won't? Is it possible you don't want to produce the first grandchild? That you don't want the Girards to have a claim on you?"

"That's not fair!"

"Or is it that you just don't want to respond to Joel? That he doesn't turn you on?"

The well of tears in both her eyes overflowed, splashing from her cheeks onto her uniform. I handed her the box of tissues.

"Who is it that you love, Julia? That you don't want Joel Girard's child?"

She dropped the box, startled by the abrupt snap of my voice. I held her eyes harshly for a moment, absorbing her startled expression of extreme denial as if it were nothing. Then, suddenly ashamed, I bent forward in my chair and picked up the fallen box.

I could not help but see the words printed on it. "For Professional Use."

My shame and guilt flamed through me. I looked at the woman. Julia was weeping, silently. Her pain arced from her like an electric force. She was helpless, and I had made her so. I thought through the fifteen minutes we had spent together, the savagery of my confrontations of her—even the accusatory coldness of my tone.

It burst over me. Shame heightened and solidified into the harsh, grating awareness of guilt. Now I knew what those feelings of irritation had been. I thought of the times when Julia's hour had run ten, perhaps even twenty minutes overtime. In flashing insights, I remembered the elation I experienced on days when Julia's session would terminate my work, the irritation when she was late, the impact of her from the first session.

It was not simply the pull of her attractiveness, though that was undeniable. It was the way in which she had emphasized the early concepts I had imagined in the woman I would someday find and love. For the first time, perhaps, I questioned my own imprinting of the dark-haired, soft-eyed woman of lean flanks, flat belly, boyish hips, and long limbs.

Being a man and not a computer, I can readily admit that I have found a number of my patients attractive, some charming, and some even the occasional object of fantasy. Yet always before I had marked the impulses for what they were—the irrational, random thoughts that were, in part, an acknowledgment of my own loneliness. Julia had become the actualization of these.

Through the years of my professional life, I had read many articles on countertransference—the involvement of the therapist's own feelings. This investment of one's own impulses in the relationship with a patient had been an item I had always treated with some contempt. Those who had reported the phenomenon, I felt (quite smugly, it turned out), were weak, vulnerable, perhaps stupid in their handling of their own needs. I had become like a driver whose skills at negotiating dangerous corners had made him contemptuous of turn radius, velocity, and centripetal acceleration.

In short, I was infatuated with Julia Girard. My questions had not been designed to lead her to insights into herself. They had been unconsciously designed to lead her to prefer me to her husband.

I could feel my face flooding as I looked at her. The color drained as my mouth went dry, then the flush broke through and flooded my cheeks again. The hairs at the back of my neck prickled. My hands soaked themselves with perspiration. I had to speak.

"I had no right to ask questions like that. I'm . . . sorry."

"I—" She broke off, unable to speak.

"I'm sorry about many things, Julia. I owe you a sincere apology."

She found her voice, strained as it was. "It's . . . all right."

"I suddenly realized, just a moment ago, that I was being deliberately cruel toward you."

"I thought you were . . . getting at something. That it had to be done this way."

I took a deep breath. "No. It shouldn't be done this way.

Not ever. I—I find that *my* feelings are involved. I wasn't ethical, professional, or anything else. I was . . . *jealous.* I didn't want to give you the chance to tell me about the man you love, because it isn't me."

Her breath was sucked in so sharply that it was nearly a sob. She lifted her tearstained face, her eyes seeking mine. She held eye contact with me for a long time, and I forced myself to stay with her searching gaze, prepared for any castigation she might wish to give me.

Instead of being angry, she asked a question. "What does that mean?"

"It means I have a 'must' thing to do. I must transfer you to someone else who can help you, or terminate your treatment. I'm not able to be very objective where you are concerned."

"Oh."

"I *am* sorry, Julia. I'm old enough to be your father. If I'm so stupid as to become infatuated, you have the wrong doctor."

"I . . . don't want to be transferred." Her voice was low and soft, somehow huskily wet with her tears. "You did find out—you did stop yourself from being cruel."

"I'm not very proud of myself about that."

"I . . . felt you liked me, and I was glad about that."

"Glad?"

"You're a lot like him."

"Joel?"

She shook her head. "No. It happened before Joel. It was the doctor I was working for in Atlanta. I . . . had to quit, over something like this."

"You had a thing with him?"

"Not *with* him—just about him. He didn't even know it. I was so afraid I'd do something stupid. I thought I'd make a fool of myself. I quit so that he'd never know I was . . . in love with him." Her last words came out in almost a whisper. "He was . . . a fine person—a very special person. He was my first boss. I had my first professional job in his office. He took me right out of school, and he trained me." She looked up. "He made me a good hema tech, Dr. Howard."

"I'm sure you're good at hematology."

"Even if I do break needles in pregnant women, and get

blood on myself." She smiled. The tension was broken. We could both feel it ease. "If Dr. Beatty hadn't trained me as well as he did, I couldn't hold my job here. I don't get along with the other people in the lab. They think I'm a snob, as I've already told you." She smiled wryly. "They're right, too. I've been more than a snob. I've been deliberately cruel, too."

"Do you still love Dr. Beatty?"

"No. I never did, really. He's someone very special, still. I was *in love* with him. I don't think I have very much ability to *love* someone. I can only be *in* love."

"What do you mean by that?"

"I'm not really sure. Only that to me, when you're *in* love, you think only about yourself—your joy, your wants. When you *love,* the only important thing is what you can give to the person you love."

"That's pretty profound, Julia."

"I mean it."

"With Joel, too?"

Her face softened. For a moment her eyes betrayed the fact that her thoughts were far away. "Especially with Joel. I do love Joel. He puts up with so much from me that I feel guilty as hell. But I do love him. I think that's what makes this thing so impossible. I love him. I want to give him a child. I can't do it. That's what makes me so furious."

"Giving Joel a baby would make him a *father*?"

Her face was strange. It was almost a Julia I had never seen. After a long silence, her huskiness was wrapped around some words. "Like my own father, you mean?"

"You tell me."

"My father. He was—*is*— something else."

"Was? Is?" I echoed her words with a question.

"He's alive and well and living in Argentina." She said the words with the edge of malice I had heard her use many times. "He didn't want to be a father. He just had to be a *salesman.* It didn't matter what he was, as long as he thought that everyone considered him his special friend."

"What happened after that night when he raised hell in front of your grandmother?"

"Nothing. There was strained silence for a day or two, then

he couldn't stand it. He acted just like nothing had ever happened."

"What had happened?"

"He damned near accused me of being a tramp! I couldn't forgive him that. He *knew* better, but he had to act the stern father."

"You pushed him pretty hard."

"He should have taken a stand long before that. By then it was too late for him to just yell at me."

"What should he have done?"

"Why didn't he haul off and knock me on my fanny? I think that's what I really needed to have him do."

I stared at her for a moment. "You wanted to be stopped, and you just kept pushing to make him stop you."

"I did. I'm not proud of it, Dr. Howard, but when you—I don't know—yes!" She said the words in a sudden burst of insight. "That's it! When I don't know, I have to try and find out!"

"Go ahead, Julia." My words were superfluous. She was plunging ahead, explaining herself to herself.

"All my life, as far as I can remember, what I was always trying to do was to get my father to take some really definite stand on something—anything. It would have let me know that it made a difference to him—that he cared about something."

"Loved you enough to stop you?"

"Yes."

"Could you have been stopped?"

"I could have at first. Later it got to be too much of a game."

" 'Stop me if you can'? That one of Dr. Eric Berne's games—the fellow who wrote that best seller?"

"I couldn't depend on him to stop me. I could do almost anything I wanted—charge clothes without permission, stay out late, drink beer—which I hate—then he'd find some way to explain it to himself and pass it by with some phony excuse."

"Didn't even *try* to stop you?"

"The time I told you about." She slowed in her relation of the events she was experiencing for a judgment of the past denunciation scene. "I was so terribly bitchy. I *shamed* him. He had to slap me."

"This isn't what you felt about it then," I observed.

"No. Not when he was coming down with the law like Moses from Mount Sinai."

"What thing do you think hurt him most?"

"The implication that I might have been in some strange bed." It came back as fast as a ricochet. "I hadn't gone to bed with Bill Phillips—or anyone else. I wasn't a successful drinker, either. I'm still not. As for my wild nights out, I'd sometimes neck for half an hour to make sure it was late enough to upset my father when I did come home. I've had third and fourth cups of coffee to make sure I'd be late."

"When you were a teen-ager?"

"Yes, during my junior and senior years. He was home most of the time then, operating the local lot. He only went to Savannah after I left for medical tech training."

She stopped, aware of the implications of this. "He . . . wanted to be home while I was home."

"Mmm."

"I know he and mother weren't getting along. She'd sit there making little clucking noises when he wasn't strict with me. Once in a while, when we were alone, she'd tell me I was disappointing him and that he was displeased. Why the hell couldn't he tell me?"

"Why the hell not?"

Her face clouded. It seemed to darken from inside. "I always thought he had *her* brainwashed into thinking he had strength. It may have been the other way around. He chose to work away from home after I left. Maybe he was trying to salvage some of his own self-respect."

"Because of how you treated him?"

"No." Her voice dropped to a whisper. "Because of how she sapped his strength. Somebody sold him on the idea that everyone had to like him. He must have felt he was a terrible phony."

"What drove her?"

"She was afraid. She had children to feed, clothe, and educate. It may well have been she who demanded that he make a friend of everyone."

Julia's voice slowed, taking on a puzzled, wondering tone. She was struggling for words to fit the returning memory. As she did, I could see the faint remembrance brighten, taking on shade and texture. She wove it into the pattern of insight she was making

238

of the relationship between her mother and father. It took shape slowly, carrying us back in time. . . .

She hadn't wanted to give up the dream. She was astride the saddle, daddy's arm clamped about her eight-year-old waist, pulling her to his hard chest. His feet were in the distant stirrups she could not reach. The wind whispered across her face as he spurred the big brown horse into a run.

It was the raised voice that broke the dream. She rolled her face into the pillow, trying to make the dream come back. Then she was awake, the dream beyond recall.

"Don't you know what it's like for me, Alice? Having people think I'm just a smiling *thief?* Haven't you any idea how much that makes me sick at my stomach?" Richard Darrell's face burned, his voice rising again. "A goddamned used-car salesman. Smile at everybody—kiss every available ass."

"Be quiet, Richard. You'll wake the girls." The admonition was followed by a softer tone. "I know that it gets to you, honey. But . . . what you're asking . . . it's too much."

The voices dropped. Julia, now fully awake, slipped from her bed, padding barefooted to the head of the stairs. She crouched there in the dark, looking down into the lighted living room where her father paced the floor. Mother sat in her usual chair, her long-fingered hands grasping at the arms.

"It's a chance, Alice. A real chance."

"We can't take chances, Richard. Not right now."

"Look. I'll get about a hundred on the GI Bill, and I can go on selling on weekends. That's when I make most of my sales anyhow. In just a little over two years, I could take the CPA exams." His voice richened. "Certified public accountant. I'd be a professional man. A couple of years with a good firm, and I could set up my own office."

"Rebecca Willis told me that Fred started with Rule and Egbert for only six hundred and fifty dollars, and he's been a CPA for three years. It's just too much of a risk."

Richard Darrell resumed his pacing, searching for arguments to close the sale of an idea to his wife. "I'm not Fred Willis, damn it. I'm me!" He turned to look at her. "We can get by on six hundred a month. I almost make that on weekend sales now.

I've got my GI insurance. I can borrow almost three thousand on that, if we get into a bind."

Alice Darrell gasped as if he had suggested murder. "Oh, *no!* We can't give up that protection."

"Alice, for God's sake! I'm only thirty-four and in good health. I'm not a steeplejack or a crop-duster pilot." His voice dropped. "I'm trying to find a way to make a good living for us without feeling like a pimp."

"I know how you feel, Richie—really I do. But can't you see why I'm so frightened? Two children and another on the way."

Julia could see her father's face freeze. He closed his eyes tightly and threw his head back. Alice Darrell rose from her chair and went to him.

"I didn't want to tell you this way. I wanted it to be a happy thing for both of us. But we might need that money desperately. When Heather was born, there was all that trouble and expense. The doctor said it shouldn't be a problem this time—but what if it is?"

She put her arm around him and lay her head on his chest. "I want you to be happy about it, Richard. I didn't know anything about what you were planning."

"I . . . wanted to surprise you. Wanted to have it all worked out."

"If there's no problem—maybe we could do it next year. If we could just put by a little money first." Her voice choked. "I'm sorry, darling. Can you stick it out another year? You've got a lot of friends. Everybody likes you. They come back to buy from you."

"Sure," he said flatly. "I make a friend of everybody. Good old Rich Darrell has elevated ass-kissing to a fine art."

"That's the way it was, doctor. He had to have a friend in everyone." Julia's expression was impossible to read.

"And why do you have to have an enemy in everyone? So that you have *nothing* to lose?"

Her face contorted, and her lip was caught between her teeth. "I . . . have to hold some kind of distance. I don't trust easily."

"Because if someone *dislikes* you, you *know* where you stand?"

"I never thought of it that way. My father always seemed like such a tasteless man. Maybe he wasn't. But he didn't show much discrimination among people."

"He needed them?"

"Like his next breath."

"And you don't?"

"No!" The word came explosively. Then she lamely changed it. "I mean, of course I need people."

"But not if you feel it's a compromise. Only if it's on your own terms, Julia. You discriminate till people prove they're worthy of being needed."

"That's pretty snobbish, isn't it?" Her voice had softened from the bright tone of discovery to the soft tone of acceptance.

"It's pretty defensive, too." I looked at her closely. "Is that why you can't bear the idea of fatherhood for Joel? Because it has always seemed like such a weak position?"

"Weak?"

"You've said your own father wasn't able to stop you—not that he didn't stop you. Earlier you remarked that fathers were never there when you needed them—that a man had to give direction as well as love."

"You're talking about Dr. Beatty, aren't you? My old boss, the one I thought I was in love with?"

"Am I?"

"He made me into a good lab technician. I learned more from him in a few weeks than in all the months of school."

"He demanded your best?"

"Nothing else would do—right down to the last decimal point."

"You gave that willingly, because he set limits for you like the ones you had sought from your father. So you thought you loved him."

She was silent for a long time. When she looked up, the tears stood in her eyes again. "Joel is the man I love, doctor. He's not my father, and he's not Dr. Beatty. He's Joel, and that's all he's ever had to be."

"Even if he's someday also a father?"

She stood up and reached for my hand. "He's going to be, Dr. Howard. I've never been so sure of anything."

It was hard to write about Julia. Not that the feelings were not powerful, nor were they dimmed by distance and the fading of my memory. Actually, she prepared me for what was to come in my own life.

There had to be a Julia, somewhere in my professional life. Looking back on my years of training and practice, I sometimes wish that she might have come sooner than she did. She was as essential to my growth as I hope I was to hers. She grew to know her entitlement to be herself, and the two birth announcements I have received from her and Joel in the years since I left Seminole were great moments of remembered warmth.

Perhaps such a situation exists for every therapist. There almost has to be a time when he becomes aware of the distortions of his own perception—of his illusions about the people with whom he tries to work. It seems to me to be an essential trial for his own development. It teaches the lesson of humility, of course. Beyond this humility lesson lies the teaching of the essential rightness of a personal approach to the problems others bring to us in their cry for help.

For the novice or the quack, the drastic recognition that "complete objectivity" is impossible may result in withdrawal from the attempt to be a therapist, or an increase of self-delusion. The first solution is ironic because people are bettered by the withdrawal of therapists who cannot let themselves care at all. In the second solution, unfortunately, people are hurt by those who make therapy a mechanical set of applications of a "system."

243

Despite the forgoing, I would not deny the need for full training, rigorous self-discipline, and some preliminary knowledge of the irrationalities of our own makeup. It is essential for any clinician. But to assume that these things can provide insulation from our own feelings and illusions is a gratuitous pretense. Without his feelings, rational and irrational alike, no therapist could ever know the feelings of those who come to him for help.

My infatuation with a woman twenty years younger than I made me into an ineffectual child seeking to help a very troubled adult. I am most fortunate that Julia was a woman of genuine strength. In spite of her own pressing needs, Julia was able to help me to know myself. It was even more fortunate that this very knowledge became the tool that enabled me to help her.

Until she reads these lines, Julia may not be aware of what I feel she did for me. What she did know, in that mute interchange of pain for two people, was that to acknowledge vulnerability did not invite destruction. We found that bit of human knowledge together, each experiencing it in his own feelings, each giving it his separate and unique interpretation.

Julia ripped my smugness from me. My training had given me a generous supply of overconfidence. I had read articles on countertransference with some contempt—not believing that an adequate therapist could ever be emotionally involved with any patient. I had considered such practitioners either foolish or flawed.

She also taught me not to withhold my genuine feelings from my patients or myself, reaffirming the human condition of all of us—that we humans are not like our neighbors, but that we are more alike than we are different, as Havelock Ellis so long ago observed.

More importantly, in confronting me with myself and my own unfulfilled needs, she prepared me for the risk of unrestrained loving by finding her way to love without restraint. I am sure that her husband and children, as well as my wife and myself, have reason for a grateful acknowledgment of this, as does my own new son.

Thus, in hundreds of "ego mills"—mental health clinics

—people move into the wilderness of their feelings, seeking to construct some more effective map for self-guidance. The therapist, as guide, has not been in that unique territory before. His function is defined by his ability to be both with and for his particular patient. This is not as a knight on a quest or anything so romantic, but as a recognizer and illuminator. That we cannot always recognize or illuminate is the constant pain of the therapist. That we are allowed the time to try is the most constant affirmation of the worth of the effort and needs of the people who cry, "Help!"

Yes, people have problems, some that beggar description. No therapist can meet and help with all troubles. I recall a childhood incident of my own, wherein my father was asked if he had "trouble." "No," he replied. "Trouble is something I can't fix. What I have is a problem."

DATE DUE